30 Personal Stories of Strength and Resilience

SHE STANDS *Strong*

HANNA OLIVAS & ADRIANA LUNA CARLOS
along with 28 inspiring authors

TABLE OF CONTENTS

INTRODUCTION

Welcome to *She Stands Strong: 30 Personal Stories of Strength and Resilience*. Within these pages, you'll find a tapestry of narratives that illuminate the power of the human spirit in the face of adversity. This collection is not just a series of stories; it's a celebration of women who have transformed their deepest fears into their greatest strengths.

Every woman featured in this book has encountered moments of doubt and despair—those daunting instances that can either shatter or empower. They are everyday heroes, not because they have never faced challenges, but because they have chosen to confront them head-on. Through their journeys, you will discover the transformative power of resilience and the profound insights that come from embracing vulnerability.

As you delve into these intimate portraits, you'll witness the remarkable ways these women have navigated the complexities of life— overcoming professional setbacks, battling personal demons, and breaking free from societal expectations. Their stories serve as beacons of hope, guiding us toward a deeper understanding of ourselves and the strength we all possess.

This book invites you to reflect on your own experiences and challenges, encouraging you to see fear not as a barrier, but as a stepping stone toward empowerment. In a world that often seeks to diminish our voices, *She Stands Strong* amplifies them, reminding us that we are not alone in our struggles.

Hanna Olivas

Founder and CEO of SHE RISES STUDIOS

https://www.linkedin.com/company/she-rises-studios/
https://www.facebook.com/sherisesstudios
https://www.instagram.com/sherisesstudios_llc/
www.SheRisesStudios.com

Author, Speaker, and Founder. Hanna was born and raised in Las Vegas, Nevada, and has paved her way to becoming one of the most influential women of 2022. Hanna is the co-founder of She Rises Studios and the founder of the Brave & Beautiful Blood Cancer Foundation. Her journey started in 2017 when she was first diagnosed with Multiple Myeloma, an incurable blood cancer. Now more than ever, her focus is to empower other women to become leaders because The Future is Female. She is currently traveling and speaking publicly to women to educate them on entrepreneurship, leadership, and owning the female power within.

A Journey Through Life's Perfect and Imperfect Storms

By Hanna Olivas

There comes a point in every woman's life when she looks in the mirror, sees the reflection staring back at her, and wonders, "How did I make it this far?" For some, the question is wrapped in gratitude, in awe of the strength that carried her through difficult times. For others, it's laden with exhaustion—battle scars from a life that hasn't always been kind. Regardless of the path that led to this moment, one truth remains: She is still standing.

I am no stranger to life's storms, both the perfect and the imperfect ones. The type of storms that sneak up on you out of nowhere, throwing you into a whirlwind you never saw coming, and the ones that you can feel brewing from miles away, inching closer and closer until they're impossible to ignore. Some of these storms I've weathered with grace, others I barely survived, but through it all, I've learned one thing—strength isn't something you find when everything is going right. Strength is what you discover when the world is falling apart.

This is my story. A story of strength, resilience, and perseverance. It's not always pretty, but it's real. It's honest. And most importantly, it's a testament to the unbreakable power that lives within each of us when we choose to stand strong through life's unexpected challenges.

The Calm Before the Storm

Like many women, I was raised with a set of expectations about what my life should look like. Society has a way of laying out a neat and tidy blueprint for women—be kind, work hard, get married, raise a family, and somehow balance it all with grace and ease. But life doesn't always follow the script.

I grew up surrounded by strong women. My grandmother and mother were the type of women who could take on the world with their bare hands and still find time to offer love and kindness to those who needed it most. They didn't have it easy—far from it—but they had this quiet resilience that I admired from a young age. Watching them, I believed that no matter what came my way, I could face it with the same strength and determination. But life, as it tends to do, had other plans.

In the early stages of adulthood, I thought I had it all figured out. I was filled with optimism and energy, ready to take on the world and build a life that would reflect all the dreams I had. I was married, I had children, and I was starting to build my career. On the surface, it seemed like everything was falling into place. But underneath, the pressure of juggling it all was mounting. As I struggled to balance being a wife, a mother, and a businesswoman, I could feel the cracks starting to form.

The First Storm Hits

Then came the first storm—one that tested me in ways I never expected. I was diagnosed with multiple myeloma, an aggressive form of blood cancer. In an instant, my world shifted. The certainty I had about my future disappeared, replaced with an overwhelming sense of fear and uncertainty. Cancer has a way of ripping the ground from beneath your feet, leaving you in a free fall, unsure of when or how you'll land.

I remember sitting in the doctor's office, hearing the words but not fully absorbing them. Cancer. How could this be happening? I was young, I was healthy, I had a family that needed me. But there it was, staring me in the face, a storm I couldn't outrun. It felt unfair, cruel even. For a long time, I didn't know how to process it. I was angry, I was scared, and I didn't know how I was going to survive—not just physically, but emotionally and mentally.

I went through all the stages of grief. I mourned the life I thought I was supposed to have, the life I had so carefully planned. I raged against the injustice of it all, wondering why this was happening to me and to my family. But in the midst of that turmoil, I made a decision: I was going to fight. I was going to stand strong, even when the storm was raging all around me.

It wasn't easy. There were days when I wanted to give up, when the pain—both physical and emotional—was too much to bear. But I found strength in my family, in my faith, and in the knowledge that I was not done yet. I still had so much to give, so much to fight for. And so, I fought. Not with perfection, but with perseverance.

The Imperfect Storms of Life

When people think of strength, they often picture someone standing tall, unyielding, in the face of adversity. But real strength—true strength—doesn't look like that. True strength is messy. It's raw. It's waking up every day and choosing to keep going, even when everything inside you is screaming to stop. It's crying in the shower because you don't want your kids to see you break, then drying off, putting on a smile, and getting on with the day. Strength is not the absence of fear or pain; it's moving forward despite them.

After my diagnosis, life didn't magically get easier. The storm didn't just pass. It lingered, hanging over my head like a dark cloud that I couldn't shake. But in the midst of that storm, I found a resilience within me that I didn't know existed. I learned that I could handle more than I ever thought possible. That I could endure the pain and the uncertainty, and still find moments of joy and gratitude. I learned that it's okay to not be okay, that asking for help doesn't make you weak, and that leaning on others is not a sign of failure.

Life is full of imperfect storms. Storms that we can't predict, can't prepare for, and can't avoid. But through each one, we have the choice to stand strong, to hold on to the things that matter most, and to keep moving forward. There is power in resilience, in knowing that no matter what life throws your way, you can survive it. You can thrive in the aftermath of destruction.

Choosing Strength Every Day

One of the greatest lessons I've learned on this journey is that strength is a choice. It's not something we are born with or something we acquire overnight. It's something we build, brick by brick, through every challenge, every heartbreak, every storm we endure. And the more we face, the stronger we become.

But choosing strength doesn't mean pretending that everything is okay when it's not. It doesn't mean putting on a brave face and pushing down your emotions. It means being honest with yourself about where you are, what you need, and how you're feeling. It means acknowledging the pain, the fear, the uncertainty, and still choosing to keep going.

There were days when I didn't feel strong at all. Days when I wanted to hide under the covers and let the world pass me by. But on those days, I reminded myself of my purpose. I thought of my children, my husband, my family, and the people I loved. I thought of the impact I still wanted to make in the world, the lives I still wanted to touch. And I got up. I chose to stand strong, not because I wasn't afraid, but because I knew that my story wasn't over yet.

The Power of Perseverance

One of the most important qualities I've learned to cultivate through my journey is perseverance. Life will test you. It will push you to your limits, stretch you beyond what you think you can handle, and force you to confront the parts of yourself that you'd rather ignore. But if you can persevere, if you can keep going even when it feels impossible, you will come out stronger on the other side.

Perseverance isn't about never falling. It's about getting back up every time you do. It's about believing in yourself, even when the odds are stacked against you. It's about trusting that no matter how bad things get, there is always a way through.

Standing Strong Through the Unexpected

As I continued on my journey through life's storms, I faced many unexpected challenges. Health scares, personal losses, financial struggles—each one tested my resolve in different ways. But through it all, I learned that strength isn't something you find when everything is going right. Strength is something you discover when the world feels like it's falling apart.

After my cancer diagnosis, there were many moments when I wondered if I would ever feel "normal" again. There's a certain innocence that is lost when you face a life-threatening illness. You can't unlearn the things you've learned about the fragility of life. But while the journey was painful, it was also transformative. I learned that standing strong doesn't mean being invincible. It means being vulnerable, open, and willing to keep moving forward, even when the path ahead is uncertain.

I also learned the power of community. As women, we often try to carry the weight of the world on our own shoulders. We don't want to burden others with our struggles, so we stay quiet and try to handle everything on our own. But there is incredible strength in leaning on others. Whether it's family, friends, or even strangers who show up in unexpected ways, the support of others can help you stand strong in moments when you feel like crumbling.

There were days when I felt like I couldn't do it anymore—days when the weight of my illness, my responsibilities as a mother, and the pressure of running my businesses felt overwhelming. But in those moments, I leaned on my tribe. I reached out to the women who had walked similar paths, the ones who had survived their own storms and were willing to walk alongside me through mine. Their strength became my strength, their resilience became my guide. And together, we stood strong.

Gratitude in the Midst of Chaos

One of the most surprising lessons I've learned through my journey is the importance of gratitude. It's easy to be grateful when everything is going well, but it's much harder to find gratitude in the midst of chaos and pain. But the truth is, gratitude is one of the most powerful tools we have for standing strong through life's storms.

When I was going through treatment for my cancer, there were days when I felt like I had nothing left to give. The physical toll of chemotherapy, the emotional exhaustion of fighting a disease that threatened my life—it all felt too heavy to bear. But in those moments, I began to practice gratitude. I started small, focusing on the little things—a beautiful sunset, a kind word from a friend, the sound of my children's laughter. Slowly but surely, those small moments of gratitude began to shift my perspective.

Gratitude doesn't make the storms go away, but it does change the way we experience them. When we focus on what we have, instead of what we've lost, we find strength in the midst of our pain. Gratitude reminds us that even in the darkest moments, there is still light to be found.

Finding Purpose in the Pain

One of the most profound lessons I've learned is that there is a purpose in our pain. When we face life's storms, it can be easy to get lost in the suffering, to feel like we are victims of circumstance. But I've come to believe that our pain can be a powerful catalyst for growth and transformation.

For me, the journey of standing strong through life's storms has been deeply connected to my purpose. After my cancer diagnosis, I felt a deep sense of calling to give back and to use my experience to help others who were facing similar battles. That's why I founded my nonprofit, Brave and Beautiful Blood Cancer, to support men, women, and children affected by blood cancers. We started with simple acts of kindness—care packages for patients undergoing treatment, toy drives for children, turkey and coat drives for local families affected by illness.

What began as a small way to give back has grown into a mission that fuels me every day. Through Brave and Beautiful Blood Cancer, we've been able to make a tangible difference in the lives of so many people in our community. We've created a space where people can find hope, support, and love in the midst of their storms. And in doing so, I've found healing in my own journey.

Giving has a way of shifting our focus from our own pain to the needs of others. It reminds us that we are not alone, that we are all connected, and that we have the power to make a difference, no matter how small. When we give from a place of love and gratitude, we create ripples of change that extend far beyond ourselves.

The Gift of Love and Kindness

If there's one thing I've learned through my journey, it's that love and kindness are the most powerful forces in the world. In the midst of life's storms, it can be easy to close ourselves off, to protect our hearts from further pain. But when we open ourselves up to love—when we choose kindness, even in the face of adversity—we create space for healing, connection, and transformation.

Love has carried me through my darkest moments. The love of my family, my friends, my community—it has been my anchor when the winds of life have threatened to pull me under. In return, I've learned the importance of giving love freely, without expectation or conditions.

Kindness is a gift we can all give, no matter our circumstances. It doesn't take much—a smile, a kind word, a small act of service—but its impact is immeasurable. In my own life, I've seen how simple acts of kindness can change the course of someone's day, and even their life. And in giving kindness, we receive it back tenfold.

Standing Strong for Ourselves and Others

As women, we often feel the pressure to be strong for everyone around us—our children, our partners, our friends, and our communities. We take on the weight of the world, often at the expense of our own well-being. But what I've learned through my journey is that standing strong doesn't mean carrying the burden alone. It means taking care of ourselves so that we can show up fully for the people we love.

Self-care is not selfish—it's essential. Whether it's taking time to rest, nourish our bodies, pursue our passions, or seek support when we need it, self-care is the foundation of strength. When we take care of ourselves, we are better able to weather life's storms and to support those around us.

Standing strong also means standing up for ourselves. It means setting boundaries, saying no when necessary, and prioritizing our own needs and desires. As women, we are often taught to put others first, to be nurturing and selfless. But true strength comes from honoring ourselves and our worth.

The Legacy of Strength

As I reflect on my journey, I am filled with a deep sense of gratitude for the lessons I've learned and the strength I've discovered along the way. Life's storms have not broken me; they have shaped me into the woman I am today—a woman who stands strong, not in spite of her struggles, but because of them.

I know that my journey is far from over. There will be more storms, challenges, and moments of uncertainty. But I also know that I have the strength to face whatever comes my way. More importantly, I know that I am not alone. There is a community of women—strong, resilient, powerful women—who are standing beside me, ready to face the storms together.

We are not defined by the storms we face, but by how we choose to stand through them. We are not victims of circumstance; we are warriors of resilience. And together, we can weather any storm.

In standing strong, we give others permission to do the same. We create a legacy of strength, resilience, and love that will carry on long after the storm has passed. And in the end, that is what matters most—not the storms we endured, but the way we stood strong through them.

A Final Word

To the woman reading this, know that you are stronger than you think. Life will throw storms your way, some that you can see coming, and others that will catch you off guard. But no matter what, you have the strength within you to stand strong.

You are not alone. You are part of a legacy of women who have weathered the storms before you, who have stood strong in the face of adversity, and who continue to rise, again and again. You are powerful, you are resilient, and you are capable of more than you can imagine.

So when the storm comes—and it will—stand tall. Stand strong. And know that you are not only surviving, but you are thriving. Your story is far from over.

Adriana Luna Carlos

Founder and CEO of SHE RISES STUDIOS & FENIX TV

https://www.linkedin.com/in/adriana-luna-carlos/
https://www.facebook.com/adrianalunacarlos
https://www.instagram.com/sherisesstudios_llc/
https://www.sherisesstudios.com/
https://fenixtv.app/

Adriana Luna Carlos is an accomplished web and graphic designer, author, and mentor with a passion for helping women succeed in life and business. With over 10 years of experience in graphic and web arts, Adriana has built a reputation as an innovative leader and entrepreneur. In 2020, she co-founded She Rises Studios, a multi-digital media company and publishing house that has helped countless clients achieve their branding and marketing goals. In 2023, she co-created FENIX TV, an online streaming platform that showcases stories of people breaking barriers, shattering stereotypes, and triumphing against the odds.

As an advocate for women's success, Adriana challenges her clients and mentees to strive for nothing less than excellence. She has a deep understanding of the insecurities and challenges that women often face in the business world and provides the guidance and resources needed to overcome them. Her success as a business leader and entrepreneur has made her a sought-after mentor and speaker at events around the world.

Through her work, Adriana has demonstrated a commitment to creating opportunities for women to succeed in business and life. Her passion for innovation, leadership, and women's empowerment has made her a respected figure in the business community, and her impact will undoubtedly continue to inspire and empower women for years to come.

Unbreakable

By Adriana Luna Carlos

There's a power within every woman that's as fierce as it is quiet. It's a power forged in the fires of adversity, one that builds up silently, layer by layer, as life tests and challenges us. I've come to understand that true strength is born not from the absence of hardship but from our ability to stand tall despite it, to face what life throws our way and say, "I am still here." This chapter is my reflection on resilience, on how I learned to stand strong, and on how each of us has the ability to rise from the ashes of our struggles stronger than before.

Growing up, I often felt like I had to be strong—sometimes because I wanted to be, other times because I had no choice. For 10 years, I lived with a heavy secret. My experience with sexual abuse from a family member left me feeling lost, small, and silenced. I was caught between confusion and fear, wondering how I could endure another day of pain but unsure how to make it stop. It took a strength I didn't know I had just to survive those years. But the day I decided to finally tell my family was the day I discovered a strength that changed me forever.

The scariest day of my life wasn't one of the days the abuse occurred; it was the day I decided to speak up about it. The thought of telling my family, of finally putting words to what I had endured for so long, was terrifying. I was flooded with doubt and fear, worried about what my words might do to my family and the upheaval that would follow. Yet, as afraid as I was, something inside of me knew that this was the moment to stand strong. Despite feeling like I might crumble under the weight of it all, I found the courage to open up, to release the pain I had carried alone for so many years.

In those moments of truth, I learned that real strength isn't about never being afraid; it's about moving forward even when fear is overwhelming.

Speaking up wasn't just about ending the abuse—it was about reclaiming my life, my voice, and my worth. And though it was the hardest thing I've ever done, it was also one of my most powerful acts of resilience.

My journey to resilience began long before I fully understood what it meant. Growing up, I learned the value of hard work and perseverance from my family. They lived by the principle, "We say what we mean, and we do what we say." But dealing with trauma changed everything I thought I knew about strength. My strength had to take on a new shape, one that allowed me to endure what felt unendurable and to stand tall even when I felt hollow inside.

Resilience doesn't mean we don't break; it means we learn to rebuild. In those moments of doubt and despair, I realized that resilience was something I would need to cultivate every day. It wasn't an achievement to check off or a destination to reach; it was a process—a journey of learning how to keep going when life felt impossibly heavy.

Resilience isn't about perfection. I've learned that it's okay to feel lost, to doubt, and to wonder how much more we can bear. There were days when I didn't know how I could face another moment, let alone another day. The trauma had affected my sense of self, leaving me questioning who I was and where I belonged. But in those moments of darkness, I discovered that standing strong doesn't mean never feeling weak. Sometimes, strength is simply refusing to give up, even when every part of you wants to.

I found healing in small steps, in moments of vulnerability that I learned to honor rather than hide. I allowed myself to be open about my pain, and in doing so, I found a community of support that lifted me when I felt low. Standing strong became less about being unbreakable and more about allowing myself to be whole, no matter how many pieces I felt I was in.

Resilience is not about never falling; it's about rising every single time we do. Life will bring us to our knees, not once, but many times. It's part of the human experience. But each fall is an opportunity to rise with even greater strength, to grow in ways we never thought possible. The moments when I felt most broken turned out to be the ones that taught me the most about myself. I learned that the cracks we carry do not weaken us; they allow the light of our experiences to shine through.

Each time I faced adversity, I discovered a new level of inner strength. I found a voice I didn't know I had, a determination that only grew with each setback. Rising after a fall is a choice we make every day, a commitment to ourselves to keep going, even when the road is hard. It's a reminder that we are not defined by what happens to us, but by how we choose to respond to it.

One of the greatest lessons I've learned on this journey is the power of standing strong together. We are not meant to walk this path alone. When we connect with others, we share not only our struggles but also our strength. We create a community of resilience, a support system that lifts us up when we feel weak and celebrates with us when we rise.

I found that sharing my story—my struggles, my triumphs, and my lessons—wasn't just healing for me; it also gave others permission to embrace their own strength. Each of us has a story that can inspire someone else, a truth that can give another person the courage to stand tall. Together, we become an unstoppable force, reminding each other of our resilience and capacity to overcome.

To every woman reading this, know that you are stronger than you think. There is a well of resilience within you that is deeper than any challenge you will ever face. Embrace it. Let go of the idea that strength means perfection, and instead, find power in your authenticity, in your willingness to rise after each fall, and in your choice to keep moving forward.

Resilience is a journey, one that we walk every day. It's the small acts of courage, the moments when we show up even when it's hard, that define us. Stand strong in your truth, knowing that every challenge you overcome is a testament to your strength. Let your story be a beacon of hope, a reminder that no matter how many times you fall, you have the power to rise.

Our journey to healing and resilience is ongoing. Embrace each step, each challenge, and each victory, knowing that you are building something unbreakable within yourself. You are a testament to the power of standing strong, and by sharing your light, you inspire others to find their own.

Wendy Broekx

Health, Fitness + Weight Loss Coach

https://www.facebook.com/wendy.broekx.9
https://www.instagram.com/wendy_broekx
https://www.wendybroekx.com/

CHALLENGE AGE, EMBRACE STRENGTH, LIVE WITH
PASSION—THIS IS THE LEGACY I CREATE.

Wendy is a Health and Fitness Coach with over 30 years of experience,
committed to transforming lives. She passionately guides women over
40, 50, and beyond to rediscover their inner strength, look amazing,
and feel radiant, powerful, and unstoppable.

As a Pro Bodybuilding Figure Athlete with Ms. Fitness Australia,
Wendy has trained celebrities like Claudia Schiffer and competed at
the highest levels.

Her fitness journey began with a love for sports like hockey and athletics,
leading her to become a certified Fitness Trainer in the late 1980s. Since
then, she has empowered countless others to achieve their goals.

Today, Wendy challenges the notion of age, proving that strength
knows no bounds. To all women: It's never too late to chase your
dreams and redefine strength. Age is just a number, enriched with
wisdom and power.

Rewriting My Story:
From Challenge to Champion

By Wendy Broekx

Embracing the Unknown

The morning air buzzed with nervous energy as I stood in front of the mirror, preparing to step on stage in a glitzy bikini and heels for the very first time.

My heart pounded with a mixture of excitement and fear, a potent blend of emotions that felt both thrilling and terrifying. At 48, I had achieved much in life, yet I was also a woman who had borne the weight of hidden traumas.

As I warmed up, I knew that this moment wasn't just about showcasing my body - it was about revealing the resilience that had brought me here and embracing the unknown with courage.

But to truly understand how I arrived here, poised and ready, you need to know where it all began.

The path to this moment was anything but straight. It was jagged and twisted, shaped by years of self-doubt, fear, and pain. My life had often felt like a series of chaotic turns, each one threatening to pull me under.

Growing up, I faced challenges that no child should ever have to endure. The trauma of sexual abuse and, at times, violence left me shattered and disconnected from the world, as if I were merely a spectator in my own life.

This deep wound followed me into adulthood, where it morphed into a pervasive sense of inadequacy. It wasn't just about what had been done to me; it was about the narrative that had been etched into my very being—a belief that I was somehow less, that I didn't deserve to chase my dreams, that my past would forever define me.

The Shadows of Childhood

We lived in a small country town, and though I was only three, I vividly remember the arguments, the shouting, and the constant fighting. The tension in the house was like a storm that never passed, always on the verge of breaking. Until one day, everything changed. I stood on the driveway, my tiny hand waving goodbye to my father. I was too young to understand what was really happening, too innocent to grasp that he was leaving for good and that our family would never be the same again.

Soon after, my mother, my two elder sisters, and I moved out to a farm, further away from the small town and even more isolated. But to me, an innocent young child, the farm seemed like a paradise. There were animals everywhere—cows in the fields, chickens clucking around the yard, and mice that ran rogue through the old farmhouse. Insects buzzed in the air, and there was always something to explore, something new to discover. The wide-open spaces felt like an endless playground, full of adventures waiting to be had. It was a child's dream, and I threw myself into it, blissfully unaware of the undercurrents swirling just beneath the surface.

But the idyllic days of exploration and innocence were short-lived. My mother soon invited her new boyfriend to move in with us, and the dynamics of our little world began to shift. At first, it seemed like nothing more than a new presence in the house. I didn't understand the implications and didn't see the shadows gathering around the edges of our new life. To me, he was just another adult in a world of adults who made the rules and decided what was normal.

Yet, there was something about him that I couldn't quite put my finger on, something unsettling in the way he watched us and interacted with us. As a child, I didn't have the words or the understanding to articulate what I felt. But looking back, I realise that those early feelings of discomfort were the first signs of the darkness that was slowly creeping into our lives.

Finding Strength in Sport

At the age of five, we settled back into the small town that had once been our home, but life was changing rapidly around me. My mother and her new partner had decided to get married, a union that brought with it a deeper sense of unease and uncertainty. The shadows that had begun to creep into our lives on the farm now seemed to envelop our world entirely, casting long, dark figures over the simplicity and innocence of childhood. Yet, amidst the growing darkness, I discovered a light that would guide me through some of my toughest years: the exhilarating world of sports.

In our family, hockey was more than just a game—it was a tradition. My mother and sisters were avid players, dedicating countless hours to the game and the club. From a very young age, I found myself dragged along to every game. Watching them play ignited something inside me, a spark of curiosity and excitement that was impossible to ignore. So, naturally, at five years old, I picked up a hockey stick and stepped onto the field for the first time.

It didn't take long for everyone to realise that I had a natural talent for the game. The moment I felt the rush of the wind against my face as I sprinted across the field, the adrenaline pumping through my veins as I maneuvered the ball past opponents, I knew I had found something special. I was fast, agile, and utterly captivated by the thrill of competition. Every game presented a new challenge, a new opportunity to push myself further, and I loved every minute of it.

School provided even more avenues to explore my blossoming athletic abilities. I consistently won sporting events, often outperforming girls twice my age and height. Whether it was running races or navigating obstacle courses, I threw myself into each event with unwavering enthusiasm. I remember in first grade when misbehaviour was punished by sending us out to the oval to run laps. While others groaned and dragged their feet, I relished the opportunity. To me, running wasn't a punishment—it was pure freedom. The steady rhythm of my feet against the ground, the fresh air filling my lungs, the open sky above—it all felt like an escape, a momentary release from the complexities of home life.

Hockey may have been my first love, but it certainly wasn't my only one. I dove headfirst into a multitude of sports, each offering its own form of solace and satisfaction. I excelled in athletics and swimming, mastering strokes and techniques with an ease that contradicted my age. Softball and tennis also became part of my repertoire, and I often found myself competing not just against my peers but against seniors, holding my own and earning their respect. Sports became my sanctuary, a place where I could channel my energy and focus, where the troubles of home faded into the background, overshadowed by the immediacy and intensity of the game.

By the age of nine, my dedication and skill in hockey had earned me a spot representing our state—a significant achievement that filled me with pride and a sense of purpose. Living in the country presented its own set of challenges, particularly when it came to attending regular training sessions in the city. To make it work, I was billeted out to a family willing to open their home to me. This meant attending a new school, adapting to different routines, and integrating into a family dynamic that was entirely unfamiliar. Despite being extremely shy and introverted, I adapted quickly. Sports had taught me resilience and adaptability, skills that extended beyond the field and into every aspect of my life.

I poured my heart and soul into every practice, every game, every training session. The accolades began to pile up—trophies, medals, sportsperson of the year awards. From the outside looking in, I was a competent and confident young girl, a rising star with a promising future in athletics. Sports provided me with a sense of identity and accomplishment that I desperately needed. They offered structure and discipline, as well as an outlet for the complex emotions swirling inside me.

Looking back, I realise that my immersion in sports was more than just a pursuit of passion—it was a means of survival. The field, the track, the pool—they were all places where I could assert control, where I could be strong and capable in ways that I couldn't always be at home. Each sprint, each goal, and each victory was a step away from the darkness that loomed over my personal life and a step toward a future where I could define myself on my own terms.

In those early years, sports became my refuge, my escape, and my salvation. They taught me lessons about perseverance, teamwork, and self-belief that would carry me through the many challenges to come.

Even as the shadows at home grew darker and more threatening, the light I found in sports continued to burn brightly, illuminating a path forward and instilling in me a resilience that would prove invaluable in the years ahead.

Surviving the Darkness

When I began high school, the subtle cracks in our family's foundation had split wide open, exposing the darkness beneath. What had once been an undercurrent of unease had erupted into something much darker and more sinister. It wasn't just me; my two older sisters were also caught in the web of sexual abuse that permeated our home. Our home had become a battlefield where violence and terror reigned.

There were things that happened during those years—things so traumatic that my mind has buried them, pushing them deep into the recesses of memory, never to be recalled. Yet, there are some things that refuse to stay hidden, memories that have haunted me in nightmares for years and have left scars that will never fully heal.

The abuse was relentless, a constant in my life that overshadowed everything else. It was as if I was living in a world that was detached from reality, where cries for help went unheard. Despite the increasing severity of the violence, no one seemed to listen, not even my own mother. The police were called numerous times, their flashing lights and uniformed presence a brief interruption in the horror that unfolded behind closed doors. But every time they left, nothing changed. It felt as though they, too, were sweeping the truth under the rug, unwilling or unable to confront the darkness that had taken hold of our home.

As my sisters grew older, they began to see an escape route, a way out of the nightmare that had become our daily existence. They moved out as soon as they could, seeking lives of their own, free from the oppression and fear that had become our norm. While I was happy for them, their departure left me alone to face the full brunt of the abuse. The isolation was suffocating, the knowledge that I was now the sole focus was a terrifying reality.

In the midst of this chaos, sports remained my sanctuary, the one area of my life where I could still exert some control. I continued to pour everything I had into my athletic pursuits, excelling in hockey and athletics. I represented my state with pride, bringing home trophies and awards that should have been symbols of triumph. But beneath the surface, my relationship with sport was becoming increasingly complicated. What had once been a source of joy and freedom was now becoming an addiction, a desperate attempt to maintain some semblance of control in a life that was spiralling out of it.

The abuse at home had twisted my perception of myself and my body. The constant need to be better, faster, and stronger was no longer just about winning—it was about survival. I began to struggle with body image, unable to reconcile the strength I displayed on the field with the weakness I felt at home. In my quest for control, I fell into the grip of Anorexia, a disorder that took root in my mind and body, feeding off my insecurities and the trauma that plagued me.

Looking back, it's clear that my eating disorder was another manifestation of my need for control, a way to assert power over at least one aspect of my life. In a world where everything felt chaotic and dangerous, controlling my body and what I put into it became an obsession. I deprived myself of food as a way to cope, as a way to feel like I had some say in what happened to me, even as everything else felt hopelessly out of my control.

Despite the physical toll the eating disorder took on me, I continued to excel in sports. I was winning athletic awards at school, still representing my state in hockey, still appearing on the outside as a competent, driven young woman. But inside, I was crumbling. The pressure I put on myself to succeed, coupled with the relentless abuse at home, was pushing me to the edge.

The darkness of those years is something that I still carry with me, even now. It's a part of my story that has shaped who I am, that has influenced the choices I've made and the paths I've taken. The resilience I displayed on the field was real, but it was born out of a need to survive, not just to win. The trophies and medals were not just achievements—they were lifelines, something to hold onto in a world that was otherwise unbearable.

As I moved through high school, the duality of my life became more pronounced. On one hand, I was the athlete, the competitor, the girl who could outrun and outplay anyone. I was popular and served as House Captain for several years. On the other, I was a young woman battling demons that no one could see, trying to hold herself together in a world that was constantly trying to tear her apart.

But even in those darkest moments, there was a part of me that refused to give in, that clung to the hope that one day, I would find a way out. The strength I developed through sport was not just physical—it was mental and emotional, a resilience that would eventually carry me through the most difficult years of my life.

And so, I continued to fight, both on and off the field, determined to survive, determined to overcome. It was this determination that would eventually lead me to where I am today, but the journey was far from over. The battles I fought during those years left deep scars, but they also forged a strength within me that would prove unbreakable.

Yet, amidst the growing turmoil at home, I found a glimmer of hope within the walls of my school. I was fortunate to have a teacher who saw something in me that others didn't—my PE teacher. He recognised my potential and pushed me to be my best, offering the support and encouragement that I so desperately needed. Physical Education quickly became the one subject where I excelled, where I felt confident and capable. It was the class I looked forward to, the one place where I could channel my energy into something positive and feel a sense of accomplishment.

A New Path Begins

In my final year, Year 12, I was introduced to the world of aerobics, and it was as if a new door had opened for me. The movement, the energy—I fell in love instantly. For the first time, I felt a clear sense of direction, a goal that I could focus on despite the chaos that still enveloped my life. I knew then that I wanted to become an aerobics instructor, and from that moment on, I was determined to make it happen. The idea of leading others, of helping them find the same joy in movement that I did, became a source of hope, a future I could cling to when everything else was so dark and uncertain.

Despite the ongoing turmoil at home, I found solace in spending time with my father or with my sisters, who were both married by then. Their homes became my refuge, safe havens where I could escape the constant tension and fear. My father, however, seemed either oblivious to or unwilling to confront the reality of what was happening, leaving me to navigate those dark waters largely on my own.

But even those sanctuaries were not immune to the pressures of life. By the time I had finished school, my eldest sister's marriage had ended in divorce. It was a painful time for her, but in that moment of upheaval, she saw an opportunity to rescue me from the toxic environment I had grown up in. She decided to move to the city, and she took me with her, offering me the chance to start a new life away from the shadows of our past.

Moving to the city was like stepping into a whole new world. My sister and I found a place to live, and as fate would have it, our new home was close to a gym. For me, it was like discovering a piece of heaven on earth. Although I was still young, extremely skinny, and painfully shy, I knew I had to join. There was something about the gym that called to me, a promise of transformation and growth that I couldn't resist. Little did I know that this decision—to walk through those gym doors—would change the trajectory of my life forever.

A New Beginning

The gym became my new sanctuary. Every session was a step away from the past, and toward the life, I wanted to create for myself. The journey was just beginning, but already, I could feel the power of that decision shaping the course of my destiny.

I was extremely fortunate and perhaps fate was at play again—that I was taken in by the owners of the gym. From the moment I walked through those doors, they saw something in me, a potential that others had overlooked. They wanted to help, to nurture that potential, and before I knew it, I was employed, and my journey to becoming an aerobics instructor was officially underway. But they were more than just my employers—they became my best friends, my mentors, and my family. Their guidance extended far beyond the confines of the gym. They taught me, supported me, and inspired me in ways I had never imagined—still to this very day.

Their influence on my life was profound, and the bond we formed was something truly special. They weren't just guiding me professionally; they were helping me grow as a person, showing me the world beyond what I had known, and helping me to see my own worth. The lessons they imparted, the wisdom they shared, and the unwavering belief they had in me became the foundation upon which I began to build a new life. They saw the potential in me when I struggled to see it myself, and their faith never wavered.

Even now, as I reflect on those early days, I realise how pivotal their presence was in shaping the course of my life. The guidance, support, and love they offered weren't just temporary boosts—they have been lasting influences that continue to inspire me to this very day. They were, and continue to be, my best friends, my mentors, and my family. Their impact on my life is something I carry with me always, reminding me of how far I've come and how much further I can go.

I learned so much under their wing. They opened my eyes to the world and the world of fitness and nutrition, where I absorbed every bit of knowledge I could. I became good at what I did, and for the first time, I started to grow as a person. I was beginning to find my voice, my confidence, and a sense of purpose. But despite the progress, there were still so many issues I couldn't push past, no matter how hard they tried to help me.

I had always been an overachiever, driven by a relentless desire to be the best at everything I did. This drive, however, was also fueled by the body image issues that had plagued me for years. It often felt like the outcome I so desperately wanted—a sense of peace and self-acceptance—was always just out of reach, teasing me, playing hard to get. I pushed myself hard, engaging in long daily runs, enduring bike rides, triathlons, and teaching class after class, with the hope that one of them would finally help me break through. But every time, it felt like I was hitting a brick wall.

My relationship with food continued to be a battleground, with my taste buds often suffering the consequences. I had moments of triumph, those exhilarating "YES!" moments when it seemed like I had finally found the answer. But they were fleeting, never sticking around long enough for me to feel like I had truly conquered the barriers that held me back. It was like being trapped in a never-ending cycle of frustration, where the goal was always just out of reach.

A Transformative Loss

But in 2014, everything changed with the profound and heartbreaking loss of my eldest sister to breast cancer and, within two years, my middle sister to bowel cancer. It was a pivotal moment that shattered my world and transformed my approach to life and well-being. Their deaths were a stark reminder of the fragility of life and the importance of health beyond the physical. I realised that true well-being required more than just a fit body; it required nurturing resilience and emotional strength, something I had been neglecting for far too long.

This devastating loss sparked a new chapter in my life, one where I began to emphasise sustainability over short-term gains and genuine well-being over mere appearance. I came to understand that real health is about balance, about nurturing the mind and soul as much as the body. This was a lesson learned at great personal cost, but it redefined my journey moving forward. No longer was I simply chasing after the perfect body or the latest fitness trend; I was striving for a deeper, more meaningful sense of health—one that honoured both my physical and emotional needs.

But this realisation also took my lifelong commitment to helping others in fitness to an entirely new level. After a deep dive into scientific research, debunking long-held myths, and embracing cutting-edge, evidence-based approaches, I emerged with insights that challenge and redefine conventional health and fitness paradigms. My mission became clearer and more urgent: to guide women on a transformative journey to get in the best shape of their lives, to build strength, boost confidence, and truly own their power.

This wasn't just about teaching fitness anymore; it was about leading a revolution in how women approach their health and well-being. I wanted to empower women to break free from outdated, restrictive norms and embrace a holistic, sustainable approach to health that honours their unique needs and goals. My work became a fusion of passion and purpose, driven by the desire to help women not just survive, but thrive—physically, mentally, and emotionally.

This mission continues to drive me today, as I work to inspire and uplift women on their own paths to wellness. The insights I've gained, the strategies I've developed, and the passion I bring to my work are all part of a larger vision—a vision where every woman can truly own her power and live her life with strength, confidence, and purpose.

Embracing the Challenge

But even as I dedicated myself to helping others, I yearned for a challenge of my own—something that would push me beyond my limits and, hopefully, help me to finally become a better, more confident person. This drive was ingrained in me, perhaps stemming from my childhood, where resilience was a necessity. It was at the age of 48 that my best friend and mentor suggested I enter a bodybuilding competition. The idea both excited and terrified me. It was a daunting prospect, and I have to admit, I nearly gave up multiple times because it was so confronting and challenging. I felt awkward, exposed, and very self-conscious. But the thought of backing out filled me with even greater fear—fear of embarrassment, shame, and regret.

On the day of the competition, I was nervous as hell. My heart raced, my hands shook, and I nearly passed out from the anxiety. But I got up on that stage, and the moment I did, something inside me shifted. It was electrifying and empowering in a way I had never experienced before. That first step onto the stage was more than just a personal victory; it was the start of another new chapter in my life.

After six years of competing, I earned my Professional Athlete Award with Ms. Fitness Australia. Nearly 100 medals and over 30 trophies now stand as a testament to my dedication, perseverance, and success. Since the age of 15, I have dreamed of being a Fitness Instructor, and I have spent my entire life working in the health and fitness industry. But this accomplishment, this journey into bodybuilding, brought my passion to a whole new level.

Empowering Others

Today, at 56, I mentor women over 40 to get fit and strong, to look fabulous, to be healthy, and to develop kickass confidence—no matter their size or shape—whether it's just for life or to step on stage. That's what I always wanted and struggled so long to achieve. This isn't just a career for me; it's my life, my passion, my everything.

My experience, like turning the pages of a deeply personal journal, has been both a revelation and a reassurance. It confirmed that facing my fears and embracing challenges head-on could lead to transformative growth and a profound sense of fulfillment.

Ultimately, I share my story to leave a legacy that impacts and reshapes how we, as women, view our capabilities and futures. It's about showing that with courage, resilience, and a little bit of grit, transformation and fulfillment are always within reach, no matter where we start.

We're not just moving through life; we're sculpting a masterpiece of experiences, each one testifying to our incredible capacity to thrive. Every challenge, every triumph, and even every setback contributes to the person we become.

This journey underscores the importance of mentoring and supporting each other, demonstrating that our experiences are not just personal victories but opportunities to empower and inspire those around us. Through our shared stories and collective strength, we create a powerful ripple effect that touches lives far beyond our own.

So, to all the women out there, here's the truth: You are extraordinary. No medal or accolade could ever truly represent the courage, determination, and spirit you carry within. The victories we don't always see—the quiet battles fought in the shadows, the moments of perseverance when no one is watching—are incredibly important because they show our resilience and grace under pressure. These are the true measures of our strength.

Our worth is immeasurable. Each of us has the power to sculpt our lives into something beautiful, to create a legacy of strength, kindness, and empowerment. Let's continue to lift each other up, to celebrate not just the visible achievements but also the invisible battles that define our journey. Together, we can embrace our full potential and inspire others to do the same.

And remember, *never give up on anyone; **especially yourself!***

Wendy xo

Caroline Guirgis

Founder of Connection 4 Ever, LLC

https://www.linkedin.com/in/caroline-guirgis-2496956/
https://www.facebook.com/profile.php?id=61552946417100
https://www.instagram.com/carolineguirgis/
https://connectionforever.com/

Caroline, an accomplished author, philanthropist, and dynamic public speaker, has significantly contributed to literature and society. With six published books, her work blends insightful narratives with compelling advocacy for change. Caroline founded a nonprofit organization supporting those in hardship, achieving milestosnes like building a library and a school in Uganda and developing rehabilitation programs for people with an addiction. She also established a mother-daughter organization focused on philanthropy, fostering a spirit of giving and volunteerism. She shares her journey and insights globally as a public speaker, inspiring others to pursue growth. Her roles as a mother and wife enrich her perspectives on love, responsibility, and connection. Caroline is driven by a passion to connect with people and empower them, embodying compassion and dedication in every aspect of her life.

My Story of Strength and Resilience

By Caroline Guirgis

Strength and resilience are often discussed together, but they stem from distinct characteristics within an individual's personality and behavior, each playing a crucial role in facing adversity and life challenges. Strength can be viewed as the intrinsic capability to endure adverse conditions or to exert force against opposing forces. It is a measure of one's grit and can be both physical and mental. In a psychological context, strength may manifest as the ability to make tough decisions, stand firm in one's beliefs, or support others despite personal hardships.

Resilience, on the other hand, plays a crucial role in personal growth and development. It refers more specifically to the capacity to recover quickly from difficulties. The elasticity of the mind and spirit allows a person to rebound from setbacks, adapt to change, and keep going in the face of adversity. Resilient individuals are not just strong now; they can maintain their core purpose and integrity amid unforeseen shocks and stresses.

While strength and resilience often overlap, they are not identical, especially when facing adversity. Strength is about withstanding pressure, holding ground, or even pushing forward. It's the emotional and physical force one can summon in a moment of need. Resilience, on the other hand, is more about the journey of recovery and growth—how one can absorb an impact, process the experience, and come out the other side, perhaps altered but unbroken. A person might be strong enough to endure pain or withstand an immediate crisis, like lifting a heavy weight or facing a sudden, tragic event. However, resilience is demonstrated over time. It is evident when someone can go through a period of stress or loss and find their way back to a state of emotional and psychological stability.

The critical difference lies in their temporal aspects and overall impact on a person's life trajectory. Strength may help someone confront a formidable challenge or carry an impossible burden. Yet, without resilience, this same individual might struggle to recover from the toll that the challenge or burden takes on their well-being. Resilience requires more than sheer strength. It involves adaptability, learning, and growth. It's about enduring a situation and transforming the experience into something constructive or at least recoverable. Resilient individuals often use their experiences as stepping stones, learning from each situation and integrating these lessons into their lives to improve their future responses. While they can be described separately, strength and resilience often intertwine and reinforce each other. Being decisive can provide the foundation required to develop resilience. Conversely, recovery and growth (resilience) can build inner strength. For example, the emotional strength to face adversity head-on can lead to quicker recovery. In contrast, recovering and learning from adversity can enhance mental strength and fortitude.

Strength and resilience are vital in life's dynamic and often challenging environment. Strength provides the immediate response to crisis and challenge, offering the fortitude needed to face adversity. Meanwhile, resilience allows individuals to navigate these challenges, learn from them, and emerge ready to face new challenges. Both qualities are complementary and essential for a balanced, adaptive, and fulfilling life. The most effective individuals harness both, using their strength to manage the immediate impacts of life's challenges while drawing on their resilience to adapt and thrive in the long term.

From a young age, I recognized my inner strength, which manifested in my responsibilities, such as caring for my younger siblings. I was their guardian, ensuring their safety as we walked to and from school, and I oversaw the daily routines at home. With our parents working long hours, ensuring everything ran smoothly fell to me, and I embraced this role with a sense of duty and resilience. This early assumption of responsibility honed my understanding of maturity beyond what was typical for a child my age. Each morning, I would ensure that my siblings were prepared for school—lunches packed, shoes tied, and backpacks ready. After school, the house became my domain, where I managed homework supervision, coordinated playtime, and sometimes, with the careful focus of a novice chef, prepared dinner. There were many tasks and significant responsibilities. Still, through this, I developed a pragmatic approach to problem-solving and an ability to stay calm under pressure—qualities that laid a strong foundation for leadership in my later life.

My role in my siblings' lives went beyond mere caretakers; I was their confidant and protector, a steady presence in a world that often felt chaotic due to our parents' absence. This dynamic fostered a deep bond between us rooted in trust and mutual reliance. It taught me the importance of compassion and empathy from a young age. As we faced life's minor challenges together, from scraped knees to schoolyard disputes, I learned not only how to lead but also how to listen and respond to the needs of others, skills that proved invaluable throughout my life. Though others might have felt overwhelmed by such responsibilities, for me, they were the very foundation of the strength I was building over the years. The demands increased during the summer months when school was out, and the days stretched long and complete. It required great energy and endurance to keep up with my active siblings, ensure their safety, and find ways to keep them engaged and content. I was too young to grasp the significance of these experiences at the time entirely, yet they quietly sculpted within me a robust resilience and a profound capacity for leadership.

Unbeknownst to me, each challenge faced and each obstacle overcome during those formative years contributed to a reservoir of inner strength. Whether it was resolving conflicts between siblings, managing the household budget, or finding creative ways to solve the myriad daily problems that arose, these experiences were invaluable. They prepared me for the complexities of adult life and instilled in me a deep-seated belief in my capabilities. Before I even understood the concept of personal growth, I was living it—building layers of strength and resilience that would support and guide me throughout my life.

The accurate measure of strength and resilience often reveals itself in the face of significant adversity. My greatest test arrived in 1988, a year that would forever alter my understanding of my capabilities. Until then, my responsibilities had seemed immense, yet they paled compared to the profound challenge that year. This event thrust me into a new realm of emotional and practical trials. In the immediate aftermath, I questioned my strength; the shock and grief were overwhelming, undercutting the very sense of stability and control I had cultivated over the years. It was a stark confrontation with my vulnerability, a feeling that perhaps I was not as unshakeable as I had believed. Yet, as time passed and I navigated through the complex process of grief and the reorganization of our family life, I began to see that strength is not just about steadfastness in the face of routine challenges but also about the ability to endure and adapt when life takes unforeseen turns.

Perhaps more importantly, this period taught me about the nature of resilience, which is not simply about bouncing back quickly or with ease but about pushing through even when recovery feels impossible. Resilience manifested in my ability to wake up each day and face the realities of a different world. This was resilience's most authentic form—quiet, gradual, and profoundly transformative. Thus, while I initially doubted my strength, I emerged with a clearer understanding that I was indeed strong, perhaps in ways I hadn't recognized before.

The journey through grief, hardship, and resilience is profoundly personal and universally relatable. My life has been a testament to the human spirit's ability to endure and evolve through immense difficulty. This narrative begins on a day that etched a permanent mark of sorrow and transformation in my life—the day I lost my father to a massive heart attack in 1988. I was 19 when the world should have been wide open to me, but instead, I found it abruptly constricted by the overwhelming weight of loss. My father's sudden departure was a sharp, brutal introduction to adult realities. The subsequent emotional turmoil wasn't mine to bear alone; the ripple effects touched every member of our family, particularly my brother, John. John did not merely grieve; he plummeted into the depths of despair, turning to drugs as a refuge from his pain. Watching his descent was like being forced to relive the trauma of our father's death every day, each moment hoping for redemption, each moment sinking further into collective misery. Those ten years were a relentless test of my spirit and determination as I fought desperately to pull him back from the brink.

Miraculously, hope flickered through the darkness when John found solace in the gospel. It was as if he had been reborn into a world of possibility and service. He transformed his anguish into a source of strength, becoming a pastor and dedicating his life to helping others. His journey from the depths of addiction to the heights of spiritual leadership was a profound testament to the possibility of redemption and renewal. Yet, just as this new chapter began to write itself, it was abruptly and tragically cut short by a fatal car accident in 2005. Reeling from John's death, I confronted my battle as my ulcerative colitis worsened, demanding more from me physically and emotionally than I ever imagined possible. At the same time, a fire ravaged our family home, uprooting us and adding to the already chaotic tapestry of our lives. Amid these crises, I grappled with my daughters' struggles—each revealing her battles with life's complexities. My role as a mother was tested as I faced the heart-wrenching reality that despite my best efforts, I couldn't solve all their problems.

Compounding these challenges were the growing strains in my marriage. The idyllic union I had envisioned seemed to crumble under the pressures of life's relentless trials. I had envisioned myself as a pillar of strength and stability for my family, but I questioned my efficacy and purpose. Despite the seemingly endless nights, I refused to succumb to despair. I discovered a reservoir of unyielding strength within—a spirit that refused to be quelled by life's relentless storms. I turned more deeply to my faith, finding Jesus' solace and a powerful ally in my quest for peace and understanding. Through my faith, I began to see the losses and challenges not as mere punishments but as part of a larger, divine tapestry meant to teach and transform. I learned to accept my father's death as part of a more excellent plan, John's addiction and subsequent redemption as a journey that shaped him into a beacon for others, and my imperfections as opportunities for growth and humility.

Armed with these revelations, I dedicated myself to rebuilding and strengthening the relationships with my daughters. I adopted a new approach, focusing on listening more and speaking less, fostering an environment where my daughters could thrive on their terms. In my marriage, I shifted from trying to mold my husband to embracing our differences and working together to forge a path forward based on mutual respect and understanding.

This journey has been neither simple nor pain-free, but it has been vibrant with lessons learned and wisdom gained. To those facing their trials, know this: resilience is not an inherent trait, but a skill honed through adversity. Embrace your vulnerabilities, seek meaning in your trials, and never underestimate the power of faith and hope. Life's challenges, while daunting, are also what defines us—they are our most profound teachers. Today, as I reflect on my path, the pain endured, and the joy discovered, I am grateful for every twist and turn. These experiences have shaped me into the person I am today and given me a wealth of insight and compassion that I hope can inspire and support others in their journeys.

Several nuggets of wisdom have emerged from the trials and tribulations of my life's journey that may help others navigate their challenging paths. Here are some insights gleaned from enduring loss, battling family crises, and finding strength through faith and resilience:

1. Embrace Vulnerability as a Source of Strength: Often, we view vulnerability as a weakness, but opening up about our struggles allows us to connect deeply with others and find support in our communities. In our most vulnerable moments, we can also be the most open to change and growth.

2. Seek Purpose in Pain: Every hardship carries a lesson. While seeing the bigger picture amid suffering is often difficult, looking for a purpose in pain can provide a pathway out of despair. Whether using personal experiences to help others or simply growing in compassion and understanding, finding meaning in misfortune can transform suffering into a source of strength.

3. Cultivate Spiritual Resilience: My faith has been a bedrock, providing comfort and guidance in times of chaos. Whatever your spiritual beliefs, developing a spiritual practice can offer a sense of stability and hope. It's about connecting to something greater than oneself, which can be profoundly grounding.

4. Acceptance and Letting Go: Accepting what cannot be changed is crucial for mental and emotional well-being. This does not mean giving up hope but instead recognizing the limits of our control. Letting go of past hurts and focusing on what can be changed helps move forward.

5. Invest in Honest Communication: Relationships thrive on transparency and understanding. Taking the time to listen and

communicate with empathy truly can resolve conflicts and build stronger bonds. Speaking and listening profoundly is essential, allowing others the space to express themselves.

6. Practice Patience and Persistence: Change and healing often take time. Being patient with oneself and with others during difficult times is vital. Persistence and patience can lead to unexpected and fulfilling outcomes even when the situation initially seems intractable.

7. Draw on Community Support: No one is an island. In times of need, leaning on community resources, whether family, friends, faith groups, or professional help, can provide additional support and perspective crucial for overcoming adversity.

8. Lead with Compassion and Forgiveness: Extend compassion to yourself and others. Forgiving oneself for perceived failures and forgiving others for their faults can liberate a tremendous amount of energy that can be redirected toward constructive healing.

9. Nurture Self-awareness: Regular introspection can help one better understand one's thoughts and emotions, leading to better decision-making and personal growth. Self-awareness is crucial in identifying the roots of issues and effectively addressing them.

10. Never Stop Learning from Life: Every experience, good or bad, brings knowledge and an opportunity to grow. Staying open to learning from each situation enhances our wisdom and equips us better for future challenges.

As we draw this chapter to a close, I offer you words of hope and encouragement. Life's journey is fraught with unexpected challenges and hardships, each with the potential to test our limits in ways we might never anticipate. Yet, precisely through these trials, the depth of our strength and resilience is revealed and refined. I urge you to embrace each difficulty as an opportunity to discover and nurture your capacities for endurance and recovery. Remember, strength does not manifest through an absence of vulnerability; instead, it is realized when we confront our weaknesses and persevere. Resilience is not about a swift return to normalcy after a setback but about the gradual process of healing and growth that follows. Seek strength in steadfastness and the courage to face the unknown. Cultivate resilience not merely as a return to form but as a transformation—a reinvigoration of spirit from having walked through fire and emerged, not unscathed, but undeniably stronger. Let these experiences illuminate your path, guiding you to a life marked not by the absence of hardship but by your remarkable ability to overcome it.

Hold onto hope, for the beacon shines during the darkest times, guiding you back to strength and resilience. And as you journey forward, remember that these qualities are not just to be discovered during trials but also nurtured in moments of peace, preparing you for whatever lies ahead. May you find in your story, as I have in mine, a continual source of strength and an unyielding resolve to emerge ever-resilient. By sharing these insights, I hope to offer some guidance to those who may be struggling. Remember, resilience is not about never faltering—it's about rising each time we fall, learning from each setback, and continuing forward with an enriched understanding and renewed purpose.

Sade Jenkins

Her Mom Story & Mom Chat Show
Podcaster & Storyteller

https://www.linkedin.com/in/sade-jenkins-/
https://www.facebook.com/sade.jenkins.31
https://www.sadejenkins.com/

Sade Jenkins is an advocate for moms reconnecting with their happiness after motherhood. She has helped other moms by sharing her journey through the highs and lows of being a mother. She is determined to shift the silence and embarrassment of not being the perfect mom into embracing your growth through the journey.

Your Story Is Still Being Written

By Sade Jenkins

The interesting thing about life is that one minute, you can feel like you're on top of a mountain, and with the blink of an eye, you're stuck in the valley.

If you would've told the little girl version of me that your dream of being a mom is going to break you one day, I'm pretty sure she wouldn't believe you. As a child, I always dreamed of having an amazing career and being a mother. I dreamed about the way my child would look, her laugh and cute little smile. I desired to experience the fullness of all the things that came with motherhood. Hearing my child call me mom. Cooking everything under the sun.

So, when I had my first child, I was over the moon in love with this beautiful baby boy of mine. He was healthy, beautiful, and officially mine. I finally was experiencing everything I dreamed of: having a husband and my first child. The only thing that was missing was having my family around me every day.

Growing up in the South, I experienced everyone knowing everyone. The majority of my family lived in Arkansas. Every day, family and friends drop by to say "Hey" or drop something off from their garden. Being in that environment, you experience lots of laughter, loud talking, and, of course, amazing food. In my hometown, we took care of each other. There was never a moment where I didn't feel loved.

After having my first son, my husband and I moved to our first duty station in Georgia. Being a country girl, I felt right at home with the location. Nothing like the smell of the country air and beautiful trees everywhere. The distance from everyone wasn't easy. No family. No friends. I knew that I wanted our child to have great memories, just like I did as a child. To feel loved and cared for and to be filled with lots of happiness.

So, with time, Georgia grew on me. The amazing food and southern hospitality made it easier. Things were getting better when we finally moved into our first home on base and found an amazing church home. After my family came to visit, I started to feel at home.

A year later, I started gaining weight and feeling lightheaded. I found out I was pregnant with our second child. Immediately, we were so excited. We started picking out names and trying to guess his or her name. We knew the baby was going to be a winter baby, which was so exciting. Around that time, we experienced snow for the first time. Of course, we ran outside to build probably the ugliest snowman ever, but we didn't care. That night was so exciting because it was our son's first time experiencing snow. He was so adorable running around with his furry dog coat. That same night went from exciting and beautiful to my worst nightmare.

My son couldn't sleep well that night, so I had him sleep next to me. For some reason, that night, he was tossing and turning a lot. His leg came towards me and kicked me in the stomach. In that moment, it was like everything stood still. It felt like my mind and body were separated for a moment. All I could do was walk slowly to the bathroom, and I started to pray. I prayed harder than I had ever prayed in my life that my baby was okay. I started to feel a slight pain going across my stomach. All I felt was panic and fear of the unknown. I placed my hands on my stomach and started to sing to my stomach. I sat on the floor singing "You Are My Sunshine" over and over, hoping that my body would calm. I walked slowly to my phone to call the emergency line, hoping that they would give me some reassurance that my baby was okay. All I heard them say was that it was a waiting game. I felt so guilty, helpless, and scared. I cried all night. I begged God to save my baby.

I tried so hard to have faith, but doubt kept creeping in. We went to the emergency room to see if they could give us any answers. They told me that because I was so early and starting to bleed, the baby may not make it. Later that day, I went to the bathroom, and my body fully miscarried. I fell to the floor, screaming and asking God why. Why my baby? Why couldn't he save my baby? Everything in me felt so broken. I felt like my body had failed me. My husband and I really struggled with the loss of our unborn child.

A few weeks later, I started to develop sharp pains on the sides of my pelvis. This led to me having issues with walking, sleeping, and carrying our son. For months, I was in and out of the doctor's office and hospitals being examined. For a while, no one had any answers. I knew something was wrong because my periods were so painful. Every time I experienced ovulation, I would experience a burst of pain throughout the sides of my body. Something had to change because I was miserable.

I decided that I was going to find someone to help me. I stayed up late researching every doctor that I could find. I finally came across a practice that specialized in pelvic health. Something in me felt like this was the answer to my prayers. The next day, my nerves were all over the place. I finally had an appointment that could potentially tell me the truth about my health.

When they called my name, it felt like my stomach dropped. I walked to the back, and they did an ultrasound. During the examination, I kept watching everyone's face to look for any signs of concern. Immediately after the ultrasound, they showed me a large cyst on my ovaries. The doctor made light of it and said that there was nothing to be concerned about. That this happens all the time, and it should go away. Something about the words "should go away" didn't sit right with me. I kept telling the man that I was in a lot of pain and that I was concerned. He didn't take it seriously, so I took my situation to someone else to investigate it further.

I was so frustrated because here I am back at square one. I just wanted to know why this was happening and what I could do to feel like myself again. I didn't want a pill that was only going to patch the pain. I wanted the full truth about my health. I started back on my research for another doctor. This time I wanted someone that has the same lady parts as me. I needed someone who understood the woman's body because they were a woman as well. I found another doctor who specialized in pelvic health. This time I felt so unsure if this would be worth the visit. I went back, and they did an ultrasound. The interesting thing about this time was that the one cyst was now ten to fifteen cysts on both ovaries. She just kept moving around, finding more and more cysts in my body. After the examination, she took my blood. I sat there scared of what all those cysts on my ovaries meant. Was it cancer? Would I need surgery?

She came back to the room with my results. I was diagnosed with a rare case of PCOS. My case was rare because I still could have kids. She explained that most women who have PCOS have struggles with fertility. I had what they call the string of pearls, which is when you develop small cysts around your ovaries. The problem with this is that it causes hormonal imbalance. She felt that the miscarriage and my first C-section may have made it worse. She wanted to start the process of creating a treatment plan to see how my body responds. First, we tried birth control, and that was horrible. I was constantly sick from the pills. Next, we tried pills to help with shrinking the cysts and a pill to balance my hormones. Baby, when I tell you that pill to balance my hormones wore me out. One of the side effects was temporary menopause systems. Oh, my goodness! I felt like my body was on fire one minute, and the next minute I was cold. I was all over the place. That was the longest week of my life. After taking the hormonal pill, I was able to just take the cysts shrinking pill. Something was off still. My periods were still so painful. Every period kept me stuck in bed. She examined me again to find that I had what was called endometriosis. Being the person that I am, I panicked and started doing research. I instantly became afraid that my dream of being a mom again was slowly fading. Between the PCOS and now endometriosis, I started to question how it would ever happen again. She told me not to give up and that we would figure this out together. After looking at my ultrasound again, she decided that the best route would be to have a surgery called laparoscopic to remove the tissue and cysts. I did all the things that she asked me to do to prepare for the big day. They removed all the cysts and tissue. She said everything looked good. If we wanted to try again for another child, we could. It might be a long journey, but it was possible.

That was all I needed to hear was that it was possible. We were willing to take that challenge. I made another appointment to tell her that we were ready. We created a plan for me to continue taking my medicine at a low dosage, eat healthy and work out frequently. She told me that if I stick to that plan, my cysts will continue to shrink, and I will experience low pain, if any at all.

Talk about filled with excitement. With all that excitement, I kept hearing those words that it may take two years or more to have another child. As time went by, I kept reminding myself that it would happen in God's time, not mine. I decided to stop focusing on when and just enjoy the journey of feeling like me again. Time went by, and my son was getting so big. I still wasn't feeling any pain anymore. I felt the best that I had felt in a long time. I noticed that I was starting to crave weird things like plain corn flakes with strawberry sauce, nuts, butter, and sugar. This was not my normal at all. What really caught my attention was when I started craving peanut butter. To some, that may not sound weird, but for me, that is weird because I have a sensitivity to it. My body normally reacts when I eat it. For some reason, that day, I couldn't fight my craving for it, and I made a whole batch of peanut butter cookies. Yes, I ate every single crumb. Surprisingly, I had no reaction. That was an immediate red flag! Am I pregnant?

I made an appointment with my doctor to get blood work. As I sat there waiting for the news, all I could think about was that it had only been two months since the surgery. She came back, looking at me in shock. You guessed right, I was pregnant. All I could do was sit there in shock with tears coming down my face of joy. I walked outside to my husband, looking at me with so much hope and curiosity in his eyes. All I could do was scream, "Yes, yes, I am pregnant!" We both just sat there in the car, excited and shocked. God showed up and showed out with this one. My doctor told me that we would create a plan to keep me and the baby healthy. Everything felt amazing. I felt no pain, and our baby was growing perfectly. After every appointment, I felt so excited with small amounts of fear. Fear that I would miscarry again. Fear that my body wouldn't be able to handle another pregnancy. To calm those thoughts, I made myself find things that I enjoyed, like cooking, playing with my son, and reading books. Of course, my top favorite was lying down and cooking new recipes so I could enjoy every bite. The bonus about the pregnancy was that my little prince was a foodie as well. We both did a happy dance when it was time to eat.

Finally, January was here, and I had our baby boy. Seeing his little face just made everything that we went through worth it. Holding him sent a rush of emotions. I felt joy, but more than anything, I felt blessed. Like God really showed up and showed out for my family.

All of those moments taught me to never doubt God and to always listen to my gut. If you feel that something is wrong, trust that gut feeling. Don't let up on figuring out what is wrong. You deserve to know what is wrong. I also learned that it is important to have the right doctor to advocate for you and your health. It is so important to have a doctor who listens to your concerns and is willing to look further into the health issue. My doctor advocated for me and the longevity of my health. She went over and beyond to make sure that I was educated, cared for, and most of all, that I was fully healthy.

What I also learned is that you never know how strong you really are until life tests you to see what you can handle. Experiencing a miscarriage and my health declining were things that I never would've expected to happen. The interesting thing about life is that you never know what it is going to throw at you. Dealing with my life and health changes made me see life as a gift to cherish. My new motto in life is to "Live Life on Purpose." That can mean getting to know yourself again. That can mean allowing yourself to be free to be fully who you are. That can mean living a life that makes you proud and excited about life.

It can mean whatever you desire it to mean; as long as it is meaningful and filled to the brim with joy, then you are doing it right!

Avery Sunshine

Sunshine Mindset LLC.
Owner, Internationally Credentialed and Certified coach,
Master Trainer & Speaker.

https://www.linkedin.com/in/averysunshine/
https://www.facebook.com/groups/1400905980351789
https://www.instagram.com/sunshinemindset_avery
https://sunshine-mindset.com/

WHO AM I?

My name is Avery Sunshine, and I am the owner of Sunshine Mindset LLC, an ICF-ACC credentialed and certified international coach, public speaker, and master trainer.

As someone who has a painfully familiar history with self-doubt, fear of judgment and intense fear of using my voice, it is now my mission to empower kids, teens and adults to fully own their voice, embrace their unique gifts and talents and to create that life their heart desires while making an impact for themselves and the world around them.

Over the past ten years, I've had the privilege of coaching hundreds of individuals, spanning various age groups and international borders and have been genuinely amazed by their transformation and positive growth.

My approach to interaction is distinctively characterized by its uplifting, empowering, loving, committed and connected nature — it's the unique magic I'm enthusiastic about sharing with the world.

"Now What?"

By Avery Sunshine

"What if your life began with the question, "Well now what?" From the moment I was born into this world as a frail, baby girl on June 21, 1977, weighing just 5 pounds and 11 ounces, it was as if I was stepping into a world that wasn't quite ready for me. The best my mom could do when she brought me home from the hospital was lay me on the bed and turn to my aunt and ask, "Well... now what?" This seemed to echo the uncertainty that would define much of my early years.

As an infant plagued by colic, I cried endlessly, my needs for comfort and connection often going unmet. This lack of attention contrasted sharply with the care my younger sister received when she arrived six years later. The differences in how we were treated highlighted a stark reality: Our early environment and the attention we received—or didn't receive—shaped who we then became.

By the time I was old enough to interact with the world, I had already earned the label of the girl who didn't speak. So, now what? My separation anxiety was intense; I would scream and cry when left with a babysitter, fixating on the garage door until my parents returned. Social anxiety made it difficult to form friendships or communicate with anyone other than my parents, a struggle that persisted into my early adulthood. Therapy became a recurring part of my life as a young adult, though I often found it hard to open up and talk.

So, now what? I moved to Los Angeles at 17 years old, eager to escape my family dynamic and the environment in which I grew up. After graduating high school in 1995, I was determined to leave. I relocated to LA to audition for a year-long intense dance scholarship program with people from all over the world. Although I didn't make it the first year, I was accepted the second year. I loved dance; it was my outlet and a way of expressing myself without having to use my voice. Even though I was in LA, pursuing what I loved, something was still missing and holding me back. What was missing was my self-worth, self-love, self-confidence, self-trust, and the ability to use my voice. Long story short, I struggled with vertigo and eventually had to let go of dance, although I continued to do a few auditions for print work and music videos, among other things.

Here comes the famous question again, "Now what?" It was only as a young adult, seeking therapy on my own, that the topic of abuse surfaced. From 18 months through high school, I have been a victim of abuse. I endured physical abuse from both my parents and that later evolved into emotional, mental, and verbal mistreatment from my mother. I made this harsh reality my normal and honestly, I just didn't know anything different. It was a life where warm, genuine, and authentic unconditional love was a rare commodity.

One therapist I was seeing regularly in Los Angeles, sensing the depth of my struggle, once said, "I hope one day you have a daughter of your own... It could be really healing for you." Her words, reflecting on my strained relationship with my mother, hinted at a path to healing that I could only begin to imagine.

At the age of 27, I met my husband and got married. Shortly after, as life would have it, here I was having a baby girl of my own at 29 years old.

Here it comes again, are you ready? This is a BIG NOW WHAT moment! I knew immediately that I didn't want what was considered my normal growing up to be the same for my daughter. I wanted to be the kind of mother to her that I had always longed for but never had. I started intentionally preparing for motherhood, learning, and reading while she was still in my womb. After giving birth to my beautiful baby girl, I was extremely in tune both emotionally and physically with her.

When she turned 3, I noticed she was different from many other kids her age. She was nervous in social settings, such as school, playdates, birthday parties, and at her kids' gym and social skills classes. My daughter was eventually diagnosed with selective mutism and social anxiety. Reading and learning about these anxiety disorders was eye-opening for me; it felt like I was describing myself as a young child, teen, and young adult. During this time I was blessed to have another baby girl. They are about 2 and a half years apart.

When it was time for my youngest to start preschool a few days a week, I began to notice she was following in her older sister's footsteps. She would become emotionless, tense, and withdrawn, even with me, in social settings. She wouldn't eat snacks at school, do art projects, play at recess, or talk with anyone. She was diagnosed with selective mutism, social phobia, and extreme separation anxiety.

Can I get a drum roll, please? Here we go again, NOW WHAT?

I knew I couldn't let my kids suffer socially the way I had. I always thought my struggles were due to my upbringing, but I realized I had a double dose working against me: a dysfunctional family, physical, mental, and verbal abuse, combined with social anxiety, separation anxiety, and selective mutism. With all these odds stacked against me and zero support, I knew I had to step up and get my daughters the help they needed to thrive and overcome these challenges.

I became a maniac on a mission. I was determined to save their lives. I could not let my kids suffer and struggle the same way I did socially. I decided to learn everything I could. They both started therapy, attended a week-long intensive camp focusing on brave exposure practice, and used their brave voice in a school class-like setting for several years. I am smiling ear to ear as I write this because they are both on the other side of selective mutism and social anxiety now. They are thriving socially and in all areas of their lives.

So, now what, you ask?

In my mission to save my daughters' lives, I ended up saving my own life as well. Seeing their personal transformation and self-confidence grow gave me confidence in myself. I knew there was a higher level for me to achieve, and I wanted to be an example for them. I began attending training in emotional intelligence and became internationally credentialed and certified as a coach. I have coached clients from all over the world ages 8 through 70 years old who have created life-changing transformations for themselves while working alongside me. I am also an emotional intelligence trainer and engaging motivational speaker. Using my voice, which was once my biggest fear, is now my greatest strength and gift to share with the world. I realized and now wholeheartedly believe at my core that we truly are best equipped to serve the person we once were.

Our past experiences do not have to define or dictate who we are today. At any moment, we can choose to rewrite our story; we are the authors of our own lives. While we may not be able to change our past experiences and events, we can change the meaning we attach to those events and how we feel about ourselves. I am not saying that this is an easy process to navigate through. It absolutely takes a ton of intentional practice, but I am proof that it can be done. I am here to tell you that there is without a doubt light at the end of what may seem like a dark and lonely tunnel. You deserve to create the life for which your heart longs.

Life is now. Tomorrow is never promised or guaranteed for any of us walking this earth. This is not a dress rehearsal. This is the real deal. I personally invite you to give yourself permission to be your authentic self and to make a choice right in this very moment that will change the way you show up in the world for both yourself and your loved ones.

My invitation is for you to boldly choose to shine, show up to shine, own your voice, speak your truth from your heart, and start intentionally becoming the star of your own life. You are 100% worth it! Embrace your inner rock star! Now is the perfect time to empower yourself to shine your light and embrace your own unique gifts, talents, quirkiness, weirdness, strengths, weaknesses, and flaws in only the way that you can.

Now is the time to authentically choose to show up for yourself and the world around you. This world needs your light that only you can bring. If you don't do you, you won't be done. Cheers to living full out and out loud!

And, THIS IS WHAT!

Life is short! Live it fully starting NOW! So much love and light straight from my heart to yours!

Dr. Shade Kolade

Founder and CEO of Leadership Synergy Institute

https://www.linkedin.com/in/leadershipaccelerator/
https://www.facebook.com/LeadershipSynergy
https://www.instagram.com/leadershipaccelerator/
https://www.leadershipsynergy.ca/
https://linktr.ee/drshade

Dr. Shade Kolade is a distinguished professor, award-winning researcher, and certified leadership coach. As a thought leader, she brings a unique blend of technical acumen and leadership expertise to her work. Dr. Shade's journey from academia to corporate roles and entrepreneurship showcases her adaptability and resilience. As a professional who faced systemic barriers and career challenges after moving to Canada, she employed leadership-based strategies to overcome them. She has inspired many with her story of overcoming adversity and empowering others to do the same. Her work focuses on nurturing trust, fostering connections, and driving meaningful change in technical organizations. Committed to elevating expertise and inspiring leadership, Dr. Shade provides practical insights and tools for overcoming common leadership challenges. Her mission is to shed light on the path for leaders, helping to build inclusive environments where every individual can thrive and every leader can spearhead transformative change.

Turning Deepest Fears into Greatest Strengths: Reflections of a Transformational Leader

By Dr. Shade Kolade

Introduction

How often have you found yourself at the edge of uncertainty, feeling fear grip you like an unseen force, and questioning whether you have the strength to move forward? It takes immense courage to turn such fear into a driving force for growth and empowerment. I know; I have been there.

I had uprooted my life and children from everything I knew and the comfort of being around those who loved and supported me to move to a new country. Like most, I came filled with a 'new country dream' of endless opportunities, a fresh start, and a better life for my children. However, this dream was immediately shattered into smithereens, and I had to face the shock of a new culture and the uncertainties that came with it.

Imagine having advanced degrees, stellar work experience, exceptional interpersonal skills, and years of excellence, but struggling to find a job. Each 'no' wounded me, eroding my confidence and instilling doubt. My three children depended on me and I couldn't afford to falter. Each step felt heavy, burdened by responsibility and the unknown future. Yet my children's faces flashed before my eyes, their innocent smiles fueling my resolve to find a way forward.

In those moments of despair, I recalled my mother's lessons. Her unwavering strength and entrepreneurial spirit have guided me through childhood and beyond. She faced countless challenges with a smile, never backing down. Her memory ignited a spark within me. Like her, I had to dig deep and find the resilience to turn challenges into opportunities.

Ultimately, recognizing that every rejection drew me closer to a 'yes' created a mindset that encouraged persistence despite seemingly insurmountable odds. That realization marked a significant turning point for me.

Looking back, the most profound lessons came not from my successes but from my struggles. Each challenge was a teacher, and each failure was a stepping stone to greater understanding and growth. These experiences have enlightened me and empowered me to face future challenges confidently.

I invite you to reflect on your own experiences with fear and resilience. How have your challenges shaped you? What strengths have you discovered in moments of doubt? This chapter will encourage self-reflection, helping you to become more self-aware and resilient in the face of fear.

The Journey

Reflecting on my journey from Africa to North America and my challenges, I gained profound insights into resilience and self-discovery.

As an academic and researcher, I won a prestigious fellowship and had the blessings of my home university to carry out a portion of agriculturally critical research. This is how my journey started in North America. Being a single mother to three very young children, I had to make the hard decision to leave my children with family to avoid disrupting their education, sanity, and routine too much. All that said, I still had to deal with the guilt of 'abandoning' my children. What good mother does that, even if it advances her career and potentially creates a better life for them?

After successfully completing the initial project, my host university proposed retaining my services and offered a contract position that allowed me to expand on the novel discoveries from my original research. This opportunity facilitated my contribution to a breakthrough in biosystems research, a field in which I had extensive experience.

Everything went very well, and after completing that project, I also got an opportunity to fill a teaching position at the university. University research positions (other than faculty) are grant-based and could change depending on the priorities of the party in power at the time, so I could not commit long-term. My struggle to integrate into real society began.

Those early days were fraught with self-doubt and uncertainty. I questioned my decisions often, wondering if I was making the right choices for my children and myself.

Moreover, accepting to extend my stay beyond the fellowship meant giving up my full-time university faculty job back home and the life of comfort I had worked hard for. It came with the decision to either extend the separation from my children (which I was not willing to consider) or relocate them to be with me. Once that move was made, I chose to stay because the kids liked it here, and uprooting them again was out of the question.

I was highly educated and skilled but faced one rejection after another in the job market. Outside the university, it was the same message—with a PhD, I was too highly qualified for any position. Imagine how frustrating it is to be overqualified.

I went through a period of resume and cover letter tweaks, endless interviews, and sometimes multiple interview stages for one position only to be told how impressed they were with my competencies but that they had decided to go with another candidate. These rejections were professional setbacks and personal blows that tested my resilience and belief in my abilities.

One particular day stands out vividly in my memory: Another rejection letter lay before me, the words blurring as tears welled in my eyes, and the weight of responsibility pressed down on me, threatening to overwhelm me. Everything I knew about career progression was challenged to its limits. I went from one job board and employment organization to another. It didn't look like it would get easier since I did not have connections outside the university.

Wiping away my tears, I resolved to persevere. It was time to forge my own path instead of relying on the conventional job market and career processes. The journey wouldn't be easy and the fear of failure loomed. Yet, I knew that my deepest fears held the potential to become my greatest strength. Thus began my quest to transform fear into a foundation for empowerment and success.

I attended workshops, networked tirelessly, and pulled myself up by the straps of my boots. Through all this, I often thought of my late mother's unbreakable spirit and leaned on what she would do. I am very grateful that she taught me that true strength lies not in never falling but in rising every time we fall.

Through a series of interviews and meetings, I convinced a manufacturing company to see the value in my transferable skills in science, laboratory research, and administration. I quickly proved myself in that job and began to rise in my career. Every obstacle I met on the job became a lesson, every failure a stepping stone. I embraced my fears, viewing them not as obstacles but as challenges.

As time passed, my stellar leadership skills, which I had continued developing, positioned me for managerial positions. One day, the Regional Director of my organization called me into a meeting quite unexpectedly to offer me a pick of the three vacant senior positions. I was overjoyed, to say the least, and knew that my determination had begun to yield results: small successes accumulated, each a testament to resilience and determination.

Eventually, I started helping other professionals, most of whom were my graduate students, enhance their leadership development skills through a series of masterminds and workshops. The transformation I observed in those individuals was heart-warming and spectacular. This led me to contemplate doing this long-term—I felt purpose calling me, and I was ready to roar!

Still smarting from the rejections, job instability, and if the burden of single-handedly raising my children in a foreign country were not scary enough, the thought of jumping into building a business and the uncertainty of it all scared me even more. I took the path of caution and started building my coaching and consulting business while working full-time.

Initially, I had tried to navigate my struggles alone, believing that self-reliance was a sign of strength. However, reaching out for help, hiring a coach, and surrounding myself with a support network of like-minded individuals proved invaluable. These connections provided practical support and emotional encouragement, reminding me I was not alone in my journey.

Slowly but surely, I started to see progress—small successes built upon each other, each a testament to the power of resilience and determination. My business began to take shape, fueled by the very fears that once threatened to paralyze me. Of course, there were challenges and painful, sometimes costly, lessons along the way. However, I realized that my experiences were not just personal victories but had universal lessons about resilience and empowerment. They highlighted the importance of facing fear head-on, turning adversity into opportunity, and drawing strength from within.

Personal Insights

Thinking through all of these with a smile on my face, I have since met and married the love of my life, and I am having my highest-grossing income year to date; surely resilience and self-discovery have great gain. One of the most significant lessons was discovering the depth of my inner strength. Before these experiences, I had underestimated my capacity to endure and overcome adversity. The challenges unveiled a reservoir of resilience within me that I hadn't known existed.

Inspired by this, I began to see my struggles in a new light. I realized that every obstacle was an opportunity to learn and grow. With renewed determination, I focused on developing new business strategies and sought new opportunities. My business began to thrive.

These experiences taught me resilience is not about avoiding challenges but embracing them. It's about finding the strength to keep going even when the odds are stacked against you. It's about turning adversity into opportunity and drawing strength from within.

Moreover, I learned the importance of adaptability. Transitioning from academia to a corporate career and then to entrepreneurship required acquiring new skills, thinking creatively, and remaining flexible in the face of change. This adaptability proved crucial not only for my professional growth but also for maintaining my mental well-being. Thankfully, I already gained substantial business management, marketing, and customer service skills while growing up with my entrepreneurial mother. Embracing these challenges and fostering a learning mindset elevated my personal growth.

It also underscored the value of a support network. These connections provided practical assistance and emotional support, demonstrating that I wasn't alone in my journey. During a particularly challenging period, when I found myself at a crossroads, the business struggled, and the prospect of failure loomed, my support systems reminded me that setbacks were inevitable and were actually growth opportunities.

From these experiences, I distilled five key lessons that have shaped my approach to leadership and life.

Lessons Learned

1. **Resilience Is Built Through Adversity:** My experiences underscore that resilience is not innate but developed through facing and overcoming adversity. Every challenge I faced was an opportunity to build and strengthen my resilience. Your struggles forge your resilience, preparing you for future challenges, and reinforcing your chances for success.

   Think about the story of Oprah Winfrey. Born into poverty in rural Mississippi, she faced a difficult childhood marked by abuse and instability. Despite these hardships, she pursued her education with determination and secured a job in radio while still in high school. She later transitioned to television and became a co-anchor for the local evening news, where she was deemed "unfit for television." She persisted through the struggles, eventually creating and hosting "The Oprah Winfrey Show," which became the highest-rated talk show in television history.

2. **Adaptability Is Key to Overcoming Challenges:** In a rapidly changing world, the ability to adapt is crucial. My journey from academia to a corporate career and then to the uncertain world of entrepreneurship required strategic thinking. I had to learn new skills and approaches while leveraging my past experiences and transferable skills. This adaptability allowed me to transform obstacles into opportunities.

   Consider the story of Jeff Bezos, the founder of Amazon, who started his career in the finance industry and in 1994 seized an opportunity of the new internet to start an online bookstore. This decision required him to adapt to an entirely new industry, quit his stable job, and embrace entrepreneurship. He started small, but his ability to adapt to market demands and emerging technologies has allowed it to expand beyond books and become one of the world's largest and most influential companies.

Staying open to new experiences and continuously seeking personal and professional growth and opportunities to expand your skill set and adapt to new environments will better equip you to navigate the complexities of an ever-evolving world.

3. **Leverage The Power of Mentorship and Community:** Isolation can amplify fear and doubt, making challenges seem insurmountable. I found strength, encouragement, and motivation to keep going by hiring a coach and building meaningful relationships.

Sheryl Sandberg became one of the most influential women in technology. She attributes it to realizing the importance of mentorship and community early on. During her tenure at Google, she sought guidance from Eric Schmidt, then CEO of Google, who became a pivotal mentor. This shaped her decision-making and career trajectory, eventually leading her to Facebook. She often emphasizes the value of mentorship and building supportive networks while showcasing the power of community.

I hope this serves as a powerful reminder that asking for help is a sign of strength, not weakness. A supportive community can be invaluable in overcoming adversity, providing practical support, emotional encouragement, and shared wisdom.

4. **Empowerment Comes from Within:** True empowerment is an inside job. While external validation and success are good, the most profound sense of empowerment comes from within. My journey taught me that believing in myself and my abilities, despite the external challenges, was crucial to my success.

Realizing that my self-worth was independent of others' opinions, I learned to trust my instincts and vision, which drove my decisions and helped me overcome obstacles.

J.K. Rowling, the author of the Harry Potter series, exemplifies this principle. Despite numerous rejections, struggles with depression, and living on state benefits as a single mother, she maintained faith in her story and her ability to succeed. She famously said, "Rock bottom became the solid foundation on which I rebuilt my life."

This highlights the power of inner confidence and self-belief. Recognize your worth, trust your instincts, and believe in your vision to overcome any obstacle and achieve your goals.

5. **Every Setback Is a Setup for a Comeback:** Each setback I have faced, whether job rejection, a business challenge, or personal disappointment, set the stage for a more excellent comeback. These experiences taught me to view failures as temporary and as opportunities for growth. You can adopt this perspective to remain hopeful and motivated, even when faced with significant challenges.

Michael Jordan, widely considered to be one of the greatest basketball players of all time, embodied this principle. Despite his legendary status, Jordan faced numerous setbacks throughout his career. In high school, he was famously cut from the varsity basketball team, but rather than seeing this as a failure, he used it as motivation to work harder and improve his skills.

His perspective on setbacks is encapsulated in his quote, "I've missed more than 9,000 shots in my career, I've lost almost 300 games. Twenty-six times, I've been trusted to take the game-winning shot and missed. I've failed over and over and over again in my life. And that is why I succeed."

This demonstrates that setbacks are not the end but rather a setup for a comeback and that your ability to view failures as temporary and as growth opportunities will propel you to unparalleled success in life and career. Adopting this mindset will allow you to remain hopeful and motivated, turning your setbacks into setups for remarkable comebacks.

Inspiration for You

Sharing my story is not just about recounting my experiences but about inspiring others. My journey is a testament to the power of perseverance, adaptability, and unwavering belief in one's potential. It serves as a beacon of hope for those who may be facing their own fears and doubts.

Many people have been part of my journey and have shared their struggles with me. From young professionals starting their careers to seasoned individuals considering a significant career shift, fear and doubt often create significant barriers. I have had to reassure them they are not alone and that their fears are not insurmountable.

One particular story comes to mind. A young woman, a single mother like me, was on the verge of giving up on her dreams due to the challenges she faced. We spent countless hours discussing strategies, exploring options, and building her confidence. Watching her transform, overcome her fears, and eventually achieve her dreams was incredibly rewarding. Her journey mirrored mine in many ways, reinforcing the belief that sharing our stories can indeed make a difference.

Reflecting on this, I often ponder on the power of storytelling in leadership. By sharing our vulnerabilities, we can create a sense of connection and foster a culture of openness and resilience. We can inspire others to embrace their fears and doubts as part of their journey, transforming these challenges into stepping stones for growth.

Think about the people in your life who might benefit from hearing your story. By sharing your experiences and insights, you can offer them encouragement, motivation, and practical strategies to navigate their own fears and doubts.

Conclusion

My journey from fear and doubt to resilience and empowerment is a testament to the human spirit's strength. The lessons I learned along the way have shaped me into the leader I am today. These experiences have strengthened my resolve to help others overcome their challenges and realize their potential.

My desire is that my story inspires you to face your fears with courage, turn your doubts into opportunities for growth, and ultimately discover the immense strength within you. Remember, every challenge you overcome adds to your resilience and brings you closer to achieving your dreams.

As you reflect on your own journey, consider how you can use your experiences to inspire and assist others. Your story has the power to make a difference, offering hope and encouragement to those who may be facing similar fears and doubts. Embrace your journey and let your story shine as a beacon of strength and resilience.

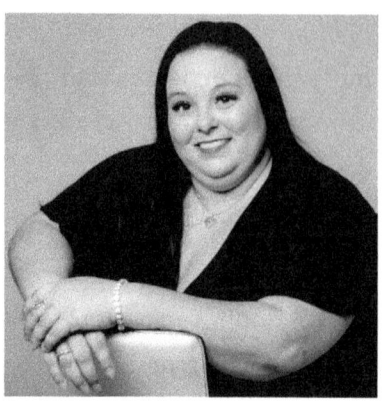

Kristen Lewis

DNP, APRN, AGPCNP-C, MSN-Ed., RN, CCRN

https://www.linkedin.com/in/drlewisdnp/
https://www.instagram.com/DrLewisDNP

I was raised by hardworking parents who instilled in me a strong work ethic and a passion for learning. As I navigated through school and various life experiences, I discovered my love for helping others and making a positive impact in the world. This led me to pursue a career in nursing and medicine, where I have dedicated my life to helping others live their best lives. Along the way, I have faced challenges and setbacks, but I have always remained resilient and determined to overcome them. My life story is a vibrant tapestry woven with triumphs, challenges, and unforgettable moments that have shaped my journey. Through my work, I have been able to empower individuals to overcome adversity and achieve their full potential. I am proud of the impact I have made in the lives of others and look forward to continuing to make a difference in the world.

My Life Story

By Kristen Lewis

When I sat down to write my story, I didn't know where to begin. How far back should I go? College? High school? Middle school? How much should I include? Just start at the beginning and write your story.

When I was 12, I joined the Civil Air Patrol, an Air Force Auxiliary Unit. I was one of the only girls so, of course, I got more attention than any girl could handle. I made rockets and flew planes. I repelled from the catwalks of the Ice Palace in Tampa, Florida. We would run hurricane shelters around the county and do emergency operations missions all over the state of Florida. I got to fly in a KC-135 and work the boom to refuel an F-18 mid-flight. It was amazing! I was a leader in the unit. I was going places.

When I was 14, something triggered me and I fell into a deep depression. All I knew was that I wanted to end it all. I took a whole bottle of Tylenol PM and threw it all up in my sleep. Somehow I survived, thank God. That's when I went to my mom to say I needed help and into therapy I went. My therapist was crazy, but I quickly learned that it's OK not to feel OK. That fact still rings true today. It's OK not to feel OK. Write it on a post-it note and put it on your mirror. Some days are worse than others, but if your good days outnumber your bad, then you're on the right track. Write that down too!

In high school, I was the drill team commander in my Air Force JROTC and I was in the top command my senior year. I was a leader, a born leader. I played upright bass and cello in the orchestra and sang second soprano in the church choir. I worked at a spa from the time I turned 16 through when I left for college. I had a key after my first week as a receptionist and spa assistant. I took online classes to fulfill the necessary requirements for graduation because I didn't want to give up my electives, JROTC, and orchestra. Then came graduation. Many students were staying home and going to the University of South Florida (USF), but I had bigger ideas. I was going to leave this town and I was going to be a doctor.

I had my future mapped out. I had a full Air Force scholarship for my choice of school. I was in the final rounds of competition for the Air Force Academy when I got my acceptance to the University of Florida. I let go of my scholarship because, well, I was 18 and stupid. I was, after all, at one of the best party schools in the South. I had interesting experiences in college. I partied with the boys Delta Tau Delta because my dad was an alumnus. I was special. I got 1 B in my first semester and then I realized it was time to get down to business. After that, I made pretty much all A's. I dated a guy for a few years and that fizzled. His mom was a lunatic. I dated an architecture major my senior year. I thought we were going to get married and live happily ever after. His parents loved me. My parents loved him. It was meant to be. Wrong. He cheated on me the summer after I graduated and dumped me my first night back in Gainesville that Fall. While I was traveling all over Europe with my brother, he was back home finding someone else.

I only stayed in Gainesville for him, so after we broke up, I focused on work and I drank… a lot! That was the beginning of my troubles with alcohol. I had a miscarriage a month later and I didn't tell anyone because I didn't want more pity after I had just been cheated on and dumped. I kept it a secret for a very long time. I started my first nursing job in the main intensive care unit (ICU) at Shands Hospital in Gainesville. I thought I was hot stuff. Wrong. I learned so much in my first year from my mentors. It was incredible what I didn't know. In September 2008, I moved back to Brandon and bought my first house all on my own when I was 23.

I worked at the local big hospital for 3 years in the Neuroscience ICU. The only reason I left was because my manager had targeted me and I was having panic attacks just going to work. I had to get out. I took the first job that was offered to me at a much smaller hospital. I told people it was so that I could go back to school and they believed me. What I didn't realize was that the resources at the big hospital were far greater than those at the local small hospital. I had to rely on all my training thus far to be the best nurse I could be with limited resources. This training would take me far later in my career.

In July 2012, one of my best friends got married and it was like a JROTC reunion at the wedding. All the bridesmaids were Bucs cheerleaders and they were jealous I got attention from the guys because I had always been just one of the guys. After the wedding, we all went to a bar by the hotel. I remember waking up in my car on a back road in Air Cargo at Tampa International Airport. I have no idea how I got there. I was lucky to be alive. I remember bits and pieces of that night. What I do remember is that I had been raped by a man from New Jersey in his hotel room. I didn't tell anyone what had happened until Monday night. I walked into work and we immediately had a Code Blue. I lost my shit and started crying and ran to the med room. That night I told my story so many times. My charge nurse who brought me to the ER, my parents, the police, and the nice nurse at the trauma center who did the exam and drew my blood. It was a nightmare. We came to the conclusion that I had been drugged at the bar with GHB and, because I'm so tolerant to medication, I remember bits and pieces. I went with the detectives from the Tampa Police Department to the scene of the crime to tell my story again. They found me on surveillance footage walking into the hotel with a man under my own power. I thought they'd actually catch him! Wrong. Not only did they not catch him, but they closed the case because I had two different semen samples removed Monday night during the exam at the trauma center. The nightmare continued. It took me a long time to trust any man after that, but eventually, I did.

After that, I started drinking heavily. I never went to work drunk, but I always drank to get numb at home, alone. My worst night was when I had 6 mg of Xanax and 12 shots of Jack Daniels. I knew I had to change. I gave up drinking completely, cold turkey, and focused on work. I took every course that was offered to perfect my craft. I did eventually go back to school in 2012. I graduated from USF in 2013 with my Masters in Nursing Education. I taught at USF for a while teaching clinicals and labs. I wrote and taught the simulation scenarios for the StarRN program put on by HCA at CAMLS in Tampa. I became a badass ICU nurse in the process. My career as a nurse and educator was back on track.

In 2014, I was diagnosed with Polycystic Ovarian Syndrome (PCOS) and I was devastated. I was told I would likely never be able to have children. It was heartbreaking to someone who just wanted to get married and have a family of her own. I was angry. But hey, my testosterone level was 4 times what it should have been, so no wonder I was angry!

In September 2015, three older women at work got together and wrote a list of complaints about me. My manager called me in and handed me the list with a write-up. No discussion prior to the write-up. She just gave me the list and said it was going in my file. I was devastated. I drove to St. Pete Beach and started drinking. My best friends, Ashley and James, a married couple, drove out to the beach and sat with me while I cried. They drank with me until I felt better and then they drove me home. I had decided I wasn't going to let those women win. I wrote out a 15-page document going over every complaint stating my opinion and an action plan as to how I was going to fix each one. I discussed the complaints with every night shift co-worker and put their statements in the document. I turned it in to my manager and she put it in my official human resources file. I had saved my career. I decided after that that I was going to go back to school to get my Doctorate of Nursing Practice so I applied to USF with a plan to start in Fall 2016.

In February 2016, I started dating John. It was hot and heavy from the get-go. He came to my house and helped me clean it up because it was a wreck. I was a terrible housekeeper. In April 2016, I found out in the same week that I was pregnant and that I had been accepted to the doctoral program at USF. Big decisions had to be made. I decided that I was going to do both because I didn't know if I would ever be able to get pregnant again. It was a miracle baby. He said I only got pregnant because he has super sperm. He was, I later found out, a violent convicted felon who was on felony probation. I let him move in with me after I got pregnant under the condition that he didn't deal drugs and he never smoked spice or did other drugs while at my house. He couldn't take it. He was high on spice when he blocked me in my room and wouldn't let me leave. Somehow I managed to get out. He was high on spice when he tried to strangle me against a wall in the kitchen and my dog, Maggie, got in between us and saved my life. I found out on July 1 that I was having a baby boy. He was NOT happy with the name I picked because he wanted a junior. Things escalated from there. He harassed me day and night with long voicemails and text messages when all I wanted was for him to leave me alone. I wound up having to evict him from my home and things just kept getting worse. He was stalking me and continued harassing me. In August, I got a restraining order. I walked into court, 6 months pregnant, with 3 copies of an 86-page document showing all the text messages, Facebook messages, and voicemail transcripts from just the month of July. I put 4 screenshots on a page and numbered them all. I highlighted the good parts for the judge. I won. In the following months, he stalked me from just far enough away that it wasn't technically a violation. I lived my life in hypervigilance on a daily basis. He did finally violate the restraining order on December 6, so he was safely locked up behind bars when I gave birth.

I had Jacob on December 12, 2016. My mom was my coach and my best friend Christie came to help. My aunt was also in the delivery room standing against the wall cheering me on. I had one more try and then I was going for an emergent C-section. I pushed like our lives depended on it because, well, they did depend on it! I remember lying there with my legs in the air not being able to move and hearing them say they had to revive him. What was happening? Why wasn't he crying? I heard the suction and I was terrified. He had swallowed meconium on my last push. Then he cried. I cried. We all cried. It was a beautiful sound.

I stayed with my parents for a few months after he was born so they could help me. My best friend Jovany stayed at my house with Maggie, my dog, and I would take Jacob over in little increments so she could get used to him. I was afraid she would bite him or something because it had always been just me and her. It worked! Eventually, I moved back home and began my life as a single mom. I was working full-time, going to school in a doctoral program, and doing clinicals on my days off. I still don't know how I did it all. The things that got me through were my faith and my family's unwavering support.

I graduated with my Doctorate of Nursing Practice (DNP) in Adult Gerontology Primary Care in December 2020 after many obstacles had been thrown in my way. My ex-boyfriend got out of prison in June of 2018, so I was back in hypervigilant mode. I had to restart my DNP project nearly halfway through because they said my project idea was "research." COVID happened, which threw another wrench in my plans to graduate on time. Despite all the obstacles, I finally finished.

During COVID, the healthcare landscape drastically changed. In the ICU, the stress level intensified trifold. COVID patients were not your typical ICU patients. They required much higher levels of care and, in the beginning, nobody knew what to do, so we were flying by the seat of our pants. It was terrifying. We didn't know if we would take it home to our families. We didn't know if we'd survive after being in the room with COVID-19-positive patients for prolonged periods of time. All I knew was that I had to help my patients to the best of my ability with the tools I had been given. In the end, I was burned out. COVID had taken its toll on me just like it had done to so many other nurses around the world. I was ready to leave the bedside and start my new career as a nurse practitioner.

It took me almost a year to find my first NP job and the one I got would teach me many lessons and bring depression and anxiety back into the forefront of my life. I went from working 12-hour night shifts in an ICU to working day shifts 8–5 in an outpatient primary and acute care clinic. Talk about a 180! I loved it. I was helping people get and stay healthy instead of treating highly critical patients. It was an incredibly high-stress environment, but I was determined to stay for at least a year because that looks better on a resume.

In July 2022, I accepted a position at a local internal medicine office and immediately gave my notice. I left that job in October 2022. I barely had an orientation and then I was on my own. I'll admit it was a bit overwhelming at first, but I knew I had to succeed. By January 2023, I was taking nurse practitioner students (all three of them). They actually appreciate me and my work ethic. At my annual review in September, my CEO told me how much he appreciates having someone he can trust. I am rocking it! I am only at the main office two days a week. Every other day of the week I run a different office all on my own. My experience in a small hospital with minimal resources has assisted me in managing an office where I am the only practitioner with little to no resources available. It is nice having a different patient population every day. Every day is different, so I never get bored. Now

I have students everyday from schools all over the country. I think I am a pretty good teacher, at least, that's what they tell me. I guess it's true because they keep coming back for more semesters!

In November 2023, I had a visit from my Quest Labs rep. She brought her national cardiovascular trainer just to come meet me. Me! I was over the moon. We became friends. Friendships blossom in the rarest of places. Anyway, she brought the NATIONAL trainer to my office JUST to meet ME! We had intellectual conversations about insulin resistance and how it plays a role in pretty much every other system of the body. I showed him the case study I made from my own lab results and he actually took it with him because he was so impressed! I am knocking it out of the park!

With my new career as a nurse practitioner thriving, I look back on all I have been through and I am amazed at how far I have come. My story is one of highs and lows, happy and sad, resilience and strength. Through my faith and the unwavering support of my family, I have been able to overcome many personal challenges and professional setbacks. What I want you to remember is that it's OK to not feel OK all the time. I hope this has given you inspiration to know that you can change the course of your life no matter your circumstances. I have had quite a life so far, but my story isn't over!

Corinne Brown

Corinne Brown Coaching
Leadership/Results Coach

https://www.linkedin.com/in/corinne-brown-36513673/
https://www.instagram.com/corinnebrowncoaching
https://corinnebrowncoaching.com/

Corinne Brown is a seasoned Leadership Results Coach with over 14 years of experience empowering professionals to unlock their potential and achieve measurable success. Specialising in executive coaching, Corinne has a proven track record of transforming leadership capabilities through personalised strategies and actionable insights. With a background in leadership/life coaching, training and assessing, consultancy and personality profiling, Corinne excels in fostering high-performing teams, enhancing decision-making skills, and driving organisational change. Known for a results-oriented approach, Corinne combines practical techniques with a deep understanding of human behaviour to inspire leaders to overcome challenges and reach their goals. Whether working with individuals or groups, Corinne is committed to creating a lasting impact by cultivating leadership excellence that aligns with organisational values and objectives.

Surviving Emotional and Financial Abuse in a Toxic Marriage and Sexual Harassment in the Workplace

By Corinne Brown

Living through a toxic marriage marked by emotional and financial abuse has been one of the most challenging experiences of my life. The emotional abuse was insidious—constant criticism, manipulation, isolation from my loved ones, and the relentless erosion of my self-esteem. Financial abuse only made things worse, as I found myself stripped of financial independence, with every decision tightly controlled and my access to funds severely restricted.

Surviving this situation required immense strength and careful planning. The first crucial step was recognising the abuse for what it was and understanding that it wasn't my fault. I reached out to trusted friends, family, and a counsellor, who provided me with the support and perspective I desperately needed.

Breaking free from a toxic marriage was not easy, but it was possible. I prioritised my safety and well-being above all else, reaching out to local organisations that specialise in helping victims of domestic abuse. They offered me guidance and assistance that were crucial in reclaiming my life.

Rebuilding my financial independence was just as important. I began by quietly setting aside money, opening a separate bank account, and seeking legal advice to understand my rights. I educated myself on financial matters and explored resources available to survivors of abuse.

The path to recovery was anything but linear. In the early years, I struggled with feelings of shame and self-doubt, constantly questioning my decisions and worth. Financially, I faced the daunting task of rebuilding from scratch. I learned to manage my finances independently, made sacrifices, and sought out resources that could help me regain control of my life. It wasn't just about money, it was about reclaiming the autonomy I had lost. Every small victory, whether it was paying off a debt or securing a stable job, became a milestone in my journey to freedom.

Emotionally, the healing process was just as challenging. Trust had been broken, and my sense of self was fragile. Therapy and support groups played a crucial role in helping me process the trauma and rebuild my confidence. Over time, I began to rediscover my passions and reconnect with the person I was before the abuse. It took years of persistence and self-compassion to heal, but eventually, I reached a place of peace and resilience.

It took me 10 years to fully recover from the financial and emotional abuse I endured in my marriage. The scars ran deep—my self-esteem shattered and my finances in ruins. Rebuilding my life required immense patience and resilience. I had to relearn self-worth, regain financial independence, and heal emotionally. The journey was long, filled with setbacks and doubts, but each step forward brought me closer to freedom. Over a decade, I gradually rebuilt my life, rediscovered my strength, and found peace.

Looking back, I see not only the pain but also the strength I found within myself to overcome it and build a brighter future.

It's been a journey, but I've learned to be patient with myself, taking one step at a time.

Today, I stand stronger, knowing I've emerged from the darkness with renewed confidence and stability.

Some years later, after going through a process of transformation, rebuilding and re-educating myself, I began working as a Leadership

Coach. It was a passion of mine, to develop emerging and senior leaders, and I thought I had finally found a new beginning to living a happy and productive life, both personally and professionally.

I had a renewed outlook on life and felt I was contributing in some way to making the world a better place. I embarked on a career in mining, working with leaders to build efficient, effective teams with a focus on emotional intelligence and self-leadership. It felt good to be able to share my experience, knowledge and skills with a diverse range of professional people, or so I thought. It was not something I envisaged happening, being sexually harassed in my place of work. Working in mining can be very challenging, you're working with people who have little to no regard for your health and well-being and toxic masculinity is everywhere around you. When it happened to me (not just once, but many, many times, my immediate response was to just resign and leave, not wanting to be in a work environment which treats women so disrespectfully), I knew I had to take action to protect myself, so I immediately called it out!

I was swiftly shown the door. I took my battle to the courts, and after 16 months, my case was dismissed. There was no apology, no support, no justice. No one in the legal profession was willing to represent me, advising me that to do so would cost me upward of $40k AUD to engage a Barrister, with no guarantee of winning my case. It was a long and lonely time for me, and again I found myself ruined financially, emotionally, and physically. The stress and pain were debilitating and those who witnessed the harassment, turned their backs on me, fearful of losing their jobs, if they spoke up.

Losing the job I loved for speaking out against sexual harassment was utterly devastating. It felt like a profound betrayal, not only by the individuals who perpetrated the harassment but also by the organisation I had dedicated myself to and believed would uphold justice and protect its employees. The experience shattered my sense of security and trust, leaving me feeling isolated, vulnerable, and questioning my own worth and the fairness of the world around me.

The aftermath was incredibly challenging as I grappled with a mix of intense emotions, anger, sadness, and profound disappointment. My career, which had been a source of pride and fulfilment, was abruptly derailed, and I was forced to navigate the difficult path of rebuilding my professional life, while also healing from the emotional trauma. Despite the pain and adversity, eventually, this experience strengthened my resolve to stand up against injustice and advocate for safer, more respectful workplaces for everyone.

Enduring both a toxic marriage and a toxic workplace pushed me to the brink, forcing me to confront deep emotional and psychological challenges. These experiences shattered my self-worth and tested my resilience in ways I never imagined. However, they also ignited a powerful desire within me to reclaim my life and help others do the same. As I navigated my healing journey, I discovered a passion for supporting others in overcoming their own struggles. This passion led me to become a Coach, where I now use my experiences to empower others to break free from toxic environments, rebuild their lives, and find their own strength and purpose.

Resilience is the inner strength that allows you to rise after each fall, to keep moving forward despite the obstacles, and to grow through adversity. It is not about avoiding challenges or never feeling pain; rather, it is about embracing those difficult moments and choosing to learn from them. Resilience is built through every decision to get back up, heal, and transform hardships into stepping stones. It is a journey of persistence, where each step forward reinforces your ability to navigate life's complexities with courage and grace. By acknowledging your struggles and using them as catalysts for growth, you cultivate a deeper sense of purpose and inner power.

Self-worth is the foundation upon which resilience stands. It is the recognition that you are inherently valuable and deserving of love, respect, and kindness—first from yourself and then from others. When you have a strong sense of self-worth, you are less likely to internalise the negativity from toxic relationships or situations. Instead, you become more attuned to what serves your well-being and are more willing to set boundaries that protect your peace. Building self-worth involves embracing your imperfections, celebrating your strengths, and understanding that your value is not tied to external validation. When you nurture a deep, unwavering belief in your own worth, you empower yourself to face any challenge with confidence and resilience.

Resetting my life to build resilience and strength began with a commitment to self-reflection and self-awareness. This involved taking an honest inventory of where I was in life, identifying the areas that were draining my energy and causing distress, and understanding the underlying patterns that have led me to this point. It required courage to face uncomfortable truths and to let go of what no longer served me—whether it was toxic relationships, unfulfilling work, or self-limiting beliefs. By acknowledging these factors, I created space for growth and made a conscious decision to choose a new path aligned with my values and aspirations.

My next step was to cultivate healthy habits that reinforced emotional, mental, and physical strength. This included setting and maintaining clear boundaries, practising mindfulness, and engaging in regular self-care routines such as exercise, meditation, or journaling. Building resilience is also about fostering a growth mindset—one that views challenges as opportunities for learning rather than setbacks. Surrounding myself with a supportive community of friends, mentors, and support groups also provided a crucial network of encouragement and accountability. By consciously choosing positivity, compassion, and persistence in my daily actions, I gradually built a solid foundation of resilience.

Lastly, a message for you, embracing the power of purpose and intention can dramatically reset your life. When you define a clear purpose—whether it's personal growth, helping others, or pursuing a passion—you create a compelling reason to keep moving forward, even in the face of adversity.

Intentional living means making choices that align with your core values and being mindful of how you spend your time and energy. Resilience and strength are not built overnight but through consistent, deliberate actions and choices that honour your journey and prioritise your well-being. Over time, this approach not only helps you overcome life's inevitable challenges but also empowers you to thrive and live a life that is deeply fulfilling and true to yourself.

"Your self-worth is not determined by how others treat you, but by how you choose to see and value yourself each day." —Corinne Brown

Gina Stockdall

Founder and CEO of Marilyn Jeanne Designs, LLC

https://www.linkedin.com/company/marilynjeannedesigns/
https://www.facebook.com/marilynjeannedesigns
https://www.instagram.com/marilynjeannedesigns
https://www.marilynjeannedesigns.com/
https://www.jesusandcoffeepodcast.online/

Gina Stockdall is a passionate advocate for survivors of domestic violence, a business owner, and a dedicated mother. After overcoming an abusive relationship in her early twenties, Gina transformed her life, becoming the CEO and founder of Marilyn Jeanne Designs, LLC, a Christ-centered marketing agency that empowers nonprofits, ministries, and churches. With a heart for giving back, Gina donates 20% of her business profits to domestic violence shelters in Kansas City. She is committed to helping others find their own strength and resilience, believing that healing and growth are possible for everyone.

From Brokenness to Redemption

By Gina Stockdall

At eighteen, I thought I had it all figured out. I had dreams, ambitions, and a sense of independence that made me feel invincible. But life has a way of humbling you when you least expect it, and my life took a drastic turn when I found myself in a relationship that would become the darkest chapter of my young adult life. The relationship started innocently enough, with all the excitement and passion that new love brings. But as the months passed, the cracks began to show. I didn't realize it at first, but the man I was with was slowly chipping away at my sense of self, my confidence, and my freedom.

The signs were subtle at first. What I initially thought were just quirks in his personality became red flags that I ignored. He was possessive, jealous, and controlling. He isolated me from my friends, manipulated my thoughts, and made me believe that I was nothing without him. It was a slow descent into a toxic environment that I couldn't see clearly until it was too late. By the time I realized the depth of the abuse, I was entrenched in the relationship to see a way out. I was emotionally, mentally, and even physically drained.

Leaving him at twenty-two was the hardest thing I had ever done. The decision to walk away wasn't just about ending a relationship; it was about reclaiming my life, my identity, and my future. But leaving wasn't the end of the struggle—it was just the beginning.

When I left, I thought I would feel free, liberated from the shackles that had bound me for so long. Instead, I found myself suspended from college, unable to focus on my studies, and living on my mom's couch with no direction, no purpose, and no hope. My life became a series of fragmented pieces that I didn't know how to put back together.

The people I once considered friends—people who had been close to me, who knew me—sided with my ex. They believed his lies, his twisted version of events that painted him as the victim and me as the villain. It was a betrayal that cut deeper than any wound he had ever inflicted on me. I was abandoned by the very people who should have stood by me, and I was left to pick up the pieces of my shattered life alone.

The loneliness was suffocating. I felt like I was drowning in a sea of despair, with no one to reach out a hand and pull me to safety. My days were a blur of work and partying, a toxic cycle that only served to numb the pain for a few hours. I drank to forget, to escape the reality of my situation, but the reality was always there when the alcohol wore off. I was spiraling out of control, and I didn't care. I was lost, heartbroken, and merely surviving instead of living.

It was during this dark time that my mom extended a lifeline, one that I wasn't even looking for. One Sunday morning, she invited me to church. I had grown up attending church and Christian private schools, but I had strayed away during high school and college. It had been years since I attended a service that was a major family milestone (wedding, funeral, baptism, etc.). Church seemed like the last place that could help me at the time, but I figured it wouldn't hurt, so I went. That decision changed the course of my life.

The service was beautiful, and everyone was so incredibly welcoming. The pastor preached about God's love, forgiveness, and the promise of a new beginning. I listened intently, hanging onto each and every word. It felt like the message was meant just for me. Through this sermon and particular church family, a seed was planted that day, even though I wasn't fully ready to accept it.

What happened after the service was what truly started to turn things around. Later that day, I received a call from one of the pastors from the church. I still don't know how he got my number—maybe my mom gave it to him, or maybe it was divine intervention. Either way, he reached out and invited me to a young adult Bible study that the church was hosting. I hesitated at first, unsure if I wanted to really be around people or if I could even face them. But I felt weird telling a pastor no (and perhaps I had a spark of hope too), so I said yes.

Attending that Bible study was like stepping into a new world. The people there were genuine, kind, and welcoming in a way that I hadn't experienced in a long time. They didn't judge me or question my past; they just accepted me for who I was in the moment—a broken soul in need of healing. Slowly, I began to open up, to share my story, and to let others into my life again. The walls I had built around my heart started to crumble, and for the first time in years, I felt a glimmer of hope.

The Bible study became my sanctuary, a place where I could be vulnerable without fear of rejection. We studied the Word of God, prayed together, and supported one another through our struggles. It was in those moments that I began to understand what it meant to have a relationship with Jesus. It wasn't just about going to church on Sundays or following a set of rules; it was about surrendering my life to Him, trusting Him with my pain, and allowing Him to heal the wounds that no one else could see.

Through my time spent getting to know the pastor and the members of the Bible study group, I began to see my situation in a new light. As we studied God's Word together and shared our experiences, I came to realize that God didn't just see my pain—He was in it with me. He wasn't distant or detached; He was right there, walking with me through every struggle, every tear, and every heartbreak.

This realization hit me deeply. For so long, I had been trying to fight my battles alone, shouldering the weight of my pain and trying to fix everything myself. But as I began to understand God's presence in my life, I saw that I didn't have to carry this burden on my own. I needed His strength, His guidance, and His love to lift me out of the darkness. It was then that I made the decision to surrender—to let go of my need for control and allow God to take over.

As I grew in my faith, I began to see the world differently. The things that once seemed so important—partying, drinking, numbing the pain—no longer held any appeal. I found joy in the simple things, in the friendships I was forming, in the peace that came from knowing I was loved by a God who would never abandon me. I started to rebuild my life, piece by piece, with God as the foundation.

One of the most unexpected blessings that came out of this period of my life was meeting my husband. He was part of the young adult Bible study group, someone I initially saw as just another friendly face in the crowd. But as we spent more time together, I realized that there was something special about him. He was kind, patient, and had a deep love for the Lord that inspired me. Our friendship blossomed into something more, and before I knew it, I was falling in love.

Our relationship was different from any I had experienced before. It was built on mutual respect, trust, and a shared faith in God. He didn't just love me for who I was; he loved me for who I was becoming in Christ. He saw my brokenness but also saw the strength that was emerging from it. He encouraged me, prayed with me, and supported me in my journey of healing.

When we got married, it wasn't just a celebration of our love for each other; it was a testimony to God's faithfulness. One of the friends we had made in the Bible study, a guy who had become like a brother to us, stood by my husband's side as a groomsman. He's now the godfather to both of our children, a constant reminder of the new family God brought into my life when I needed it most.

Looking back now, it's hard to believe how far I've come. The girl who was lost, broken, and spiraling out of control is no longer the person I see in the mirror. Instead, I see a woman who has been redeemed, who has found her worth in Christ, and who is living a life full of purpose and joy. I'm now seven years sober (will be eight years on December 31, 2024), something I never thought would be possible when I was in the midst of my darkest days. I've earned not one, but two college degrees, a testament to the strength and determination that God has placed within me.

But more than the external achievements, it's the internal transformation that I'm most grateful for. I've learned to trust God with every aspect of my life, to lean on Him when things get tough, and to believe that He is working all things for my good, even when I can't see it in the moment. The journey hasn't been easy, and there are still days when the scars of my past threaten to pull me back into the darkness. But now, I know where to turn when those moments come. I turn to the God who has never left my side, who has guided me through every storm, and who has given me a life that is more beautiful than I ever could have imagined.

To anyone reading this who might be going through their own season of pain, I want you to know that you are not alone. I know how easy it is to feel like you're the only one, to believe that no one could possibly understand what you're going through. But I also know that there is hope, even in the darkest of times. Life will knock you down, and sometimes it will feel like you can't get back up. But you can. Not by your own strength, but by leaning on the One who created you, who loves you, and who has already fought your battles.

The road to healing is not a straight path. It's filled with twists, turns, setbacks, and challenges. But every step you take is a step closer to the life that God has planned for you—a life full of peace, joy, and purpose. Trust Him with your pain, your fears, your doubts, and your dreams.

He is big enough to handle it all, and He is faithful to bring you through it.

You got this. Not because you're strong enough on your own, but because you serve a God who is. A God who sees you, who loves you, and who has a plan for your life that is far greater than anything you could ever imagine. So, hold on to hope, lean into His promises, and know that you are never alone.

Marta Suchomska

Founder of Thriving Women in Business

https://www.linkedin.com/in/suchmarta/
https://www.facebook.com/suchmarta
https://www.instagram.com/such_marta/
https://thrivingwomeninbusiness.newzenler.com
https://linktr.ee/such_marta

The visionary and creative mind behind behind the monthly digital magazine "Thriving Women in Business".

Through Marta`s leadership, magazine stands as a beacon of empowerment and inspiration in the digital landscape, dedicated to spotlighting the remarkable journeys and accomplishments of women across diverse industries. With unwavering commitment, the magazine provides a comprehensive platform that amplifies the voices and experiences of women entrepreneurs, executives, innovators, and leaders worldwide.

Each issue is meticulously crafted to offer an enriching blend of insightful, thought-provoking, impactful features, all tailored to resonate with the aspirations and challenges faced by women in business.

Through its global reach and inclusive approach, it strives to break down barriers, challenge stereotypes, and inspire the next generation of female leaders to pursue their ambitions with confidence and resilience.

"Thriving Women in Business" is not just a magazine; it's a movement—a powerful force that celebrates the achievements of women in business!"

Barriers Are Meant to Be Broken, and Dreams Are Meant to Be Realized

By Marta Suchomska

Ever heard that

"Life is a journey filled with unexpected twists and turns"?

Well, my story is no exception. In fact, it is a perfect example that such a saying is true!

My story is one tale of perseverance, determination, and the power of embracing opportunities that came my way.

So, let the story begin!

My journey began in a relatively small city in west-north Poland, where I grew up, far from the busy cities and opportunities that lay beyond. Like millions of others, I went to school (gosh, such an average student I was!), graduated, worked during summer holidaysbasically living normal, "box standard" teen/young adult life.

Then, the first big opportunity came along.

My dad`s brother allowed me to come over to stay at his, in the UK for the summer holiday. Not only that, but also he massively helped me to secure a job more or less from day one!

For me, at age of nearly 22, that already sounded like a dream! Whoooooooaaaa, I could work in the UK for two months, earning better money than I would in my hometown!

Surely at that point, I couldn`t ask for more!

I didn`t care much that my English was… well… let`s put it nicely… on a very basic level!

On 23rd June 2010, I landed in the UK.

I had a huge combo of positive emotions thanks to my supportive parents, they didn't spread their own, typical parental fears to me, so I landed here without a heavy heart!

I wasn't sure what to expect. All I remember is that I felt grateful for such a possibility. Excited to see a totally different world. Amazed to see so diverse cultures. For me, all of that was a little bit like *a candy floss for the toddler when eats it for the first time and instantly falls in love!*

Little did I know that I was about to embrace the challenge that literally changed my life! Gosh, I started adulthood!

Attended interview—tick.

Secured a job as a housekeeper—tick.

Open bank account—tick.

Registered for NIN—tick.

It felt good!

Day by day flew, week by week…

Work took a huge chunk of my time and energy, however, due to (what I thought then) limited time in the UK, I was exploring the city and surroundings daily.

Did I feel brave? Not at all!

I felt small! I knew my value, but at the same time, I felt limited.

I couldn't articulate everything I wanted to, nor could I understand people around me much.

I felt frustrated, some of the basic tasks were a huge challenge for me: How do I approach someone to ask for directions? How do I explain in the shop what I am looking for?

Sometimes I felt isolated because I wasn`t able to share my excitement with people around me, e.g., during a live Jazz music festival. It was very hard to explain to coworkers where I had been during my day off, what I had visited, and how impressed I was with what I had experienced.

There were moments when I felt confused too.

Funny examples for you: "free cash machine"—I mean…cash for FREE?!

Another one: "Heavy plant crossing"—is there any big plant going to cross the road?! HOW?!

Or "Free House" above the pubs… say what?!

Oh, and one thing that I do not understand… Why do British people call dinner a TEA?!

In 2010, not many had nice shiny phones with instant internet access, so I couldn`t just Google things, use maps on the phone, or translate on demand.

You see, again, thanks to the way that my parents raised me, I didn`t let those negative emotions win. I allowed them to get to me, play on me, and then I snapped and decided that I was the boss here, and I was not going to be dependent on negatives.

So, I turned it all by 180 and went to squeeze positive out of negative, realizing the importance of learning English, I embarked on a dedicated journey of learning and self-improvement.

I have spoken with my parents about it, and after gaining their permission to stay in the UK for a year, I enrolled in a language class at local Matthew Boulton College in Birmingham.

It was a very affordable option, and I was able to combine three days a week at the college with four days of working.

Thanks to my amazing teacher, I spent countless hours practicing pronunciation, vocabulary, and grammar. Each day at college presented its own set of challenges, but my determination to overcome them fuelled my progress. With the support of a patient teacher, who understood how it is to learn a foreign language (he was from Syria) and the encouragement of my peers, I slowly but steadily began to communicate in English.

I felt more confident.

While my language skills were improving, I needed a job to sustain myself. Cleaning hotel rooms seemed to be a practical option, and I embraced it with an open mind. Though it was physically demanding and often thankless, I approached my work with a sense of pride and diligence.

Each room I cleaned was a step closer to my dreams, a lesson in humility, and a reminder of the importance of hard work.

Gosh, if you have never done this job, let me tell you this: It is extremely hard work!

Yet, I had a goal of learning English in my head and that job was a tool that allowed me to do so.

After a year in college, I passed my exams and again asked my parents for permission to stay one more year to learn English even better.

Again, being as supportive as always, they allowed me to do so. They have always believed in me and in my choices. I am more than sure that they were full of worries, but they both put a brave face on. Were they scared that something bad could happen to me? More likely, we are from a small city, there is no real crime around, and their middle daughter was in a multinational metropolis on her own. Were they scared that I would like it so much that I would stay? Possibly.

Little I knew that that they were right!

I met someone whom I fell in love with, and after not long, we moved in together.

Then, we decided to build a family together and by the time that I was taking exams at the end of second year in college, I was pregnant with our first child. I passed exams, gave birth to a baby boy and while on maternity leave, I started hunting for a new job. You see, I didn't have to search for a job at that point. I had a job to go back to if/when I wanted to.

However, due to personal circumstances, I wanted more in life. I wanted to prove to others that I was more than those that I was surrounded by at that point were thinking about me. Due to a lack of day-to-day support at that point in my life, I needed a break, and I needed something for me as me, not as a mom.

I couldn't vent out too much to my parents as they were 1000 miles away and couldn't help me in person. I didn't have many friends yet. I still felt "brand new" in the country and, even more, to the role of a mother.

I was an emotional mess, and I knew that environmental change, even slight, would do me great.

I was ready to move on.

I have applied for various jobs, and despite limited work experience, I have been invited for an interview. Due to circumstances, I had to attend it with my child—gosh, you wouldn't believe how bad I felt, unprofessional, stupid… you name it.

Thankfully, I had a great, compassionate, empathic person who was interviewing me and… I ended up with a better job offer than I applied for!

Can you believe it?!

It felt great!

Despite obstacles, I achieved something, and it felt phenomenally great!

This was one of those moments when I reminded myself that I was born to play big!

After a few years at the workplace, another opportunity came along. I finally passed my BA degree in Poland (I was able to take part online and submit all my assignments online too, yet had to fly often to attend all exams in person), and I was able to apply to study for a master's degree at University College Birmingham, in International Hospitality Management.

I was in a zone to move the world—well, at least my little world—to achieve something that no one in my close family had done before. You know, for years, I was told that I would never learn English. And now, I was ready to study for a Master's degree at the British University! I wasn`t scared; I felt proud, and I could sense that finally, slowly, I was stepping into my own powers.

My (then) boss agreed to totally change my contract, from set hours to zero hours, so I could adjust working days to Uni. Combining this with raising a child who was attending school, keeping household "up and running" and million other daily tasks was extremely challenging. But was well worth it, and that was another reminder that learning English started paying off!

I graduated and kept working, life was going well and steady. And happy.

And then the pandemic hit.

The outbreak of the COVID-19 pandemic brought about unprecedented challenges that reverberated across industries, economies, and individual lives. It forced many to reevaluate their paths and strategies, adapt to new norms, and pivot towards unexpected opportunities.

Long story short…

Like millions, I had to choose: I could use that time to moan and feel sorry for myself, or I could use it as an opportunity for a change or upgrade.

Totally unplanned, I have entered a limitless world of online opportunities.

And I sank in.

I started spending hours and hours every evening discovering online options and possibilities, teaching myself a lot of things that I never thought I would be interested in!

Tried and tested many things…

Freebies, webinars, low-cost masterclasses, courses.

You name it.

I was curious and wanted to constantly explore possibilities. I was amazed to find out that there is another world in an online space that could be a better solution for many in terms of working style—their own hours and days. Adjust work to kids' schedules, not the other way around. Adapt time spent at work to other commitments, not the other way around.

It blew my mind that things that I was previously scared about (technology, anything on the laptop) started bringing me joy and money!

Over time, I watched a few women grow from "unknown" to six-, seven-figure earners as I learned from them, and it constantly amazed me,that online success really is possible!

You "just" have to learn a bit and find out what it is that you want to do, what brings you passion and joy.

Oh, and it is totally fine to change direction as you go!

As a result of my self-guided learning, I offered a wide array of services for female business owners, including:

- designing websites
- establishing membership systems for others
- developing courses on behalf of others
- designing social media graphics
- crafting graphics for e-books and printed books
- assisting female entrepreneurs with diverse technical backend responsibilities associated with managing an online business.

I kept busy in an online world, and after countless trials and errors, I created a digital magazine plan in my head and own membership!

Fuelled by a burning passion for storytelling, which I actually never knew I had, I decided to launch my own digital magazine purely for and about women in business: *Thriving Women in Business.*

With determination, I taught myself the basics of online publishing. The early weeks were filled with challenges, from technical glitches to learning the art of content creation. However, with each issue, I grew, gradually building a readership that resonated with the stories I shared.

It struck me that so many women straight away trusted me with the project! It gave it an extra boost to get up and running. A few months later, it is still in constant improvement and under changes, yet more and more women are reaching out to share their stories, and for me, that is a massive achievement because I can help them become visible.

I have discovered that, as much as I like serving, even more I desire to amplify the voices of women in business. So, my vision was to create a platform where their stories could shine, a space where women's accomplishments were not only acknowledged but celebrated. It was a vision rooted in empowerment, aiming to inspire not only aspiring women entrepreneurs but also the broader audience to recognize the invaluable contributions that women are making to the business landscape.

The magazine is a tribute to resilience, ambition, and the unbreakable spirit that is pushing women forward despite the odds stacked against them. I wanted to shatter the glass ceilings, one story at a time, and create a ripple effect that would reverberate through the business world.

I believe that women have the power to inspire, evoke empathy, and ignite change. I am constantly searching for phenomenal women in business, to showcase the diversity of experiences, from the challenges they conquered to the strategies they devised to overcome obstacles.

Women who had faced their own trials and emerged stronger than ever.

The stories I shared began to resonate with readers who saw themselves in the journeys of these remarkable women. The impact already is tangible—messages of gratitude and inspiration pouring in, reinforcing the significance of the platform I had created.

In my case, it is not about numbers as participation is complimentary; it is about the connections forged, the conversations sparked, and the ideas ignited.

The process of curating such stories had an effect on my own confidence. As I empowered others through their narratives, I found myself transformed—from someone who once grappled with language barriers to a confident communicator who is unafraid to voice her vision.

It reminded me that

> *barriers are meant to be broken, limitations are meant to be challenged, and dreams are meant to be realized.*

Running a digital magazine requires more than just compelling content; it demands a network of like-minded individuals who believe in my vision. These connections not only expanded my knowledge but also provided opportunities for collaboration and growth. Together, we share insights, learn from one another's experiences, and uplift each other on our respective journeys.

And then, after hundreds of conversations, I realized that many readers are still held back in their businesses. The majority is due to two aspects: lack of techy "know-how" and finances.

I realized that I had tools in my hands for a deeper connection with my audience. This led to the transformation of my platform into a membership-based model.

And at that point, I decided to transform the courses that I had available into one, extremely affordable multi-passionate membership,

SEVEN

It is aimed at beginners as well as those wanting to extend their knowledge and skills. It is a premium membership site, a world of exciting benefits, valuable resources, and unparalleled support that is designed for women in business, whether you want personal or professional growth.

Looking at the evolution from only hosting a digital magazine to a membership-based platform, I am reminded of the power of adaptation. As an entrepreneur, I learned that the journey is marked by evolution—a willingness to pivot, innovate, and respond to the needs of the audience. The transition wasn't just about business strategy; it was a reflection of the intrinsic human desire for connection.

From sharing stories to cultivating a space of belonging, my journey encapsulates the evolution of a vision into a reality. The transformation from readers to members, from content consumers to an engaged community, is a testament to the impact of embracing change and stepping into the role of an entrepreneur. It's a reminder that the path to success is never linear, and that sometimes, the most unexpected turns lead to the most remarkable destinations.

Looking back on my journey, I find a deep sense of fulfillment in how far I've come. From a place of not knowing English and cleaning hotel rooms, I have transformed my life into one of purpose, creativity, and entrepreneurship. Through dedication, hard work, and a willingness to learn, I defied the odds and turned obstacles into stepping stones. This narrative serves as an inspiration for anyone facing challenges on their path, highlighting the potential for change when one embraces opportunities and believes in their own potential.

Oh, and did I tell you that, in the meantime, I have landed my perfect dream daily job too?!

I feel proud of my journey, and I am extremely grateful for everyone who has crossed my path, either for a bit or to walk together. I will be forever thankful for all the amazing women I met in the online world and their trust in me. Because of them, I have gained so much knowledge, new skills, and expertise!

Because of the constant belief in me from many, especially from my mom and Julie, I keep going, even when lows occur!

I hope that my story highlights how individuals, driven by a blend of necessity and ingenuity, can navigate uncharted waters and create new avenues of impact. It's a reminder that even amidst challenges, the human spirit can rise, adapt, and forge pathways that lead to unexpected horizons.

I believe, that from now on, you will turn challenges into possibilities!

I STAY STRONG,
YOU STAY STRONG.
SHE STAYS STRONG.

Contact details:

thrivingwomeninbusiness.newzenler.com

thrivingwomeninbusiness.newzenler.com/f/books

linktr.ee/such_marta

facebook.com/suchmarta

Natalie Dolan

Ginger Fox Media
Digital Marketing Consultant & Certified Mindset and
Neurogetics Transformation Coach

https://www.linkedin.com/in/natalie-dolan-ginger-fox-media/
https://www.facebook.com/profile.php?id=100009162518264
https://www.instagram.com/gingerfoxmedia
https://gingerfoxmedia.com/

Natalie lives in England, UK with her family and rescue dog Arnie.

Natalie founded Ginger Fox Media and Nat Dolan Coaching and has Certifications in Web Development, Digital Marketing, Mindset Coaching and Neuro-Energetics Coaching.

Natalie has ADHD and a child with high-functioning Autism, which she Home Educated until September 2024, in which her son then enrolled at college to study Animal Care.

Natalie has many interests and passions including Family time, Time in Nature, Animals, Foxes, Writing, Technology, Spirituality, Psychology, Art and Human Design.

Natalie's main life core values include:

Joy, Satisfaction, Creativity, Love, Connection, Communication, Exploration, Contribution.

Natalie loves the vibes and aesthetics of 1980's, 1990s, Boeheim, Alice in Wonderland, Princess Peach, Care Bears, Jim Henderson's Labyrinth.

Quotes Natalie loves includes:

That what does not kill you only makes you stronger.

The definition of Insanity is doing the same things over and over and expecting different results.

A Journey of Resilience: Embracing Empowerment Through Life's Challenges and Triumphs

By Natalie Dolan

It's 42 years since I popped out into the big wide world of Humanity. With four decades on this planet, I have had plenty of time for experiencing challenges and grow stronger.

She Stands Strong is the concept and belief that women around the world live a life of resilience, empowerment, and inner strength despite whatever experiences and situations are thrown at them.

"Never doubt that you are valuable and powerful and deserving of every chance in the world to pursue your dreams."

Female empowerment and personal growth are the concepts and actions that help drive us towards growing and standing strong.

Life is a journey full of not only beautiful experiences but also difficulties, lessons, and challenges. When we take steps to move into our empowerment, face up and learn from our difficulties and challenges, step into more empowered embodiment, mindset, and paradigms by undertaking various activities and using various tools such as breathwork, journaling, shadow work, and more, we are evolving into the Power of She Stands Strong.

She Stands Strong when:

She lives with anxiety.

Develops asthma aged 9.

Develops autoimmune disorders and arthritis aged 13.

Suffers from chronic fatigue.

Suffers from low self-esteem.

Experiences high school bullying.

Meets the love of her life and finally feels accepted for who she is.

People try to sabotage her happiness and relationship.

Suffers from broken friendships.

Experiences ill health and job challenges.

Experiences marriage.

Becomes pregnant, after thinking she never would.

When she births her baby boy into the world and knows that life will never be the same again.

When she experiences family estrangement.

When her first and only ever child goes to school.

When she deregisters her only child from primary school and embarks on a home education and unschooling journey, with all the judgements and negative comments.

When other home education parents turned sour and ostracized her and her son.

When she gets her son assessed and gets a high-functioning autism diagnosis and an EHC plan.

When she sends him to a high school after 5 years of home education.

When COVID hits and brings her son back into unschooling.

When she sends her son back to school to only go and register again seven weeks later.

When her son is now ready to attend College and sits there looking back at the wonderful memories she has had with her one and only child.

When she monetises her online businesses despite her neurodivergent brain and health challenges while home educating her son.

When she experiences tons of health challenges.

Those are some of the challenges and experiences where I stand strong.

What are the challenges and experiences you have been through that allow you to step into the "She Stands Strong" energy?

Life began as a happy-go-lucky baby, toddler, and child. Home life was great, and I had a close family connection with the majority of my family members. I have lots of happy childhood, family home-based memories.

I feel that my experiences with growing stronger started around nine years old.

My first experiences with health challenges hit me at nine years old when I was diagnosed with asthma, then followed by autoimmune disorders, arthritis, and chronic fatigue. For most of my childhood and a lot of my adult life, I have not only had asthma, autoimmune health issues, neurodiversity and fatigue, but also big bouts of depression and anxiety.

I don't have many memories of primary school, but bullying mostly happened in high school for me. Combine bullying with puberty and severe health challenges, and it becomes a very challenging time and experience. The fatigue, depression, anxiety, and not being able to focus and function much in a classroom environment, along with the verbal and emotional bullying, mostly gave me chronic self-esteem issues along with the anxiety and depression. I knew that this was a temporary experience and once I left the hell hole that was school, things would be much better, and they were, don't get me wrong. I did experience a whole heap of other challenges but I did feel so much more empowered, so much more freedom, so much more connected to life and people, but there was still much more work I needed to do on myself.

There is not enough space in this chapter to explore bullying in depth along with the other experiences within my life that I would love to share, but several people's names are clear in my head. I was a shy and timid girl in high school, a hermit who kept to herself, trying to remain invisible to the world around her. Yet it did not seem to work out that way as it seemed to make me stand out more like a sore thumb.

I remember one girl, who did not join our high school until Year 10, I will call her Mandy (name changed for legal purposes). I remember this other girl I was hanging around with quite frequently, who I really liked and felt I got on really well with, she was fun and down to earth, let's call her Nadine. Mandy befriended Nadine pretty quickly and many classroom lessons all three of us shared together. She spoke quite nicely to me and was friendly enough to begin with, but as time passed, her whole persona changed.

One day she totally flipped her lid, I can't even recall where we were or what we were doing, but all I remember is her approaching me and yelling out, "Fuck off, don't come near me and stay away from Nadine, she doesn't like you, she does not want to know you, but she won't tell you to your face, so I am, stay away or I will kick your head in!"

I remember shaking inside, caught off guard, like, was I really that much of a cunt, nope that would be her, was I really that much of a burden or annoyance, I rarely fucking spoke and mostly fucking listened.

I remember going to the head of years office, and I was experiencing a fully blown panic attack. I remember this lady helping me to regulate my nervous system and calm down. She also spoke to both Mandy and Nadine at some point. I remember Nadine coming up to me some weeks later and apologising and saying that she never felt those things about me or wanted me to feel this bad, but that she also had to do her best to fit into school. I never once received any apologies from Mandy.

Years later, I received a friend request on Facebook from Mandy. Still, no apology. I accepted the friend request because I was in a much more healed place and also because I was in the attitude of "The Past is in the Past." It would also be interesting to see if she had changed much; she had 4 kids now, she was a mother, she will have likely matured greatly.

I was friends with her on Facebook for a while; however, she has since disappeared from Facebook or blocked me. She was married with two kids, but then divorce happened, and she was a single mother. She then started dating a guy who was in our year at school and had two more children with him. Their relationship seemed steady for years, then eventually, she was putting out social media posts about him being abusive. Not only that, but prior to that, she put out a Facebook post about her oldest daughter having anxiety and mental health issues and being bullied at school. "Wow, now that is fucking Karma," was my first initial thought, yet after several minutes of reflection and great difficulty biting my tongue and avoiding commenting on the post, I thought this is truly dreadful. Her daughter is not responsible for the way her mother behaved at school. I often wondered if what she experienced with her daughter's bullying experience or her domestic violence relationship made her feel guilty about her behaviour in high school, and if she ever reflected on what a cunt she was.

After finishing High School, I spent two to three years at college, studying in different subject areas each time.

I still had major health challenges but just went along with life on autopilot, combining college and working part-time for a few years. I also started going clubbing and to bars with a friend called Emily, pretty much every weekend. My confidence was huge, especially after several drinks, I felt so free, and I was exploring myself and finding myself. I met a few guys along the way, but nothing serious ever became of them. Dating felt super awkward, and I got bored of people really fast. I was still young, still finding myself, and possibly hanging around the wrong places with the wrong people.

I met my current husband, aged 19. We actually went to the same high school together, but he was in the year above me. My first memory of him, when I didn't even know his name, was when I was 11 years old and he was 12. I was in Year 7, the first year of high school, and he was in Year 8, the second year of High School. I remember seeing him, blonde wavy hair, brown eyes, and dimples, with the most cheeky and mischievous grin ever, running around the school corridors looking like he was a right mischievous little shit. I remember seeing him over the years in the school talent show singing, but we never really saw each other close enough to speak properly and we never spoke or knew each other in high school.

We first properly got speaking as we went to the same local pub, my husband, then boyfriend, also knew my cousin Angel and auntie Eden, and one day he saw me walk to the local shop with my cousin, and he must have seen my cousin at a later date and asked about me. Anyhow, months went by, and one night at the local pub, I was standing with my auntie, and he came over and spoke to my auntie Eden and said, "It's my birthday next month. Will you invite your Angel and her boyfriend at the time out to my birthday night out?" My auntie said, "Yes, sure, can my niece come along also?" Wayne said, "Yes, sure," this is when we got officially introduced and briefly started speaking.

We dated for about a year before we moved in together, then lived together for one year before getting engaged, and then got married three years after that. Then, I fell pregnant one year after getting married and had a positive pregnancy test on the 3rd of September, 2007. Our baby boy entered the world on the 9th of May, 2008. I remember the day I got my positive pregnancy test so vividly, it was 3rd September 2007. It was three days after my 25th Birthday, it was also the seventh year anniversary of my beloved Grandad passing away. I remember getting a very strong Intuitive urge this day telling me: "I'm Pregnant" so I did a test, I wasn't even late for my monthly period at this stage.

I had a lot of health challenges during my relationship, and my husband was there for me through it all. There was even a time he had to give up his job to care for me when I went through an extreme case of illness lasting for months on end. Other than the health challenges, I have also experienced a few broken friendships and some family estrangement, again, there is too much I could talk about here that could probably fit a 12-to-15-chapter full book.

There was a lady I went to college with one year called Frankie, we were friends during the college course we studied together and then kept in touch afterwards. I remember I used to go to her apartment, and we would drink wine and chat. Most of the girls at college tried to warn me off hanging out with her, but I did not listen. She was a little eccentric but was a nice lady deep down. She introduced me to a few guys, but nothing became of that. I also felt she was much older than me. I was 18, and she was in her late 30s or early 40s. She was single and seemed lonely. She had a son who just came over now and then to dump his washing off. I remember encouraging her to join a dating agency. At first, she brushed it off, but eventually, she did. She went on a few dates, but then there was this one guy with who she went on several dates. I remember one day in college, she said she was going to stop seeing him, I encouraged her not to and said that she should give it longer. They dated for around a year and got engaged. We were still very much friends, but she moved out of her apartment and went to live in a lovely house with her fiance. He gave her a lovely sports car, and he had a successful building business. I attended the wedding and was friends for a while afterwards until one day, I received a text message.

"Making new friends, don't contact again."

Well, the rage in my heart was like it had been set on fire, like a knife had been stabbed right through my heart, utter shock. I would have rather been completely ghosted and had my number blocked. Here was this rejection again, it brought back high school trauma friendship rejection. Here was some ADHD rejection sensitivty coming into play.

When our son was born, I was so wrapped up in a world of love and adoration. This was like a love I had never known before. Life went on as normal. He went to nursery, then reception year, then did one term of year one, and then it was January 2014, and we officially deregistered our son from public school and he was now to go into a journey of Elective Home Education.

I was not initially sure how long this would last. Maybe it was only for a year or two, but it pretty much lasted over a decade, with a brief spell in high school for several months.

So many amazing memories and we pushed through it despite all the negative naysayers.

I look back on photographs now and this week he literally started post 16 Education at a local college doing an Entry Level in Animal Care course along with Maths and English. Only two days in and he is loving it and absolutely thriving.

I spoke with my husband and also my mother when we had concerns for my son's well-being and experience within a school setting and had the teacher call us in on a couple of occasions. The stuff they brought us in about was all very petty, and they were not putting anything in place that we had previously spoken about. I spent a good few weeks, if not months, researching Home Education and Unschooling, joining Facebook groups and speaking with others who had already experienced this journey. We deregistered him in January 2014.

I remember the first ever day he would have been in school, we took a walk to a local park, and while we were there, we just took in the whole environment, feeding the ducks and having conversations about anything and everything; it all just felt so natural and flowing. We talked with the dog owners, and Conner's favorite thing would be to see how many dog owners he could get to allow him to pet their dogs, throw a ball for them, or find out the dog's name, and he also loved to guess the dog's breed.

We got into a very good flow with the Unschooling and Elective Home Education lifestyle, with no pressure, no expectations, and just loving life and learning as it flowed to us naturally. So many resources, so much community, so many meet-ups and social activities. From Chatterbooks local library sessions where stories would be read, questions answered, learning activities relating to the books that were read within the group, creative activities, and puppet making. There were home education PE sessions, Practical Science workshops, and so much more. We mostly loved just doing the outdoor nature stuff, whether it was a group park meet-up or forest school-type event, and our favorite for a while was The Incredible Farm, which was full of hay, fun and adventures.

As Conner got older, and after several years of visits from Annemarie, the Elective Home Education Officer, we discussed him trying out high school. This was also after a couple of years of being under CAMHS, now Healthy Young Minds, and getting a diagnosis of Autism Spectrum Condition with Sensory and Information Processing issues. We applied for an Educational Healthcare Plan and decided as a family, he would experience high school life. He really took pretty well to it, and he had developed a strong connection with his main teacher, a male named Imran. Several months passed, and then COVID and school closures hit, so it was back to Home Ed. Thankfully, we had a head start, so it wasn't such a shock to our system. When they started to take the children back to school, Conner went back to Year 8, but it was only around 2 or 3 months later we were deregistering him again. It was not the same at all. He had a different teacher he did not connect well with. There were many things they did I did not agree with, and I felt they did not really stick to his EHC plan. So, back to Elective Home Education, it was, which was a very Unschooled approach, creating learning activities around his interests such as animals, films, video editing, food, etc. It wasn't as easy during his teenage years, and he had become more ostracized from the home education community. His social interactions were limited due to anxiety and a change of interests and preferences for spending time with family members and a few very selective friends.

Time has flown, and it's now September 2024. Conner has attended his welcome week at college, he is now studying Animal Care with Maths and English.

I have been working from home as a Virtual and Personal Assistant whilst also Home Educated my only child.

I have also worked hard every single year on my personal growth and soul discovery.

Not only has my home education and unschooling experience with my son been a huge learning journey for me, but it has also encouraged me to be connected to my personal care, personal growth, self-education, and self-discovery needs.

I have also undertaken several courses and certifications over the years whilst being a full-on mum. I don't feel I would have been able to do any of this without the amazing support of my husband and parents.

I have done certifications in make-up and nails and then went on to certifications in digital marketing, web development, mindset coaching, and Neurogetics Energetics Coaching.

To wrap up this chapter, I want to talk about the use of some great tools and concepts that you can use to help with your self-care, soul discovery and personal growth to allow you to step into your She Stands Strong energy even deeper.

The tools I have used along the way include:

- Breathwork
- Meditation
- Journalling
- Life Auditing
- Paradigm Shifting
- Neuro-energetic and embodiment tools and techniques.
- Mindset and personal growth tools and coaching
- Tools for a Neurodiverse brain.
- Human Design Principles.

What are the signs you are a strong woman, even if you don't feel you are one:

1. You embrace your vulnerability.
2. You stand up for what you believe in.
3. You are not afraid to Love.
4. You celebrate your femininity.
5. You take care of your mental health.
6. You're financially independent
7. You value your alone time.
8. You don't let failures define you.
9. You are not afraid to ask for what you want.
10. You are a reliable person.

11. You are not defined by Societal standards.

12. You set boundaries and respect them.

13. You are always willing to learn.

14. Your resilient and learn well from mistakes.

Thank you for reading my chapter.

To connect with me further please visit the following links below:
https://guns.lol/nataliedolan
https://linktr.ee/natdolan82
https://www.gingerfoxmedia.com/resources

Val Tan

Healthcare and Information Technology Consultant

Val Tan is a native of New York City. Aside from establishing a remarkable career, she also owns several businesses ranging from career coaching to real estate. In her spare time she volunteers on the board of a non-profit organization, serves as a missionary and mentors healthcare, engineering and/or business majors from her alma mater. Val is a mother to child performer and liturgical dancer, Alana Simone; and most recently adopted a pit bull terrier named Luna-Riley.

Faith. Love. Grit.

By Val Tan

It was a calm Sunday afternoon, and we all were heading home after church. My husband and I drove up in front of our newly leased apartment, along with our two-month-old daughter sound asleep in her car seat. Prior to moving into our new home, we were kicked out of our previous place of residence due to a disagreement with the landlord, which resulted in us being told to leave immediately. My daughter was only a few weeks old, and for the first time in my life, I was actually homeless. A close friend of mine offered for us to stay in her unfinished attic that night. We ended up staying in the attic for a few weeks, having to live out of our bags with a newborn and sleeping on a mattress on the floor. So that's why it felt really good to finally be able to call someplace home again—we sat in the car some more, took a deep breath, and looked at the front of our home a little while longer. After talking through what will be prepared for Sunday dinner that afternoon, my husband looks at me and says, "You're such a great person, wife, and mother; however, I no longer want to be married."

Faith.

"Do not be anxious about anything, but in every situation, by prayer and petition, with thanksgiving, present your requests to God." Philippians 4:6

Lord, do I forgive and stay or do I forgive and leave? Shortly after my husband told me he didn't want to be married anymore, I discovered he had been having affairs with other women as well. More particularly, a colleague from his workplace and the next-door neighbor were the two women I was more readily aware of. I could recall one particular incident, while nursing my daughter one afternoon, his mistress called the house phone asking to speak with him. I learned that this woman also had a daughter, so I asked her how she would feel if her daughter ended up also having an affair with a married man. She hesitated a little before answering then said that her daughter would not be in that situation. She then asked me how come I was not yelling or cursing her out or even crying uncontrollably while speaking with her. I told her I prefer not to for something that is presumably over. We actually spoke on the phone for quite some time surprisingly about topics unrelated to the situation. She even told me under different circumstances she would be open to being my friend since I sounded like a good and reasonable person. I told her 'absolutely not' and instructed her to not ever call the house again. Although the situation overall was very difficult to face, I relied on my faith to keep me grounded and hopeful that someday things would get better.

At this time, my daughter was two and a half months old, and I was still trying to navigate being a parent while not having a mental breakdown. The hurt and the pain I felt from being loved on to being rejected the next. I honestly didn't know what to do. I had moments where I couldn't see a light at the end of the tunnel —I just wholeheartedly had to believe that all things would work together for my good despite how bleak. I heard the Lord say, clear as day, to forgive him and leave. I immediately stopped being sad, wiped away my tears, packed up our clothes in whatever I could find- boxes or garbage bags, researched divorce attorneys and then started looking on Craig's List for apartments to rent. The clarity in that moment was refreshing and reassuring. A family member actually advised me to not leave since being a single mother was very hard, from their experience. They meant well; however, I knew that I did not want to be with someone who no longer wanted to be with me. I had to put myself first in order to be the person my daughter needed me to be. Without asking too many questions, the next day, four of my brothers and two male cousins helped me collect the rest of my belongings, with so many unanswered questions and no definitive path forward, I left our newly acquired home.

Love.

"Let all that you do be done in love" 1 Corinthians 16:14

I left and never looked back. I chose to focus on making sure I was in a sound position emotionally, mentally, and physically so that my daughter could be afforded some sense of normalcy despite no longer being a part of a nuclear family. I would clean up the house while my daughter took a nap, with gospel music playing softly in the background. I would try to recite affirmations out loud whether she understood what I was saying or not. She was born 10 pounds 21 inches long with a sweet and peaceful temperament that made loving her so much easier. While going through so much unexpected heartache and pain, I made a conscious effort to remain positive no matter what since it wasn't my daughter's fault that this was occurring. For instance, since I was nursing and didn't want my breastmilk to be sour due to stress, I would find joy in the little things to make it through the day. I would be grateful that we were reasonably healthy and surrounded by loved ones. I would celebrate the fact that at times strangers who were unknowingly angels looked out for us without fail. I would not dwell on anything that didn't make sense to or feel good at the end of the day. I chose to focus on the present, which was this beautiful, intelligent, and talented little girl before me that I was given the opportunity to raise.

I leveraged my support system, whether it was a close friend, a family member, someone from church or daycare personnel. My daughter also hand selected her village even from a young age. When she was four years old, she drew a cake on a piece of paper and presented it to her uncles on Father's Day. That's probably one of the only times I saw my brothers shed a tear. Her level of awareness and knowing who chose to be in her life was something she instinctively embodied. Aside from having our support system, I sought out a psychotherapist when my daughter was five years old. Between the ages of two months to five years old, I was raising her in pilot mode in a sense. Tunnel vision- making sure I could provide for her , giving her what she needed, supporting her acting career and any other activities that contributed to her being well rounded. When she was five, I felt I had to release the burden, own up to the weight I've been carrying; to take the time to work on me. Talk through how I felt that Sunday afternoon when my life suddenly changed forever. Talking through making tough decisions without anyone else to bounce ideas off of. Talking through trusting myself as a mother. Talking through how I chose to raise her, for instance, although she was aware that her father wasn't in her life, I never bad-mouthed him. When I forgave him, I released any anger, confusion, or bitterness. Talking through being a divorcee. Talking through coping mechanisms based on what I went through day by day. Talking through fostering an environment for her to be the best version of herself despite our circumstances. Talking through how talking it through was the beginning of a new self love on a whole 'nother level.

Grit.

"Commit to the Lord whatever you do, and he will establish your plans." Proverbs 16:3

"Val, I commend you for having the courage to leave; please know that I can watch her for you whenever you need," which is what my mom told me when she too realized I suddenly had to care for this newborn alone. After graduating from university as a Biological Sciences major, I also started contracting per diem -helping various hospitals in the inner city transition from documenting in paper charts to documenting in the electronic medical/health records. When I had my daughter, I was employed as a preventive case planner with Child Protective Services, since that was a full-time opportunity. Earning less than $35,000 a year, I had to scramble enough money to move out of our marital residence while coming up with the security deposit to secure another apartment for my daughter and me. I always worked side jobs along with any full-time job, such as bartending or being an after-school part-time teacher. I was out of undergrad for about five years when I started exploring graduate school programs. I first needed to take some courses to reorient into being in school again. After undergrad, I wanted to remain in healthcare; however, I still had to find my niche. I was accepted to a local prestigious private institution where I took non-matriculated courses as a Physical Sciences major on a pre-engineering tract. Even though I did not have it all figured out, I wanted to try what felt right, even without a guarantee. I was still working in social services at the time and decided to resign when I experienced a situation where my life was endangered. Not having another backup full-time job and still trying to care for a preschooler led to falling behind in major bills; in particular, I was not able to pay my rent for three months. I went through housing court and faced a pending eviction. I told the judge I would find a part-time job or take on temporary jobs until I could pay back my rent arrears.

During those times, I literally felt like the more I tried to move forward and simply create the space for a better life for my daughter and there was, something that happened that would cause me to want to give up. I recall telling my daughter during this difficult time that I did not have enough money to buy half a gallon of milk. A half gallon of milk! There were nights that I cried and prayed; prayed and cried over and over again. I would send my resume several times a day, go on several interviews, apply to work for several temp agencies until I was able to pay down my rent arrears–which led to not getting evicted. Once I was able to pay down my arrears, I could actually start attending classes at that private institution. In parallel, I continuously applied to engineering graduate programs- however was receiving rejection letters left and right. Imagine trying to take steps to become better but facing more hardships. One day I saw that my alma mater had an executive master's program that combined engineering and healthcare, which felt like a calling. I applied; and did not get accepted right away, but rather I received a phone call from the program lead, Dr. K. He asked why should we accept me into this program, being that I have been out of school for quite some time and GRE scores were average. I told him that I've always had a desire to work in healthcare and wanted to learn the necessary skills in order to take what I can offer to another level. After the phone call, I did not hear back from Dr. K nor my alma mater on whether or not I was accepted. There were moments of doubt since I haven't received any acceptances thus far. Despite that, I remained prayerful and believed that God will set me on a path that was custom-made solely for me.

About two weeks went by after the phone call with Dr. K when I received a letter in the mail stating I was accepted into the program on a conditional basis- where I had to earn a GPA of 3.5 the first semester of the course. I was working as an Early Intervention Service Coordinator full time while attending an accelerated engineering program full-time. After the first day of class, I sat in the lecture hall and cried—just thinking to myself, how am I going to do this? I persevered, had the support of my mother to watch my daughter when needed, told my daughter that I would be tired most times, but school was temporary. My mother was working full time 12-hour shifts before I started grad school. She ended up not working for the entire year I was at school just so she was available to take my daughter to school in the mornings where I had to be at work really early, pick my daughter up from the after school program and keep her for me until I got back from work. That level of sacrifice she made for us was one of the reasons I knew my path was orchestrated for greatness. I successfully completed the accelerated program that allows practitioners to apply lean principles, data-driven analytics and strategy to improve health systems. I graduated magna cum laude and contributed to increasing female representation within STEM. Upon earning my degree, the first job offer I accepted was double my previous salary. I've been making faith moves like that ever since. I've shaped my career by finding specific ways to help healthcare systems be more efficient and implementing standards where applicable with intentionality, confidence, kindness and creativity. I never had the desire to compare myself to anyone else. I simply remain authentic to who I am, even as I evolve throughout different seasons of my life- and extend grace to myself always.

I had to take a step back and sit with the fact that I am now a single parent. It sounds basic and foundational but it helped. As parents, we automatically go into being there for our children and making sure they have a good life, but in a sense also end up compartmentalizing. They are able to have a good life because WE are intentionally being an active loving parent. I had to remind myself that she is a part of me and the better I become as a person then, the better she will be. I evolved into a better and stronger version of myself because of my daughter. Being a single parent felt like a burden most times. However, I chose to be just that—a parent, although I had to play both roles. I continued to fill myself with faith, love, and determination since you cannot pour from an empty cup. Adversity and challenges are inevitable, however, how you respond to them will set the tone for your life. I've been homeless, went through a divorce, was even laid off while making a six-figure salary- all while raising a child on my own. Throughout it all, giving up on myself was never an option. I had to find ways to shape a perspective that outweighed any difficulties, doubts and fears.

Anything you are faced with, anywhere you decide to go or whatever you decide to do will be that much more special because of *you*. You're the 'it' factor in your life at all times. It was faith that sustained me. It was love that guided me. It was perseverance and grit that reminded me to never ever let any struggle defeat my purpose.

Dr. Luiza Raab-Pontecorvo

Atomic Tae Kwon Do & Empowered Coaching
CEO & Peak Performance Strategist

https://www.linkedin.com/in/dr-luiza-raab-pontecorvo-9196864a/
https://www.facebook.com/drluizaraabp
https://www.instagram.com/drluizaraabp/
http://www.luizaraab.com/
https://atomictaekwondo.com/

Dr. Luiza is a Peak Performance Strategist, International Performing Artist, Speaker, and Entrepreneur, owning four businesses in NY including Atomic Tae Kwon Do, Music School, Coaching and Rental Real Estate. She has been a professor at SUNYSB, Hofstra, and Adelphi Universities for over 13 years. Holding Black Belts in Tae Kwon Do and Jiujitsu, she also earned a Doctorate in Musical Arts and a BA in Social Studies and French Language. A graduate of Tony Robbins Leadership Academy, Life Wealth Mastery and Business University, Dr. Luiza is also certified in Neuroscience and NLP. She has toured internationally, performing in prestigious venues like Carnegie Hall and Lincoln Center, and appeared in the award-winning film "Breakthrough." Her Women Empowerment Program continues to transform the lives of thousands of Women around the World helping them unleash inner Strength and Confidence, design Empowering Life Vision, Ignite Entrepreneurial Spirit and Elevate their Careers.

From Proving to Becoming: The Power of Resilience, Vision, and Spiritual Strength

By Dr. Luiza Raab-Pontecorvo

Introduction: The Early Struggles

Growing up in the 1980s and 1990s in communist Poland—one of the poorest countries in Europe at that time—I felt blessed to be able to pursue my passion for music, a passion that often seemed like a distant dream in a place where many aspirations never became reality. Despite the odds, I embarked on my musical journey as a young girl, practicing for hours each day with unwavering dedication. Some said I "never had a childhood," but I believe I had something far more valuable: a vision. I held tightly to my dreams, always believing in something greater. My parents, who worked tirelessly to support my aspirations, instilled in me the belief that achieving anything meaningful required becoming "the best of the best."

Their love, support, and what I recognize today as unconscious programming, developed in me a strong drive to excel. To those who observed my dedication, discipline, and many achievements, I appeared to be a gifted child. But little did they know that I was quickly becoming a perfectionist—a young woman who achieved much but often suffered in silence. The pressure to succeed was overwhelming, leading me to sacrifice my health and many friendships in the pursuit of my dreams. Despite the harsh socio-economic environment and the scarcity of money, my love for Poland remained unwavering. I adored my country, with its rich history and resilient spirit, and I was determined to represent Poland on the world stage. I wanted to show that despite the poverty and the lingering shadows of communism, our nation was educated, strong, and full of potential.

However, this deep love for my homeland made the challenges I faced even more painful. When I moved to Warsaw to pursue my studies, I dreamed of entering a world where music would heal souls, bring peace, and offer strength. Instead, I was met with a harsh reality: The world of music that I revered was tainted by jealousy, bitterness, and attempts to crush my spirit. It was a world far removed from the beauty and purity of the art form to which I had dedicated my life. The contrast between my love for music and the toxicity I encountered became a source of deep suffering.

Little did I know that, as I grew up, I would become a threat to the male-dominated world of classical music, particularly in the brass section as a French horn player. The weight of discrimination was heavy, and the pressure to prove my worth was exhausting. I found myself in a world where some believed that a woman's place was in the kitchen, bedroom, or managing traditional household tasks. But I dared to challenge those expectations. I never imagined that my choice to play the French horn would lead me to confront not only the technical challenges of the instrument but, more significantly, the deeply rooted egos and prejudices of men who couldn't accept that I, a woman, belonged in this field.

As my life unfolded, I came to understand that true success and fulfillment are not about overcoming others' limitations or proving oneself to others. It is about embracing who you are, setting your own vision, and pursuing it with relentless resilience, a positive mindset, and a deep connection to something greater. This is the story of how I transformed from a woman fighting for her passion and driven by the need to prove her worth into a woman who knows her value and shapes her own destiny.

The Foundation of Vision: The Influence of My Parents

Long before I embarked on my journey of resilience, vision, and spiritual growth, I was shaped by the unwavering support and guidance of my parents. My parents were dreamers, like me, but they grew up in a different world—a world where communism, poverty, and a lack of opportunities kept their dreams from becoming reality. Despite these hardships, they never let go of their vision for a better life, and they instilled that same sense of possibility in me from a very young age.

My parents may not have had the opportunities to fulfill their own dreams, but they saw the potential in me, and they nurtured it with all the love and encouragement they could muster. They helped me see my vision clearly, even when I was just a little girl with dreams that seemed impossible. It was my mother who particularly influenced my mindset, teaching me the powerful lesson that I decide who I become, what I am capable of, and that anything I set my mind and heart to is achievable.

When many of my male colleagues, and even some teachers, doubted my abilities, it was my parents who stood by me, believing in my love for music and my potential to achieve greatness. Their belief in me became my shield against the negativity and doubt that I encountered along the way. My mother's words echoed in my heart during the toughest times: "You decide who you become. You are capable of anything."

This foundation of belief and encouragement was crucial in shaping the resilience that would carry me through countless challenges. It was their unwavering support that helped me see a vision for my life that was bigger than the circumstances I was born into. My parents' dreams, though unrealized, became the fuel for my own, and their strength became my strength.

Part 1: The Power of Resilience

Resilience is about transforming obstacles into stepping stones toward your goals. My journey from Poland to the United States was fraught with challenges. Even before I left my home country, I faced discouragement. Many times, I heard from male colleagues, "You're just a girl; you're too ambitious. Forget your dreams." They didn't want to work with me because, in their eyes, my ambitions were unrealistic for someone like me. These words were not just casual dismissals; they struck deep, coming from people I considered my peers—my Polish people, my own community.

The sadness, disappointment, and anger that brewed inside me because of these words fueled a relentless drive to prove them wrong. But that drive was not without pain. My own teacher, who guided me through my master's program, didn't believe in me. I vividly remember attending a concert by the Vienna Philharmonic, where I was mesmerized by the horn section's performance of Robert Schumann's "Konzertstück." I returned to my lesson filled with excitement, telling my teacher that one day I wanted to play that very piece. Instead of encouragement, his response was, "You have to be born to be able to play something that difficult."

Those words lodged themselves in my heart, adding weight to the burden of proving myself. The painful realization that someone who was supposed to support me didn't believe in my potential pushed me further into a path of validation through achievement. When I finally arrived in the U.S., I not only played that particular piece, but I also won a competition and performed it solo with an orchestra. Yet, despite achieving this long-held dream, I couldn't fully enjoy it.

Carnegie Hall became like a second home to me, where I spent countless hours on stage, living the very dreams I had once been told were impossible. Yet my broken mindset, scarred by the past, didn't allow me to savor these moments. Instead of feeling triumphant, I felt hollow, even as I was admired by those who saw me as a "superwoman" with six degrees, fluent in five languages, holding a Ph.D., Master Black Belt in two Martial Arts, running a successful Martial Arts business, and performing on Broadway and at Carnegie Hall.

This realization was a turning point in my life. I had spent so many years trying to prove myself, driven by anger and hurt. But what was the point of success if I couldn't enjoy it? It was time to make a change.

Part 2: Vision and the Power of Visualization

As I continued to grow, I realized that resilience alone was not enough. I needed a clear vision of where I wanted to go, a vision that guides us through life's storms and keeps us focused on our goals, even when the path seems impossible.

From a young age, I envisioned myself performing on the world's most prestigious stages, showing the strength and the resilience of my homeland through the power of music. This vision became a driving force in my life, pulling me forward even in the darkest times. When I eventually found myself playing concert after concert in Carnegie Hall, it was a realization of that childhood dream—a manifestation of the vision I had held onto so fiercely.

Even when I began my Martial Arts journey, which at first served as a way to release the anger I felt inside, I visualized myself mastering each technique, feeling the strength in my body, and the confidence in my mind. That vision became so real to me that it pulled me forward and one day helped me earn Black Belts in both Tae Kwon Do and Jiu Jitsu.

Visualization is not just about seeing your goals; it's about feeling them, tasting them, and embodying them. It's about creating a vivid picture of what you want to achieve and holding onto it with unwavering belief. This is what I teach my students and coaching clients today—how to create a vision that is so powerful that it propels you forward, no matter what obstacles you face.

Part 3: The Importance of Mindset

As I worked on my vision, I began to understand the crucial role that mindset plays in achieving success. Our thoughts shape our reality, and the words we speak create the world we live in. For years, I lived with a mindset of proving myself to others, and it left me feeling drained and unfulfilled. But as I began to shift my mindset, I started to see changes in every area of my life.

Realizing that my mindset was holding me back, I began to change the way I thought about myself and my achievements. I recognized the destructive power of negative self-talk and the belief that I was only worthy if I achieved something grand. I learned to replace self-doubt with self-belief, to speak words of affirmation rather than criticism, and to focus on what I wanted to create rather than what I feared. This shift in mindset was transformative and allowed me to enjoy my successes in a way I never had before.

Today, I coach others on the power of mindset, helping them to understand that they are the authors of their own stories. By taking control of their thoughts and words, they can shape their destinies and create the lives they desire.

Part 4: Letting Go of the Past

One of the most challenging but liberating parts of my journey was learning to let go of the past. For many years, I carried resentment and anger towards those who had hurt me, particularly the men who had tried to hold me back in Poland. I thought that by proving myself to them, I could heal the wounds they had caused. But I was wrong.

Holding onto resentment only kept me stuck in a cycle of pain and frustration. It wasn't until I began to let go of that anger and forgive those who had wronged me that I truly began to heal, and I enjoy what I do: my music making, my public speaking, and sharing Martial Arts with others. Forgiveness doesn't mean forgetting or excusing what happened; it means releasing the hold that the past has on you so that you can move forward with freedom and peace.

Letting go of the past allowed me to fully embrace the present and step into my power. It freed me to pursue my dreams without the weight of old wounds dragging me down. It was a crucial step in my journey towards becoming the woman I am today—a woman who is not defined by her past but by her vision for the future.

Part 5: The Spiritual Journey and Divine Power Within

As I continued to develop resilience, refine my mindset, and strengthen my self-belief, I found myself on a path that was leading me somewhere even deeper—into the realm of spirituality. The global pandemic, which upended life as we knew it, brought this into sharp focus. My Martial Arts business, like many others, faced existential threats. The families and children who remained loyal to us during those dark times were more than just clients; they were my extended family. I felt an immense responsibility to stay strong for them, to be a pillar of support in a world that was suddenly unstable and frightening.

But as I poured my energy into keeping the business afloat and caring for my community, I found myself drained and exhausted. The physical and mental demands were overwhelming, and for the first time, I felt the weight of carrying so many others on my shoulders. It was during this time of deep exhaustion that I began to turn inward, seeking not just the strength to endure, but also peace—a peace that I realized could only come from a spiritual source.

This was the beginning of a profound spiritual awakening. I started to connect more deeply with my faith, realizing that the divine power I had always sought externally was, in fact, within me. The divine wasn't something distant or unreachable; it was an integral part of who I was. This realization gave me a new kind of strength—a spiritual strength that complemented the mental and physical resilience I had developed over the years.

As the world slowly began to reopen, I attended a meditation retreat that would further transform my understanding of life, energy, and the Divine. It was here that I discovered the incredible power of energy, frequencies, and self-healing. I learned that each of us carries within us a divine power, a source of strength and healing that can be accessed through intention, focus, and faith.

This understanding of energy wasn't new to me; it had been a constant presence throughout my life, even if I hadn't fully recognized it. A vivid example of this occurred during my journey to earning my Black Belt in Martial Arts. One of the requirements for my test was to break a cement block with my bare hands. This was not just a physical challenge—it was a test of mindset, faith, and energy. I remember practicing in my garage, preparing myself mentally and spiritually more than physically. To ensure I was ready, I didn't just set up one cement block—I stacked three on top of each other. With absolute focus, channeling all my energy, I struck the blocks. They shattered effortlessly, almost as if I was caressing them rather than breaking them. I didn't feel the impact; instead, I felt my energy flow through me and into the blocks, breaking them apart with ease.

In that moment, I realized that my entire life had been an experience of energy, even if I hadn't always recognized it. As a young girl playing music, I would often feel a powerful sensation in my body, a vibration that coursed through me as I played. Today, I recognize that same sensation during meditation when I feel energy flowing through me, a vibrational force that connects me to something greater.

The experience of breaking those cement blocks was a profound affirmation of the inner life force that exists within all of us. My hands, which I had always protected because they were vital to my music career, became instruments of this divine energy. There was no hesitation, no doubt that I could break the blocks. I knew I would be safe, and I knew I was capable of the impossible.

This spiritual journey has become an ongoing part of my life. It strengthens my faith, heals my body, and brings a profound peace to my mind. It has taught me that true resilience is not just about enduring challenges, but about thriving through them by connecting with the divine power within. This connection has allowed me to face even the greatest challenges with a sense of calm and purpose, knowing that I am supported by something far greater than myself.

The spiritual aspect of my journey has also deepened my commitment to my vision for my life. It has given me the clarity and the courage to continue nurturing that vision, even when the path forward is uncertain. Spiritual growth, I have learned, is not a destination but a journey—one that enriches every aspect of life and enables us to live with greater faith, loyalty, and dedication.

Conclusion: Living with Vision, Purpose, and Spiritual Strength

Reflecting on my journey, I see how each element—resilience, vision, mindset, self-belief, and spirituality—has woven together to create a life that is both meaningful and fulfilling. The spiritual strength I have gained has become the foundation upon which everything else is built. It has allowed me to approach life with a sense of peace and purpose, knowing that I am guided by a divine power that is always within me.

To the women reading this chapter, I want to share this: You have within you a reservoir of strength, resilience, and divine power that can carry you through any challenge. Embrace your spiritual journey as a vital part of your growth. Trust in the divine within you, and let it guide you toward the fulfillment of your dreams and the realization of your highest potential.

You are stronger than you know, and more capable than you can imagine. Your past does not define you; your vision for the future does. Embrace your resilience, cultivate a powerful mindset, and believe in yourself with all your heart. Let go of the need to prove yourself to others, and instead focus on becoming the best version of yourself. When you do, you will find that there are no limits to what you can achieve.

The power to create the life you desire is within you. Hold your vision close, feel it, taste it, and live it every day. And when challenges arise, as they inevitably will, remember that you have the resilience, the mindset, and the belief to overcome them. This is your story, and you have the power to shape it into something extraordinary.

Sarah Cox

Founder and CEO of Sarah Cox Marketing

https://www.linkedin.com/in/sarahcoxmarketing/
https://www.facebook.com/sarahcoxmarketing/
https://www.instagram.com/sarahcox.marketing
https://sarahcoxmarketing.com/

Sarah Cox is a leading UK funnel & automation expert. For the past 7 years, she has been the official automation expert for the Mastermind Clients of one of the UK's top business growth experts, Nick James.

Sarah works with established 5, 6 and 7 figure coaches, experts and service-based business owners to attract more high calibre leads and clients, leverage their time and scale their business, so they can experience money and time freedom.

Sarah offers her "Leads On Autopilot" and "Clients On Autopilot" 1:1 Done For You services, group programmes and courses to decide on and implement the best funnel and automation strategy for their business and the goals they want to achieve.

In a field dominated by men, Sarah is one of the top women in funnels, automation and systems in the UK.

Control Your Destiny Or Someone Else Will

By Sarah Cox

That is what my boss said to me when I worked in Human Resources. It hit a chord straight away. It stopped me in my tracks. I hadn't really thought about it before. I had gone down the typical school, university, career path and hadn't considered anything else.

In that moment, I realised if I didn't decide what I wanted, someone else would—which area of the business I supported, whether I got the promotion I'd been promised, who my boss was, when I could take holidays—all of these decisions were being made for me by someone else.

I never really stopped to ask myself whether it was what I *wanted* to do long-term. I enjoyed the work, liked the people I worked with, and felt a sense of achievement.

But as I sat with my boss's words ringing in my ears, I had an epiphany. I realised I needed to take control of my future. If I didn't decide what I wanted and go after it, then someone else would do it for me. And I would be living a life that wasn't truly my own.

Not long after that conversation, there was a significant change of management at my company, and suddenly, my role shifted as the level beneath me was removed. My job title hadn't changed, and my pay remained the same, but the type of work I was doing was a step backwards. I was no longer growing in my role, and it left me feeling restless and dissatisfied.

I decided to explore other HR opportunities, and it wasn't long before I found a more senior role with another company. I was doing well and was recognised as one of the top HR people in the company. I liked being seen as one of the best.

But over a couple of years, the long hours, travel to and from work and pressure of corporate life began to wear me down and take its toll. I often worked late into the evening after most people had gone home and then was waking up early to do it all over again.

It all came to a head during a business trip. I wasn't feeling well before I went, but as so many of us do, I put on a brave face and pushed through it. I wanted to go as I had been selected to attend, and it was a great opportunity, so I kept going, telling myself I just needed to get through the trip.

But by the time I got home, I was completely wiped out. I called in sick on Monday, thinking I just needed a few days to recover.

A few days turned into a week, and then a month. No matter how much rest I got, I couldn't seem to shake the overwhelming exhaustion. It was more than just being tired—it was a deep, bone-weary fatigue that left me unable to function. My head felt like it was full of cotton wool and I couldn't concentrate on anything for very long.

I was diagnosed with chronic fatigue syndrome, and it became clear that this wasn't something I could just push through and recover from quickly.

The next few months were a blur. I spent most of my time at home, trying to recover and get back to some semblance of normality. But every time I thought I was ready to return to work, I would relapse. I went back too soon—twice—and each time, I ended up off sick again.

This cycle continued for nine months. During that time, I had a lot of time to think. My boss's words kept playing in my mind, "Control your destiny, or someone else will." I realised that my corporate career, which I had worked so hard to build, was at risk because of my health.

I started to think about what else I could do, what else I would do if I couldn't go back to work, if my health stopped me from pursuing my corporate career.

After nine months, I managed to go back to work part-time. It was hard. I didn't feel great. I wanted to do a great job, but my health wasn't allowing that. And as hard as it was to admit, I wasn't sure if I could continue on this path. It wasn't something I had planned to give up, but my health was affecting my ability to do my job well.

I needed to make a decision. Do I stay or do I go?

The decision to leave my HR career was not an easy one. It was tough, for sure, to give up everything I'd worked for over 19 years and a great salary for the unknown. But the reality was that my body wasn't allowing me to continue, and I needed to listen to it.

I could have taken some more time off or moved into a different HR role or moved to a job closer to home.

But I realised this was my opportunity to shape my own destiny. I decided now I had the opportunity to do something for myself and help other people.

And you know the saying "every cloud has a silver lining"? That was definitely true for me.

So, in 2011, after much soul-searching, I made the decision to leave my HR career. It wasn't just a career change—it was a complete life overhaul.

I had long been interested in alternative therapies, having used them to overcome my chronic fatigue, and I began to think about how I could turn that interest into a new career.

At the same time, I realised that I wanted more freedom in my life.

I hadn't had the freedom to do what I wanted every day as an employee.

I used to drive to work, see people in the park and the local cafes and wonder what they did that meant they weren't travelling to work like me.

I decided I didn't want to wait until retirement to do what I wanted.

I dreamt of doing my own thing: being my own boss, working when I wanted to, enjoying what I was doing every day and getting fitter and healthier.

I thought about learning reflexology, but the thought of dealing with people's feet every day made me think again.

I decided I wanted to become a Pilates Teacher. The funny thing about this? I'd never done Pilates in my life. I just intuitively knew it was what I wanted to do. After all, my mum and brother did Pilates and enjoyed it, so I thought, "Why wouldn't I?"

I took a leap of faith, as it felt like the right path forward, and a new chapter in my life began. I could never have predicted it happening before I became ill. I thought I would always work in HR.

But now, a new opportunity had arisen—a chance to control my own destiny; to be my own boss.

It was all really exciting, and I couldn't wait to get started…

But I had no idea how to build a business, how to tell people what I was doing and how to find clients.

I was googling business events in London and found The Business Show 2012. This massively changed my life. I came away on a high – hugely motivated and keen to learn more about online marketing.

It led me on an incredible journey into the world of entrepreneurship and online marketing. Neither of which I knew existed before this.

In that first year of business, I threw myself into learning as much as I could about entrepreneurship and online marketing. I attended business events, read books and invested a lot of money in working with coaches to help me develop my Pilates business.

But do you know what I realised? Yes, it was great, but I still didn't have complete freedom.

Teaching Pilates meant that I had to work evenings and weekends as this was when my clients wanted to do classes, and I had to teach in the area where I lived—I couldn't work from anywhere without starting all over again.

I had a dream—a dream to live by the sea. It's the ultimate dream for a lot of people I speak to, even now.

I dreamt of being able to work from anywhere and having the freedom that allowed me to structure my day however I chose to.

I wanted to make this dream a reality. And do you know what? A few years later, I did just that.

I had uncovered a passion I didn't even know I had for online marketing. It was something I had never considered before, as I didn't know it existed. In fact, I found myself more excited about learning how to market my business than actually teaching Pilates! I loved the process of figuring out how to attract clients, build an online presence and create automated ways to book clients in for classes.

A couple of years into my Pilates business, I went to a business event all about online marketing and business growth. The two guys hosting the event introduced a five-step framework for attracting and converting leads into clients. I loved what they shared and I knew that I wanted to learn more.

At the end of their talk, they offered a Strategy Day to implement their framework, and I jumped at the opportunity to do this for my Pilates business.

This decision changed everything for me once again.

The Strategy Day was great fun. The strategy we came up with was great and I really enjoyed the process we'd gone through to create it.

I left thinking: "I'd love to be doing this. Wouldn't it be great if they needed other people to teach this to their clients?"

And do you know what happened?

About a week later, I got an email from them saying they were looking for a handful of people to train in their Strategy Day approach. They wanted to expand their business and couldn't reach enough people on their own. They offered a Discovery Day at their office to find out about the opportunity to do this with them.

I signed up straight away, and this was, unbeknownst to me at the time, the start of my journey into becoming a Marketing Automation and Funnels Expert.

I've only learnt about the law of attraction and manifestation in the last few years, but now I think this is what happened here. I thought about the idea, visualised it and then the opportunity arose. Then, I set to work to make it a reality.

Ten years later, I am an experienced Marketing Automation And Funnels Expert. I still use what I learnt on the Strategy Day in my business today. I have honed my skills and worked with countless clients, helping them grow their businesses by creating automated, scalable systems and funnels.

And the guy I learnt from is still my mentor today.

In 2016, he asked me to be the "go-to" automation expert for his mastermind clients as he needed someone who could support his clients with implementation, whilst he focused on strategy. I still do this today at the same time as growing my own brand and business.

And I am so grateful as without him, I believe I wouldn't have the business and lifestyle I have today.

In 2017, I achieved my dream of living by the sea. I moved to the south coast and traded in my London two-bed flat for a four-bedroom house with a water view, just five minutes walk from the water.

This is another example of the law of attraction at play, as the dream I had been visualising for years had become a reality.

Whilst becoming burnt out in 2011 was very hard at the time and put my life on hold for a year, it turned into a blessing in disguise. If that hadn't happened I may well still be in a corporate job making someone else rich.

Instead…

I wake up every day with a sense of freedom and fulfillment that I never thought possible when I was in my corporate career.

I now work when I want to work.

I get to choose who I work with.

I get to decide when I take time off.

I get to structure my day to suit me.

I get to be my own boss.

I determine how much money I make by the actions I take.

I am truly in control of my own destiny, and I love it!

Lessons from an ex-career girl turned entrepreneur

Looking back on my journey, I realise just how far I've come—not only in terms of my career but also in the way I approach life. The burnout I experienced in 2011 was one of the most difficult times in my life, but it also led me to where I am today. It forced me to re-evaluate my priorities and take control of my destiny.

If there's one key lesson I hope other women, who are facing challenges, in a job they don't enjoy or living a life that doesn't fill them with joy, take from my story, it's this: You are in control of your life. No matter where you are right now, no matter how stuck you feel, you have the power to change your path. It won't be easy, and it won't happen overnight, but it *is* possible.

Here are the lessons I've learned along the way:

1. **You have to control your destiny, or someone else will.** Don't let life happen to you.
2. **Trust your intuition.** When something doesn't feel right, it probably isn't. Listen to your inner voice, and don't be afraid to make changes.
3. **Your health and happiness are the most important things in life.** Take care of your body and mind. If you don't, nothing else will matter.
4. **You can always reinvent yourself.** It's never too late to start over or pivot in a new direction.
5. **Visualise your dreams and take action.** You can achieve your dreams as long as you take consistent action toward your goals.
6. **Don't be afraid to invest in yourself.** Whether it's time, money, or energy, the best investment you can make is in your personal growth.
7. **Every cloud has a silver lining.** What seems terrible at the time, often turns out to be a blessing in disguise. We can only see it in hindsight.
8. **You can achieve your dreams**—you just have to have the courage to go after them.
9. **Time is precious.** Use it to do what you love.
10. **If you're not doing what you love, change it.** Decide what you want to do and do it.
11. **Don't let fear get in your way.** "Feel the fear and do it anyway"

12. **Don't let someone else decide what you do and when and where you do it.** You decide.
13. **You are in control of your life.** Be your own boss.
14. **Create and live the life you truly want and deserve**—and don't let anyone get in your way.
15. **You are the author of your own story.** Don't let anyone else write it for you.

My journey has been a rollercoaster, but every twist and turn has led me to where I am today—a place of freedom, fulfillment and doing work I'm passionate about.

If I could leave you with one final thought, it's this:

If you want it, you can do it.

I'm rooting for you.

Lisa "LiLi" Young

CEO of WorkSource Consulting, LLC
Author

www.linkedin.com/in/lisa-young-pmp-sphr-shrm-scp-92982985
https://www.instagram.com/lisa_lili_young/
https://www.worksourceconsulting.com
https://www.theincredibledreams.com
https://10000cards.com/card/lisa-young

Lisa Young is an experienced Human Resources professional and has successfully worked in all HR functional areas including developing processes and policies, executive coaching, employee relations, performance management, talent acquisition, compensation, compliance, training, vendor management and employee on-boarding/ engagement. With prior professional work experience ranging from recruiter to executive director, she's worked in a variety of industries and has managed cross-functional teams and supported up 30+ business units with more than 1200 employees.

Lisa has a passion for writing and has authored a children's educational book with supplemental materials. She enjoys working to scale and elevate organizations and volunteering with non-profit endeavors. Lisa

has sat on various advisory boards that focus on education, human/
women rights and economic equity. She has a passion for organizations/
projects that focus on initiatives that serve women, children, and the
underserved/BIPOC communities.

My Story of Strength and Resilience after Heartbreaking Loss

By Lisa "LiLi" Young

Everyone has pivotal events in their lives. Many random and unexpected events occur, and there is one that turns your life totally upside down or smashes it into many tiny pieces. In attempting to share one story I asked myself, what is one pivotal event in my life that caused me to find a strength that I did not know that I possessed? Like most women, I have had more challenges than I wish to recount. This particular event that I will discuss further is one in my life's story that was significant in my development and my current state of calling and direction. Before we get to the story, there are a few things that you need to know about me first.

Who Am I?

Just like the topic of strength, I am many things. And just like you, I am complex and have many different facets. I am a mother and a daughter. I'm a partner and a friend. I make a conscious effort to be kind, caring, fair, trustworthy, courageous, respectful, and a light to the people. Those are all very important characteristics to me that I strive to uphold. I'm an entrepreneur and an author. Like most women I know, I am intelligent, ambitious, educated, thoughtful, appreciative, spiritual, compassionate, hard-working, loyal, optimistic, and empathetic to the plight of others, and yet oftentimes, I can be aggrieved, frightened, and frustrated which can lead to feelings of general despair. In this world, having expectations of a fair and just society may seem optimistic to many people. I expect much of myself, and I expect much from others too. I can not wait for the day that societal norms include fairness and inclusion for all. I was born Black to a world that has not only failed to honor my race but has decided that we are here to be exploited in various ways and to be used as pawns for profit. I was also born a woman. The world has historically considered women to be second-class citizens who should only exist in the shadows of men. These are two very prevalent conditions that bring obstacles that one must be confronted with daily. Being assigned to a hierarchical system that is arbitrarily based on anatomy and skin color is a very difficult situation to navigate. Placement on the bottom of a system, in which that placement is not based on merit, skill, or character, can be very deflating to the spirit. It can be a very sobering plight, and if you let it all in at once, it can also feel debilitating. This societal placement requires you to find the strength to survive. Regardless of who you are and what you do, to have your existence and future opportunities placed in the hearts and hands of others who do not have your best interest at heart is a condition that no one will ever find comforting. The act of practicing gratitude for the smallest of things to the greatest of blessings that I have received provides me with much-needed balance and fuel for my strength.

How Do I Define Strength?

Strength, in the lives of women, often embodies a multi-faceted concept that extends beyond physical power. It represents resilience, adaptability, and the ability to overcome challenges; and oftentimes, to be able to overcome them despite societal expectations and constraints. Acquiring strength for women can mean:

1. **Empowerment:** Gaining the confidence and autonomy to make decisions about their lives, careers, and bodies. This empowerment can come through education, financial independence, or simply asserting their voices in spaces where they have historically been marginalized.

2. **Resilience:** Women often face unique challenges—whether it's societal pressures, gender discrimination, or balancing multiple roles. Strength means developing the resilience to navigate these obstacles, turning adversity into opportunities for growth.

3. **Solidarity and Support Networks:** Acquiring strength can also involve building and participating in supportive communities where women uplift one another, share resources, and advocate for each other's rights.

4. **Breaking Stereotypes:** In many societies, women are often confined to traditional roles and are vastly underestimated. Strength means challenging these stereotypes, breaking barriers, and redefining what it means to be a woman in various fields.

5. **Mental and Emotional Fortitude:** Beyond physical strength, women often cultivate emotional intelligence and mental toughness, balancing vulnerability with assertiveness and caring for others while also prioritizing their own well-being.

6. **Advocacy:** For many women, strength is linked to advocacy—fighting for equality, justice, and the rights of future generations. It can mean taking a stand against injustice, whether on a personal level or within larger societal structures.

In essence, strength in the lives of women is not monolithic; it's a blend of internal resolve, external action, and the continual pursuit of growth and equality.

My Pivotal Event:

Though opportunities provide for continued growth, I believe that challenges, and how one handles them, have the greatest impact in shaping and changing the trajectory of a person's life. I attended college, an opportunity that neither my mother nor father had the chance to experience. This was a major feat when one understands the financial disadvantage from which I came. I am a mother, which is a true gift from God. The birth of my son changed the meaning of the words love and commitment. I have traveled and seen places that I once only imagined that I would experience in the books that I loved as a child. I am very blessed and I am very thankful for what I have had the privilege to see and experience. I've had many wonderful experiences that have given me great opportunities to grow, but it has been the challenges, the things that occurred that I did not know how I would make it to the next day, that have made the most lasting impressions. There has been one such challenge that would cause me to become entirely dependent upon God.

The year 2009 was a good year. After making it through a few prior very hard years everything seemed to be turning out for the best. The previous year, my mother had gone through chemotherapy, followed by a series of radiation sessions as one last precaution to eradicate any remaining cancer cells. Dr. Schorge, her oncologist, had been a true Godsend as we navigated this very scary, brutal, and unfamiliar territory. He would willingly explain treatment plan options, dialogue about new research, and outline the pros and cons of them all. Most importantly, he saw her humanity, and he genuinely showed concern both about her mental and physical well-being, and most importantly, about the actual care that she would receive. One day, in what seemed to be a statement that came out of the blue, he announced to us that he needed to move back to the East Coast. He said that he had been struggling with this decision but knew that he needed to go home to be closer to his family. He told us that my mom had done so well through these treatments and that he was so proud of what we had managed to bring her through. He assured us that the hospital would automatically disperse his caseload to other physicians in the oncology practice to complete the end of her treatments. Because I took her to every appointment, we all developed a great relationship, and we would love to playfully banter back and forth about how good he thought he was at his craft. He gave us the date of his last day in office and asked me if we were going to come see him to say goodbye. I said nope, that he was just trying to get another co-pay from us, and we laughed. I said that instead of saying goodbye, we would come to visit him in his new practice when we felt that my mother was strong enough to take the trip.

As he stated, she was appointed another physician. His name was Dr. M., and he was far from Dr. Schorge. There was not the same care or communication that existed before. My mother and I even talked about his demeanor, and we raised our eyebrows and "wondered" why he was so non-communicative with us. He made us feel invisible. I even asked my mother if she wanted to find another physician. She stated, "We have gone through the worst of it already. I'm really tired so let's just finish the process, and we can think about that later." We did finish the protocol that Dr. Schorge outlined for us. We ended 2009 on a very high note. Though radiation therapy was rough on her body, our thought was that it was well worth it if it worked. She finished radiation, and there were no signs of cancer cells on any test. She completed her therapy in the Fall, and Thanksgiving was great. We cooked a great feast of gratitude. At Christmas, everyone was still healthy, and we had an amazing holiday. We even got through the new year without issue. We were now in the year 2010, and we were very ready to start a brand new year. We were still in January, and it was just a few days after my birthday that we noticed an issue. My mother complained of stomach pains and could not keep food down. This was a very unusual occurrence considering she had completed her treatments. We had managed her cancer treatment side effects very well throughout her journey to wellness. Her nausea and vomiting were not severe but still enough to cause us to take extreme caution because of her previous health condition. We just didn't want to take any chances. We both thought, let's catch this issue early to avoid any greater ones later. We came to the conclusion that it would be best to take a trip to the hospital in which she had received all of her oncology care. They would undoubtedly be the very best option for her care, and this issue had to be a minor one compared to the previous illness. Side by side, we walked into the hospital to address her symptoms of nausea and vomiting. She could walk, talk, and even smile when we walked into the facility.

During the next few days in the hospital, which felt like several weeks, I personally witnessed the medical negligence that occurred in relation to my mother's care. I saw that she was considered to be a subpar citizen who did not warrant the benefit of a caring physician. I saw that they administered over-the-counter drugs, items that anyone could walk into a pharmacy and buy, instead of taking her pain and symptoms with the seriousness in which they should have been addressed. I witnessed that no tests were being run and there was no treatment plan discussed. I saw her body shutting down, and I saw the extreme pain that she was in. I longed for her original doctor, who had moved to be near his family. When I asked questions of the resident who was "tasked" with doing a daily check of my mother, I was dismissed and told that just by asking questions, I was being obstinate. The care for her health, her life, and her pain were not held as critical nor even as important. After the first few days of being admitted into the hospital, her physical decline was so immediate and extreme that it worried me to even transfer her to another location. She went from walking and talking to a state in which all of her organs were shutting down. She was not even able to breathe on her own. The care, or lack thereof, that she received shed an even brighter light on how racism permeates every system in this and most countries. It showed me that a person of color, even with a middle-class standing, a loving advocate, and great insurance, is a life that is not considered valued or worthy of great care in the eyes of all medical professionals. It was evident that she was perishing and they chose to not see what was before their eyes. It was not until I contacted an attorney and then hospital administration, that I saw what great medical care could be. A team of expert physicians: cardiologist, pulmonologist, hematologist, gastroenterologist, nephrologist, and all the specialists in every field, came to assess her, but by then, it was far too late. The plan, which should have been a very common surgical procedure to remedy the issue, was no longer an option, and at this time, nothing else was either. I didn't see the resident again that called me obstinate for asking questions and I never saw Dr. M once while there. Devastatingly, I saw my mother lay limp, dehydrated, unable to breathe, and in pain for days with no real care administered. One evening, she turned her head slowly and looked up toward the ceiling. I knew that she was seeing spirit and that the time was near. I also knew that she was trying to hold on for me because I was not ready to let her go. I called family members and my friends so that they could say goodbye. In disbelief and in need of God, we formed a prayer circle. Even though I knew in my heart that it would not work, I required "the team of experts" to perform the surgery that she should have received a week earlier. I was even allowed in the surgical room with them, and I held her hand, until it was over and I had to let go. We all knew that she would not make it, but in my younger mind, they had to try as hard as she did. I required them to resuscitate her twice and then I had to let her go. In my heart and mind, I knew those attempts were futile, but again I had to feel like we tried as hard as she had. My mother and I were together when I transitioned into this world and I had the opportunity to hold her hand while she transitioned away from it; and for that, I am very grateful. That moment has been, and hopefully will be, the one that most shaped my life and my call to leadership. I had an excellent mother, and even in her death, she gave me a great gift.

My Analysis:

For anyone who has experienced an "ism" in their life, whether it be racism, sexism, or some other -ism, you come to recognize it very well when it shows up. Even as a young girl, I knew that racism existed, but I was still a bit naive about the depths and darkness of its negative impacts. Prior to the death of my mother, I thought that the battle against racism was mostly an internal one to make peace with; an individual journey for each one of us to navigate. My thought was to just be excellent and then race, gender, and socio-economic levels won't be a factor. I felt that each person had to find the best way to navigate these systems for themselves by just merely becoming an excellent being, and unfortunately, the truth is that excellence is sometimes actually regarded with much disdain. My mother's death, and how she died from neglect, changed my viewpoint that confronting systems should be done primarily for oneself. Battling racism, sexism and systems that are degrading in their design cannot effectively be done in isolation. It takes a full community of caring, fed-up, good-intentioned, and active people to make substantial and impactful change to demonstrate that there should be respect for humanity regardless of race, age, gender, color, sexual orientation, disability, and the list continues.

My greatest outcome from this experience is that I decided that her life would be as meaningful as possible through me and my actions. I would voice the things that I see that are not just regardless of the possible consequences to self. I will be an advocate for not only myself, but for those who might not have a voice. I will do what is right even when I am afraid or intimidated. I will see the world and look for the connectedness in us all. My heart has changed. My heart is fully open. I love others with the love of God because she showed me so much mercy and grace to get me through the darkest period of my life. My mindset is different. My main focus is not on either appearance or pleasing others. My mind is at peace when I feel that I am pleasing to God. My obligation to the community is heightened. We are definitely our brothers and sisters keepers, and I believe that God placed us on earth to do good works for men and women. My obligation to self is different. I value myself, my soul, and my spirit much more than world admiration. Most importantly, my relationship with God is elevated because it has become a relationship that I can not live without. God's existence is intertwined in everything that I do.

Through so much grief, depression, and anger, and even after so much guilt, the breakthrough happened. I am thankful that I got through this time in my life without self-medicating, without inflicting pain upon myself or others, and without becoming so bitter and callous that I could not rebound from it. I am thankful that I knew God and that God was willing to be there for me. I understand now that this challenge and the outcome of it has prepared me to face many other difficult situations in which I had to fully put my trust in God, even when it was frightening and uncomfortable. I am completely certain that my relationship with God is what carried me through those very challenging years and it is still carrying me to this day. In order to feel protected, we are taught the importance of self-sufficiency. I have learned that self-sufficiency is not nearly as important as having the faith to rely on God for all of your needs. I have learned to ask for guidance in everything that I do. This act of asking and seeking God's guidance comes as readily as breathing to me. My walk with God is strong and constant and will be for always. The thing that has changed the most for me is that I have learned how to surrender myself to God in order to do his will and works, in leadership, and in every aspect of my life. I advocate for others as I wished that someone in that hospital would have advocated for my mother before it was too late to make a difference. I have written a book, "Grave Mistakes", in her honor so that no other family is left without knowing the proper steps to take to potentially save their loved ones if they are in the hands of those who have taken an oath to heal but fail to do so.

Women are such amazing beings. We are the life-givers and the caretakers. We are the strength, and not only for ourselves but for all those that we know and love. Women are genuinely caring and amazingly strong individuals who often push aside their needs and shoulder far too much as if we don't know that we too can possibly break. We often bear the unbearable and keep moving forward. It is so important to share our stories so that we know that we are not alone in any situation, whether it be that we are experiencing exhaustion, pain, grief, or depression. Women need to know that it is allowable and that they should lean on others when they are in need. Throughout history, women have shown the capability to accomplish many great things against all odds. What the world would describe as ordinary women have found various ways to eliminate barriers and make miracles happen in this world. Even in struggle, you must remember that you are still strong and the ultimate goal is to get to the next day. While you are in battle, all the days that we are blessed to see should be considered as good days; days in which we are learning and becoming even stronger. In order to stay resilient you must find ways in which your strength is renewed. When you realize that it is paramount to also ensure that you implement self-care by allowing in the support that you may need, while giving yourself grace in the interim, you will become stronger and more resilient beyond what you could have even imagined.

Dr. Sonya McKinzie

CEO of ThriveHER Inc. & ThriveHER Movement Coaching
Trauma and Recovery Coach

https://www.linkedin.com/in/sonyamckinzie/
https://www.facebook.com/ThriveHERInc
https://www.instagram.com/thriveherinc/
https://linktr.ee/thriveherinc

Dr. Sonya Alise McKinzie is a remarkable individual whose life story embodies resilience and empowerment. Raised in Brunswick, GA, she is a proud single mother to her beloved daughter, McKinzie Alise Baker. Her journey through domestic violence resulted in PTSD and anxiety; however, instead of breaking her, it has made her a symbol of strength. Her transformative experience led her to pursue extensive education, earning degrees in Business Administration and Human Services Counseling, with a focus on Addictions & Recovery. She holds multiple certifications, including Victims Advocacy and Six Sigma (Green Belt). In June 2024, she will receive a honorary doctorate in Humanitarianism for her commitment and heart to serve the community.

As the Founder of ThriveHER Inc. and ThriveHER Movement Coaching LLC, Dr. McKinzie was honored with a proclamation for ThriveHER Day in the city of Brunswick, Georgia. She is also a serial author and appreciates all things creative.

Courage Unveiled: The Journey of Triumph and the Birth of Hope

By Dr. Sonya McKinzie

Reflecting on my initial encounter with domestic violence brings me back to when I was just eight years old. The scene is etched in my memory: my stepfather's violent outbursts toward my mother, and his chilling threats. It's as vivid now as it was then, and I'm left pondering, what could have possibly justified such aggression and cruelty from him?

I remember the confusion first—the loud voices that shattered the stillness of our home, the sound of things breaking, and the sudden, sharp cries from my mother. I was eight years old, and these noises were foreign to the world I knew—a world of playgrounds and storybooks, where the biggest worry was what Mom would pack for lunch.

The first time I saw it, the violence was like watching a scene from a movie, except it was in our living room, and the actors were my parents. My stepfather, a towering figure, loomed over my mother. His voice was thunderous, his words like lightning strikes. My mother was a strong woman, but in those moments, she seemed to be so small in comparison, trying to shield herself from the storm.

I hid under the covers of my bed, clutching the covers and my teddy bear, praying that it was all just a bad dream. But the fear in my mother's eyes was too real, the danger too imminent. I couldn't understand why.

I kept asking myself, "Why was he so angry?"

What had Mom done to make him want to hurt her?

In my eight-year-old mind, I thought maybe if I had kept my room cleaner or gotten better grades, this wouldn't be happening.

As the years passed, the violence became a shadow that followed us everywhere. While my mother never spoke about it, the memories of the incident were engraved in my mind. It was in the hushed whispers of neighbors, the unexplained bruises on my mother's face, and the nights we spent eating dinner quietly at the table for fear of saying anything that would be upsetting to my stepfather. After a while, I learned to walk on tiptoes, to speak in whispers, and to never ask questions, even when I wanted to scream them.

The day my mother signed the divorce papers, I imagine that we both felt a mixture of relief and an inexplicable emptiness. The man who had cast such a long shadow over our lives was gone, but the darkness didn't leave with him. He had not gone much further than the residence of my Grand Aunt. I could not understand how she could open her home to a man who had hurt and inflicted pain on her niece. I suppose this is one of many reasons why the darkness lingered in the corners of our home, in the silence that filled the rooms where laughter should have been.

Witnessing this abuse had helped grow me up much too quickly, learning lessons no child should ever know. I learned that love could be conditional, that safety was a luxury, and that sometimes, the people who were supposed to protect you could be the ones to cause the most pain. My mother, once vibrant and full of life, became a shell of her former self. She worked tirelessly at a pulp mill, wearing steel-toe shoes and working twelve-hour shifts to provide for us, her spirit bent but never broken.

Fast forward, as I entered adulthood, the patterns of my childhood haunted me. I found myself drawn to relationships that echoed the past. I mistook control for care and jealousy for passion. Often triggered by the memories of the walls of our home as they had absorbed the echoes of violence—the sharp words, the sounds of a fist to flesh, and muffled cries. My mom and stepfather, once lovers, were adversaries, locked in a battle that left scars etched into my young heart. Their love had curdled into something dark and malevolent, and I was caught in its crossfire.

As an adult, I vowed never to let love hurt me like that. But life has a way of mocking our intentions.

Enter Marcus—a tempest of contradictions. He was a storm cloud, brooding and unpredictable. His hazel eyes held secrets, and his touch was both tender and cruel. Marcus was a drug dealer, a user, and a man who wore his scars like badges of honor. We were two misfits, drawn together by a gravitational pull that defied reason.

Perhaps it was our shared sense of isolation that forged our connection. Marcus had been to places I could only imagine—the cold, unforgiving prison cells. His letters arrived like lifelines, inked confessions of longing and regret. Ten-minute phone calls became our lifeline, the static-filled conversations bridging the gap between freedom and captivity.

I am confident that it was Marcus who helped me trust and let down the barriers that the abuse I had witnessed as a young girl had built. His letters were sweet and endearing, and his calls were comforting. His voice was strong, and the way he would say, "Hey Beautiful, what 'cha doing" made me feel that he loved me despite his bad habits. He was in prison for years, and during those years, he helped heal my heart, or so I thought.

Marcus's release from prison was a turning point—a fork in the path of my life. When the prison gates swung open, he stepped into a world cloaked in shadows and secrets. I had known him through ink and paper, our words weaving a fragile bridge across the chasm of our differences. But now, he stood before me—a living, breathing enigma.

Our first meeting after his release from prison was awkward, like two strangers fumbling for common ground. Marcus's eyes held stories—

of pain, of survival, of a life lived on the edge. He was a drug dealer, a man who peddled poison to the desperate and the lost, including himself. But I didn't know that then. All I saw was vulnerability—the cracks in his armor, the hunger for connection and to feel protected from the pain I had been running from since I was eight years old.

We spent hours talking, our words dodging the truth. Marcus was a master of evasion, revealing just enough to keep me intrigued. His laughter was a siren song, pulling me deeper into his orbit. And I, the naive dreamer, believed that love could heal even the darkest wounds.

The veil of illusion settled over us—a web that hid the jagged edges of reality. Marcus's letters had been poetic, his voice on the phone a balm for my loneliness. We were star-crossed, bound by fate and circumstance. But love, my dear reader, is a fickle muse. It blinds us to the flaws, the warning signs—the jagged rocks lurking beneath the surface.

Months passed, and Marcus became a fixture in my life. We navigated the treacherous waters of intimacy—the stolen kisses, the whispered promises. But the veil was thinning, and I glimpsed at the truth—the darkness that clung to him like a second skin. His eyes held shadows, and his touch was no longer gentle. Verbal barbed wires replaced sweet nothings, and I flinched at the venom in his words.

Then came the first blow—a slap across my cheek that left me reeling. Marcus's apologies were hollow, his eyes haunted. He didn't mean it, he said, with heavy sweat on his brow. Stress, frustration—it had all boiled over. And I, the fool, believed him. I nursed my bruised face, convinced that love could mend what was broken.

The physical abuse escalated—a twisted waltz of rage and remorse. Marcus's hands were weapons, and I was the canvas for his anger. But I clung to the illusion—the belief that he was a wounded soul, lashing out in ignorance. He didn't know what he was doing, I told myself. He didn't mean it.

The veil grew thicker, casting a shadow over the truth. Marcus's drug addiction surfaced—a demon that gnawed at his insides. He would vanish for days, leaving me to wonder, to worry. But when he returned, hollow-eyed and desperate, I welcomed him back. Love, you see, is a desperate gambler. It bets on redemption, even when the odds are stacked against it.

I became his caretaker—a nurse tending to a wounded soldier. I cleaned his wounds, both visible and hidden. I listened to his confessions—the deals, the highs, the lows. Marcus was a drug dealer, a man who traded in misery. But I was blind to it all. I believed that love could save him—that my softness could temper his hardness.

The physical abuse intensified—a symphony of pain and apologies. Marcus's fists were relentless, and I wore my bruises like badges of honor. He didn't mean it, I whispered to the mirror. He was lost, broken—a ship adrift in a storm. And I, the lighthouse, guided him toward salvation.

But love, my dear reader, is not a savior. It cannot mend shattered bones or heal fractured souls. Marcus's darkness consumed us both, and I realized that I was drowning. The veil lifted, revealing the monster beneath—the drug dealer, the abuser. And still, I clung to hope—the fragile belief that love could rewrite our story.

I was wrong.

It would take me several years of him in and out of prison, substance abuse clinics, and going back to his other lover, drugs, before I would build the nerve and power to break away from the relationship.

In late 2005, after Marcus was convicted for another drug-related incident, I decided that it was time to let go of the dream that had become a nightmare. My relationship with Marcus reached its breaking point when the veil of illusion shattered completely. The cycle of abuse—both physical and verbal—had worn me down. I realized that love, no matter how intense, could not save him or us. One day, I sat in my mess, looking into the mirror and staring back at a stranger—a woman who had lost herself in the labyrinth of a toxic love story turned bad dream.

The turning point came when Marcus's rage escalated beyond anything I could bear. He slapped me down onto the floor, and I fell against the wall, his eyes wild, and I knew that this was the end. The soft place of comfort I had once been for him had become a battleground. I found strength in my vulnerability—the same vulnerability that had drawn me to him in the first place. Ironically, several days after the incident, he was convicted, and that was when I began to plan my exit.

No, it was not a dramatic exit, no tearful confrontation—just a quiet decision to save myself. I waited for my income tax check to arrive, saved up my two months' worth of paychecks, packed up my home, and made my way to Atlanta, leaving behind the letters, the memories, and the broken promises. When Marcus called me from prison, I told him that it was over, and his pleas followed me, but I changed my cell phone number, and walked away, my footsteps echoing the finality of our love.

In the aftermath, I sought refuge in writing, and therapy—a lifeline for unraveling the knots of trauma. I learned that love should never hurt and that protection should never come at the cost of my well-being. Marcus remained a phantom—a chapter closed, but its echoes lingered.

And so, I rebuilt. I stitched together the frayed edges of my heart, weaving resilience into the fabric of my existence. Marcus's darkness had left scars, but they became my battle scars—the proof that I had survived and eventually thrived.

For years, I wondered about him and how he was doing. I often heard whispers on the wind that he was still following the same patterns, abusing women, using and selling drugs, and, yes, in and out of prison. In 2021, I learned that he had died in prison, just four days before my birthday. I wondered whether he had found his way to God and asked for forgiveness before he passed away. I was grateful that I had told him several years prior that I had forgiven him for the pain that he had caused me. Unsure of how I should feel, I felt empathy and thought, that no one should ever have to die that way, his demise was one that I would not wish on anyone.

At that moment, I vowed to be my soft place, my protector. Love, I realized, begins within—the gentlest touch, the kindest words, the unwavering belief in one's worth. Thinking back, I began to put in the hard work of rebuilding myself, piece by piece. Therapy sessions became my sanctuary, a place where I could unravel the knots of my past and weave a new future. I learned to set boundaries, to recognize red flags, and to trust my instincts. I discovered that my voice, once silenced by fear, was powerful and deserved to be heard.

I won't say the journey was easy. There were setbacks and days when the weight of my past felt too heavy to carry. But with each step forward, the shadow that followed me grew fainter. I found strength in vulnerability, courage in facing my fears, and a deep, unwavering love for myself.

Leaving Marcus was like a volcanic eruption—a rupture that altered the path of my existence. The echoes of our thunderous love affair echoed through my days and nights, leaving both scars and lessons in their wake.

How did I work towards rebuilding the broken spaces that my experiences with abuse left behind?

1. **Self-Discovery and Healing**:

   ○ **Embraced Solitude**: In the aftermath, I cocooned myself in solitude. The silence was both my refuge and my battleground. I learned to listen to my heartbeat, to decipher its rhythms.

   ○ **Therapy**: Seeking professional help became my lifeline. Therapy unraveled the knots of trauma, teaching me that healing was not linear. It was messy, nonlinear—a dance of tears and revelations.

   ○ **Reclaiming My Identity**: Mark had blurred the lines between us. Leaving him allowed me to reclaim my identity—the girl who loved fiercely but deserved more.

2. **Rebuilt Trust**:

   ○ **In Others**: Trust had been shattered, but I refused to let it calcify into cynicism. Slowly, I extended my hand to others—testing the waters, learning to trust anew.

   ○ **In Myself**: Leaving Mark was an act of self-trust. I believed that I deserved better and that my heart could mend. I became my soft place—a sanctuary against storms.

3. **Broke the Generational Curses**:

   ○ **Recognized Red Flags**: Mark's abuse had etched patterns into my psyche. Leaving him forced me to confront those patterns—to recognize the signs of toxicity.

   ○ **Made Different Choices**: Moving forward, I vowed to

choose differently. No more broken knights, no more battles. Love should lift, not weigh down.

4. **Forgave and Obtained Closure**:

   ○ **Forgave Myself**: I forgave myself for staying, for believing in redemption. Guilt was a heavy cloak; I shed it, piece by piece.

   ○ **Closure**: Closure was elusive. Mark remained a phantom, but I wrote letters—unsent missives that released the ache. Closure, I realized, was an inside job.

5. **Worked to Take Back My Strength and Resilience**:

   ○ **Warrior's Scars**: My bruises became badges—a testament to resilience. I wore them proudly, knowing they were proof of survival.

   ○ **Boundaries**: Leaving Mark taught me the art of boundaries. I learned to say no, to protect my softness.

6. **Reframed Love**:

   ○ **From Savior to Companion**: Love was no longer a savior. It was a companion—a hand to hold, not a crutch to lean on.

   ○ **Self-Love**: I watered the garden of self-love, tending to its fragile blooms. Love, I realized, began within.

7. **Focused On My Spirituality**:

   ○ **Worked to Better Understand My Faith:** I opened the Bible, attended church, and began to seek clarity on how my faith could help me take back my life and voice.

In 2016, I established my nonprofit organization, ThriveHER Inc., the trademarked name for an individual who has surpassed surviving and reached the epitome of thriving in their survivorship. Through the organization, I shared my experience with domestic violence and how it had affected my life. I wrote about it in several books, "Including Heaven Rain on Me, Perfectly Imperfect, ThriveHER, Unstoppable ThriveHER, and coauthor projects". However, this is the first time that I have spelled it out with such depth and breadth.

As I am sitting here writing, I realize that I am thriving. You see, the way the words flow and each detail of what started 40 years ago is being painted on these pages. Today, I can stand before a room filled with strangers and share my testimony, speak life into those who are going through abuse and seeking an escape and healing, and feel confident in knowing I am making a difference in the lives of others.

You see, now I stand tall, no longer a victim of circumstance but a ThriveHER, a warrior. From that confusion, from that pain, I learned compassion. I learned to listen, to help, and to heal. And now, I use my voice, once small and frightened, to speak for those who still hide behind their couches, clutching their teddy bears, waiting for the storm to pass. I tell them that it's not their fault, that there is hope, that they are not alone. Because no child nor adult should ever have to understand domestic violence, and no child should ever have to carry its weight.

I've learned that the cycle of abuse can be broken and that the scars we carry can become the roadmap to a life filled with respect, kindness, and genuine love.

My past will always be a part of me, but it does not define me. I am the author of my story, and I choose how it continues. I choose to continue to grow and learn to be a stronger, confident me, a ThriveHER, and a living testimony that domestic violence does not always have the last word.

Angeline Chan

Founder of Angeline Chan Coaching

https://www.linkedin.com/in/angelinecy/
https://www.facebook.com/AngelineTheCoach
https://instagram.com/angelinethecoach
https://angelinechancoaching.com/

Angeline Chan is intimately familiar with the weight and negative consequences of Imposter Syndrome. From the start of her IT career, she battled with self-doubt, fuelled by years of subtle messaging. The turning point came when she joined a company filled with brilliant minds, which only intensified her struggle. Determined to reclaim her confidence, Angeline embarked on a transformative journey to overcome these feelings and become more authentically confident.

Today, Angeline is a certified life and career coach with credentials from the International Coaching Federation (ICF) and the Imposter Syndrome Institute (ISI). With her background in the tech industry and her personal triumph over Imposter Syndrome, Angeline empowers tech professionals to break free from their own imposter feelings and unlock their true potential.

If you are ready to start your own journey toward authentic confidence, visit her website and take the first step toward overcoming your Imposter Syndrome.

Am I an Imposter?

By Angeline Chan

For years, I felt like I wasn't doing good enough, even when others told me otherwise.

I struggled with imposter syndrome in my career in tech, and I thought I overcame a lot of those feelings and self-sabotaging behaviours.

Then, I made a decision a couple of years back to move to a different country to finally close the distance with my husband, and transitioned to a different career as a life and career coach. This transition to a coach and entrepreneur, and then a mom, just triggered my feelings of feeling like an imposter again, stronger than ever.

For better or worse, this was a pivotal point in my life, where I started to work even more actively on my imposter feelings. Through my coach training, books and a variety of courses, I not only applied my learnings to my own life, I also reflected on what worked best. As an Imposter Syndrome-Informed coach, I also embarked on a journey to help others deal with their own imposter feelings in their careers.

In this chapter, I will share my 6 biggest lessons from dealing with imposter syndrome. If you are going through similar challenges, I hope you benefit from my learnings.

Life is not a school exam. 100/100 perfection is unattainable.

According to research by leading experts on Imposter Syndrome, Dr. Valerie Young, as well as Imes and Clance, there are 7 types of coping mechanisms (Young, 2011) that people with Imposter Syndrome may unconsciously engage in, in order to avoid the anxiety and the negative feelings of possibly getting "exposed" by others for being less competent than they actually are. Overworking and over-preparing is one of these 7 coping mechanisms and is definitely something that I engaged in. In fact, many of the people I spoke with on the subject, including my coaching clients, engaged in this behaviour.

I attribute this to the education system in many places, where there is extreme pressure to get good grades, and good grades are defined by how well you are able to regurgitate the content of the textbooks you had to study.

All through my education, I have been conditioned to study and prepare for school exams, spending all my mental capacity just trying to get as close to a 100 score as possible. I was taught, as were many others, to keep studying over and over again, and continuously check my paper during the exam until time was up, to ensure that I caught as many mistakes as possible.

Looking at some of my clients' behaviours, as well as my own, such as going through a presentation or email over and over again, way more than necessary, I can't help but see the parallel between these situations in school and at work. I mean, who can fault you for carrying over these behaviours that supposedly served you for many years of your life, into how you do your work?

Except, there is no perfect score in life and at work. These behaviours, which brought me some form of comfort and likely did reduce my chances of messing up, also meant that I often spent a disproportionately huge amount of time, effort and stress on a task that may not warrant that. That is time, effort and emotional capacity that had been taken away from something else, possibly something more important. That could be another task at work, time and presence for my family at home, or just time for self-recuperation and charging my own emotional battery.

And ironically, putting such a great toll on myself trying to attain perfection actually robbed me of the opportunity to become more resilient. When things inevitably don't turn out perfectly, I spend a lot of time just spiralling and blaming myself, thinking that I didn't prepare enough, instead of extracting my learnings and moving forward. I have lost count of how much emotional energy I've wasted as a result.

The thing is, if you have an open mind and keep learning through life, you will always come across situations where you don't know something, and someone else, even someone who may be way younger than you are, may know something that *you* don't. And while it may be possible to hit your extremely high standard from time to time, it's almost impossible to do it 100% of the time.

Be at peace with what you can't control, be smart with what you can – you have the power to change your narrative

I was told that sometimes, a job listing might be put out when the hiring decision has already been made prior.

Imagine you're a hopeful applicant, applying for the job. Your skills and experience match the job description, and this is the perfect job for your current situation; it pays well, it's near where you live, and the company has a good reputation.

You prepare for the interview and leave it feeling pretty confident. You feel like you will get the job, but a couple of days later, you receive the news that, well… you didn't.

You feel terrible. You thought you had aced it, but apparently, you didn't. You spend the rest of the day, the week, and a little more than that, just replaying everything over and over again. What did you mess up? You thought you did well, so maybe that means that you're really just incompetent. You're not as good as you thought you were, or as good as your coworkers think you are.

If you had the ability to zoom out and take a look at what was happening, you might notice that all your time and effort spent on blaming yourself and feeling bad could have been better spent in other ways, like interviewing with other companies. If you *did* mess up, the time would have been better spent learning that mistake and taking action to make sure it doesn't happen at the next interview.

This tendency to spiral after a hiccup used to happen to me all the time, and I realised that this was not only my perfectionist mindset talking. It was also a tendency to think that everything was within my control. If I failed, that had to be entirely my fault, right? I failed to realise that in the real world, a lot of things weren't actually in my control. School hadn't prepared me for that.

The decision on who the company would hire was out of my control. Yes, I could influence them by preparing for the interview the best I could, but perhaps they were looking for an extra experience that they had not shared, perhaps there was bias on their end, or perhaps, like in my friend's scenario, the decision had already been made long before she walked through those doors.

That being said, there are things that you *can* control, and that is your mindset and your responses to such situations. This requires intentional work on your inner narrative and actively working on understanding, intercepting, and changing your responses to such events; essentially, strengthening your mental fitness.

This lesson is something that I learnt by accident. I was training to become a life coach, and a classmate told us about another programme on mental fitness that intrigued me. I went through the programme, and I was surprised at my own self-discovery and improvement as the weeks went by. This training, along with additional coaching and courses, gave me the tools and guidance to strengthen my mental fitness, gain more self-awareness about what was happening in situations that made me feel small, and respond in healthier ways that served me better.

When I first transitioned to become a life and career coach, my imposter syndrome did *not* make things easy. It didn't matter that I had graduated from a really great training programme, coached over a hundred hours, got great feedback from my clients, and got my certification with the International Coaching Federation. Whenever I felt that I didn't do as good a job as I wanted to, I felt inadequate, and that had very real consequences, especially as an entrepreneur. I didn't dare to put myself out there because I didn't believe in myself, and every step forward felt like I was trying to do so while having a foot chained to a boulder. It was mentally exhausting, and physically pulled me back.

Taking deliberate action to strengthen my mental fitness, however, definitely helped me. As long as I applied my learnings, I was able to focus on the right things and set the right intention for myself to take the necessary steps forward.

Needless to say, I now teach these techniques to others as well to help them with their own inner narrative and mental fitness because doing so can be a real game changer in a world where you feel like you can't seem to stop sabotaging yourself.

Not all feedback is helpful

I had great feedback in the first company I worked in. However, there was also not-so-great and not-so-helpful feedback that made me doubt myself.

I remember writing up a requirements document for my project in the capacity of a software developer and business analyst, and at one point, my project manager told my supervisor in surprise, "Wow, did you look at the document Angeline wrote? That is really well done and incredibly detailed!" I was really happy that my work was appreciated, and it was the first time I had gotten feedback on my work. My happiness didn't last long, though, because my supervisor's response was simply, "It's not good enough."

Immediately, I felt inadequate. I was happy with the work I did. I had no idea what I did wrong, just simply that it "wasn't good enough". I felt small after that conversation. My takeaway then was simply that I wasn't good in my role, and that I shouldn't get ahead of myself.

Even when I excelled in my performance reviews and got promoted, it was like that voice was still stuck somewhere at the back of my mind.

Years later, when I moved to a company with a much better feedback culture, I was passionate about obtaining feedback to help me get a better sense of my capabilities and what I needed to improve. Through the years, I learnt more about how to give better feedback and also how to ask for and receive feedback in a more effective manner. I learnt that many people aren't very good at giving or receiving feedback, but that it is a skill that *can* be honed.

In hindsight, "it's not good enough" really wasn't feedback I could do anything with. Why was it not good enough? Were the expectations behind that comment realistic? What action could I take to make an improvement? That "feedback" gave answers to none of those questions, and as a result, could not help me become better.

Now, I know how to better elicit and make sense of feedback, so if I could turn back time, I would have responded differently.

Confidence isn't just about what you know, but also what you don't

The reality is that you will never know everything about anything. Even if you're a top expert in your field. The world is constantly changing, and there are many ways to look at things.

If I'm supposed to be the "expert" in the room, it can seem like a huge sign "INCOMPETENT" has been hung over my head if someone else shares something that I had no idea about on a topic related to my area of expertise.

However, this will happen at some point, sooner or later. This doesn't mean that your years of experience and accomplishments suddenly mean nothing. It just means that you're human.

What I've learnt through many years, is that true confidence and authenticity come when you accept that you *don't* know everything, even in your area of expertise. In seeing how 'experts' interact, I have nothing but respect for the one who tells a workshop attendee, "I did not know that! Can you explain a little more?". Conversely, an 'expert' loses my respect when he or she gives a completely incorrect or unhelpful answer to a question asked, simply because they wanted to come across as having all the answers.

I find that having the right mindset and a healthy intention allows me to put on an explorer's hat of curiosity. That, in turn, helps me engage with others in a healthier manner, even if the other person seems hostile at first.

During drinks that I had with some coworkers one day, someone shared about how my reaction to stakeholders shooting down the work my team was showcasing, or complaining about what we did, stood out to them. While some of my team felt small, defensive, or even angry, I simply took a post-it pad and pen, asked about their concerns with curiosity, made sure to write their concerns down, and promised to follow up on them.

In the moment, my thought was simply, "Perhaps there's something we missed, and there's something important we might need to address". I then made sure I received those concerns so we could figure out what we needed to do (or not).

Their comments did make me realise, however, that in the past, my reaction would have been exactly the same as theirs. I remember sitting in meetings hearing such comments, and just feeling small, annoyed, or frustrated. However, as my focus and mindset changed, so did my thoughts and behaviours.

I wasn't going into the meeting to show that we understood everything perfectly, with the aim of getting a thumbs-up. I was going in to show what we had done, share what we had learnt, align on our plans and expectations, and get feedback on whether we needed to course correct.

When I realised the power of setting the right intention, I actively started applying it to situations where I felt I needed it, and I cannot tell you how big a change it can have on my entire mindset and behaviour!

Feeling like an imposter can happen anywhere, not just at work

My journey of learning about how to deal with Imposter Syndrome was multifold. I got better at dealing with my imposter syndrome while in my tech career, then as a life and career coach, as an entrepreneur, and then, the most surprising of all, when I became a mother.

After becoming a mother, I felt like a fish completely out of water. I had tried preparing for motherhood, including reading up on breastfeeding, and what I can expect as part of the baby's development. I even made sure I got support during my first month postpartum, but not only did I feel like I was completely unprepared, I often felt like I was failing. My mental health took a huge hit.

There was no manual that came with the baby, and any manual that seemed to work with others didn't necessarily apply to me.

If you've gone through this or know someone who has, this may all seem very familiar.

Months later, even when my husband and mother-in-law told me that I was doing a good job, I felt like I definitely was not. Later, I realised that, yes, while I was going through the usual struggle and what was an *extremely* steep learning curve, imposter syndrome was definitely also at play.

Again, I found myself applying my learnings, including a framework that I adopted for my own career growth and learning, to my own journey through parenthood. It helped me focus on what I needed to do and prioritise what I wanted to work on improving and learning. So, while I definitely don't think I'm the best parent in the world, I no longer think I'm a "bad mum", and I don't question why I decided to be a parent.

Sure, there are times when my imposter feelings come up again, whether it is in my career or as a mum, but instead of taking on an "imposter identity", I experience an "imposter moment", and take action to move past it.

You can do it, too, with the right support

It's important to not only have the skills to identify and prioritise what to work on, but to also be able to find and get the necessary support and resources you need. You may have noticed through what I've shared, that many of my breakthroughs came about when I had some sort of support.

What I have not shared is how I went through my own journey of not looking for support at all or getting the wrong type of support, before I was able to find the right type of support to help me overcome the challenges I faced.

A 2020 study showed that up to 82% of people experience imposter feelings (Bravata et al., 2020) and engage in self-sabotaging behaviours as a result, whether it is giving themselves unnecessary stress and pressure by taking an action that works against them or holding themselves back from taking on opportunities that are actually aligned with what they want.

I've also spoken to people who have struggled with it for so long, that they think it's just something they have to live with, and that nothing can actually be done about it.

However, if my experience is anything to go by, this is definitely not true. One thing I've learnt is that it *is* possible to change, even though it may be difficult. I was my worst critic to the point that I really hated myself as a child and young adult, and I had really strong people-pleasing tendencies. I was in a hierarchical culture for so long that when someone with some authority told me that I was lacking in something, I'd feel like a complete failure. This permeated every part of my life.

The me back then would probably never imagine what I'm doing right now, nor imagine that I would be able to handle my imposter feelings.

So if I can do it, so can you.

* * *

References:

Bravata, D. M., Watts, S. A., Keefer, A. L., Madhusudhan, D. K., Taylor, K. T., Clark, D. M., Nelson, R. S., Cokley, K. O., & Hagg, H. K. (2020). Prevalence, Predictors, and Treatment of Impostor Syndrome: a Systematic Review. *Journal of General Internal Medicine*, *35*(4), 1252–1275. https://doi.org/10.1007/s11606-019-05364-1

Young, V. (2011). The Secret Thoughts of Successful Women: And Men: Why Capable People Suffer from Impostor Syndrome and How to Thrive In Spite of It. Crown Currency.

Paula C Lamb

Health & Personal Development Coach & Podcaster

https://www.linkedin.com/in/paulalamb/
https://www.facebook.com/groups/beyondtofreedom/
https://www.instagram.com/beyondtofreedom/
https://linktr.ee/podcasterpaula

Meet Paula Lamb, a South African expat now residing in the beautiful City of Vancouver, Canada. A retired personal exercise trainer and nutritional consultant, Paula now specializes in one-on-one health and personal development coaching, helping others embrace their wellness journeys. Through her podcasts, "Knowing Me, Knowing You with Paula" and "Beyond to Freedom," she seeks to entertain, empower, and inspire listeners to take actionable steps in their lives.

Paula enjoys reading autobiographies, soaking up the sun, playing pickle ball, nature walks, and spending quality time with her husband. With extensive travel experience, she believes that exploring various cultures greatly enriches our lives. Paula is passionate about living with gratitude and kindness, believing that these values contribute to us becoming our best selves and that reaching our hand across borders, leading with patience and tolerance contributes to a better world.

Courage Beyond the Shadows

By Paula C Lamb

I can distinctly recall instances when fear has stealthily crept into my life. In some cases, fear's friend doubt has been present and has set off the inevitable alarm bells of wait, stumbling my progression and sometimes halting my dreams. In those moments, the dreaded questions have arisen: Will I be okay? Am I capable? Is this the right step? What will my friends think? With my eyes slightly glazed over like a deer caught in headlights, I was left in a state of angst, procrastination, and uncertainty about my next step. I've glanced at others and wondered why I second-guess myself, why don't I have the courage or strength that others possess.

Conversely, I vividly recall moments when I lifted my gaze forward, riding the waves of fear and doubt. Leaning into my faith, and with feelings of excitement, certainty, and optimism, I leaped over boundaries like an Olympian hurdler. I felt proud of moving out of my own way and saying 'yes' to myself, overcoming obstacles, and tuning out negativity.

While society often steers us toward the belief that strength, courage, and resilience are mostly gained by facing hardship and pushing us out of our comfort zone, I disagree. I believe these qualities are innate; we already possess these gifts from God. These innate qualities are further developed through small and large challenges, observing others exhibit strength and courage through their personal life stories, challenges, and accomplishments, embracing a growth mindset, achieving goals, experiencing losses and wins, and saying 'yes' to opportunities despite doubt and fear. Every human being, regardless of origin or background, will face challenges and leave this earth having been tested.

No matter the path, it's all character-building. For me, I've survived tough times and I'm still here. I've faced fearful and uncomfortable situations from childhood into adulthood, made mistakes, learned hard lessons, all while boosting my courage and resilience, often without realizing it. I've also discovered along the way my likes, dislikes, strengths, and limits.

When I applied to write this chapter, I was instantly excited. What a wonderful opportunity to share parts of my life story, lessons learned, challenges, and triumphs. But guess what? It took me two sittings to finally press send on the application. Why? As soon as I felt the excitement and said 'YES' to myself, my friend doubt showed up. I began to second-guess myself and got stuck in "wait mode," feeling imposter syndrome, fear of rejection, and doubts about my ability to accomplish this goal. This is a common experience for many of us, right? Passing through those obstacles of doubt is where lessons, courage, and strength bloom.

When I think of fear and the need to garner strength and courage, I'm reminded that fear appears in various forms throughout our lives. It's a complex emotion that shows up in everything from everyday situations to extreme circumstances. We experience fear when facing life-threatening situations, health issues, financial hardships, changes, letting go, phobias, anxiety, relationships, and the unknown. I'm sure you could add more to this list.

Courage and strength seem to fit like puzzle pieces with fear and its companion, doubt. No matter who you are, I guarantee that, in some way, you have faced fear or doubt. You have had to summon courage at some point, maybe not to the same extent as the person next to you or a passerby. While it's often advised to focus on the present and look to the future, I believe our past holds a wealth of wisdom and lessons. Reflecting on what we have overcome and accomplished can offer valuable insights and strength.

This reminds me of my early childhood, where I began my first lessons in facing the many forms of fear. I was raised in a single-parent home in Salisbury, Rhodesia, now Harare, Zimbabwe, and later in East London, South Africa. My mother was the primary breadwinner, while my father was absent and did not contribute positively during my childhood or initial upbringing. I have somewhat fond memories of my early childhood in Harare during the '70s and early '80s. I attended five different primary schools, which might explain why I only remember the names of two of my teachers. My childhood included after-school sports and spending time with friends doing the usual kid stuff of my time: climbing trees and fearlessly racing down suburban hills in a makeshift go-kart with hardly any brakes.

As a family, we enjoyed various activities together. My mother always organized exceptional birthday parties for us at our local putt-putt, or as some might know it, mini golf. I have fond memories of these celebrations. On weekends, we often joined my mother's colleagues and friends at their homes or various spots around the city, enjoying music, food, and sometimes a refreshing swim if there was a nearby pool. During school holidays, I regularly attended art camp and spent countless hours honing my ice-skating skills at the local rink, went to the cinema, and enjoyed sunny days with other revelers at our local public swimming pool. I remember us not wanting for much, and I certainly felt like my life was full.

Reflecting on those cherished childhood memories brings me joy, yet there's also a hint of sadness. Amidst the carefree moments, there were times of unease, fear, and upheaval. It's a reminder that appearances can be deceiving; our lives, like books, often hide depths beneath their covers.

Part of my childhood was lived through a tumultuous time in Zimbabwe: civil unrest, trade sanctions, a war fought on our borders, and the constant threat of bombs in shopping centers, theaters, hotels, and tourist holiday sites. The constant threat to the lives of all peoples of Zimbabwe, long road trips, including across borders for business or pleasure, were often in convoy with armed force protection. I witnessed and experienced some of the most frightening and uncertain times in African history.

During the independence struggle, I vividly recall a moment when my family faced profound situational fear for survival. Amidst the civil unrest, we ventured to the infamous Victoria Falls Hotel for a family vacation. The Victoria Falls Hotel, a popular tourist destination, was renowned for its historical significance and access to the Falls, one of the Seven Natural Wonders of the World. It was December 1977, summertime in Zimbabwe; there was significant unrest and intense Security Force activity to secure the border crossing into neighboring Zambia. As children frolicked in the pool, during the late afternoon, the surrounding trees and terrace would often become a favored hangout for the local monkeys, much to my dismay. I found myself frozen in the shallow end of the pool, waiting for a waiter from the restaurant or my mother to come to my rescue.

During one of the evenings, as we slept peacefully, our tranquil visit was shattered by a mortar attack from neighboring Zambia. The thunderous sound of mortars echoed in what seemed like the distance, and my mother wondered if the elephants knew to avoid the landmines meant to deter insurgents from crossing the border. Suddenly, a deafening blast awoke us from our peaceful slumber. A mortar ripped through a tree just meters from our room, striking the adjacent hotel room. My mother sprang from the bed, while I stood frozen, my eyes locked on her, waiting for direction. We knew the drill and understood the situation well: keep lights off and stay away from the windows. We knew these actions might keep us alive. Still clothed in our sleeping attire, my mother carried my young brother, with me close behind. Her steps faltered for a moment at the room doorway in fear and shock. From within the hotel corridor, a voice guided us through the darkness down a spiral stairwell to a darkened hallway filled with other guests and staff seeking safety. Military personnel dotted the corridors, and an armored tank was stationed at the hotel entranceway for protection. In the hushed darkness, we sat among others, hearing sporadic whispers and the crackle of the armed force radios as we waited out the mortar blasts and distant gunfire. The knowledge of courageous armed forces on our borders and around the hotel, fighting to protect us, gave us strength during that terrifying night. This attack was just one of many unfolding in our home country, and now our family, like many others, had become a statistic. My childhood in Zimbabwe was filled with many more similar moments.

The fear and terror of that moment, and others, were unlike the usual childhood fears, which you might resonate with, like the fear of monsters under your bed or the fear of creepy crawlies. Our life in Zimbabwe during the Rhodesian Bush War meant constant "fight or flight," with fears about our security, our well-being, and our future ingrained from early childhood.

I've rarely revisited many of my childhood tales of conquering fear, summoning courage, and nurturing resilience. They have remained tucked away in my memory. However, as I reflect on these childhood memories, as much as my memory serves me, I realize that fear is a universal companion.

These experiences remind me that the challenges we face can leave lasting scars that shape our character, mindset, decision-making, and perception of the world. Some fears can breed anger, resentment, depression, anxiety, low self-esteem, regret, stagnation, and a scarcity mindset.

Confronting these challenges offers invaluable lessons, shaping our character in profound ways, both positive and negative. Traits like resilience, adaptability, perseverance, and humility emerge as strengths, while resentment, despair, selfishness, pessimism, and cynicism can also manifest, influencing our life journey from youth into adulthood.

For me, those times provided lessons in understanding the ravages of war, appreciating the gift of security, and summoning inner courage during tough times. They underscored the importance of community and resilience, as well as navigating the waves of fear as they surfaced. The scars from that time of my life remained with me as my family was forced to transition to a new life in the coastal town of East London, South Africa, in 1983, a period for my family marked by huge adjustments and financial insecurity.

If I could converse with that little girl today, I wonder what she would recall about those formative times.

As I reflect on my past, thinking about fear and the need to garner strength and courage, I'm reminded of how our past shapes our lives and who we become. One vivid memory is of our preparation for migration to South Africa. I clearly recall the day we packed our belongings into large metal boxes, or "trunks," with handles and places for padlocks. We packed them with the hope that we would be reunited with our possessions in our new home country. Sadly, that day never came. The deep sadness of saying goodbye to my homeland, cherished childhood memories, and closest friends is still distinct. I sensed that we would never return to the place we once called home, marking the end of a chapter. At just 13 years old, I began to grasp profound life lessons. I initially understood the concept of "survival fear," but now I was experiencing firsthand the unpredictability of life, the inevitability of change, letting go, and the fear of the unknown.

No matter who you are, isn't it interesting that fear and its sidekick, doubt, often show up at the most inopportune times? This takes me to my entrepreneurial journey, a totally different type of fear from my childhood memory of the fear for safety, sometimes feeling out of control and facing the unknown. The 1990s were not only challenging but also profound and triumphant for a woman in her 20s.

My early employment years were riddled with financial vulnerability, stress, and restlessness. I felt like a boat without a rudder. The jobs I held left me doubtful that I would find a career I could be passionate about, and fearful that I would always live with the constant threat of financial instability while stuck in an unfulfilling 9-to-5 job. At the same time, deep-seated issues from my upbringing and conditioning prevented me from living a peaceful life. I was a well-oiled machine at being reactive, unapologetic, and angry. A young woman who, at times, felt hopeless and out of control. I now realize that this stemmed from a conditioned past where I lived in constant fight and fear, fear for my future, fear of the unknown, fear of loss, fear of living with financial instability, and now fear of having to match up to the expectations of society, which left me once again feeling out of control of my own life.

Reflecting on that time, I now see that all along I was learning valuable lessons. Each moment propelled me forward, honing my skill set, enriching my toolkit, and laying the foundations for the pivotal moment of becoming an entrepreneur. I thrived when I was the captain of my own ship, I valued a flexible work schedule and enjoyed talking to people. I recognized and appreciated my positive personal characteristics and preferred work environments. Wisdom has shown me that every moment, from childhood challenges to adulthood, every decision made, whether good or bad, and each career step presents an opportunity for growth and pursuing excellence in our lives. Along the way, yes, I've made mistakes, but these experiences have bestowed invaluable wisdom. After all, we know that a life well-lived isn't defined by smooth sailing alone, right?

I think you will agree that it takes strength and courage to embark on a new journey, and my childhood and early adulthood experiences provided the foundation from which I could draw the strength to take the plunge and become my own boss. The idea of becoming my own boss never prominently occupied my mind during my years of employment. Owning a business seemed outlandish, requiring substantial financial investment and a good business sense to succeed. However, I learned that this isn't entirely true. As I shifted my focus toward a career in the wellness industry, I discovered that strategizing, planning, dedication, focus, and execution are key.

My entrepreneurial vision, outlined in a step-by-step strategic plan with the aid of my mentors, demanded dedication and focus to overcome the inevitable fears and doubts during execution. Through these experiences, I learned that embracing discomfort and navigating through both small and significant life challenges can strengthen our innate courage and help us move past fear and doubt.

A white envelope containing my resignation letter was handed to my employer, and thirty days later, I returned the company car keys. I remember the overwhelming emotion that filled my body as the reality set in of having to let go and say goodbye. Just as quickly as I had bid farewell to my employment safety net, guess who showed up?

Fear and its sidekick, doubt. I stood in front of one of my mentors, fear engulfing my entire body, squeezing my chest, and leaving me slightly breathless. Tears streamed down my face as I battled to silence fear's attempts to keep me safe: "Are you sure you made the right decision? What if your business fails and you can't support yourself?" Meanwhile, doubt also began to chime in: "Do you truly have all the skills to be successful? Are you sure you can handle the challenges that lie ahead?" At that moment, I knew if I didn't get a grip on this toxic mindset, I was going to be in trouble.

I had faced fear in its various forms. I had overcome hardship and challenges. This moment, yes, was terrifying but also liberating! One I knew to be embraced with my "I will persevere" attitude. And guess what? Four months into my inaugural entrepreneurial venture, I had tripled my previous monthly income, an outcome I had never dared to imagine. My months of planning and strategizing were blossoming. I built a dedicated client base I was proud of. I admit there were days when fear came to visit, keeping me vigilant and alert. During those early days, my fears primarily centered around finances, possibly something that is permanently present for an entrepreneur, and the scars from my childhood and my family's financial hardship. Nonetheless, I embraced my role as the pivotal puzzle piece in my entrepreneurial story, trusting myself to make it a resounding success!

Fear, often an unwelcome presence, serves a crucial purpose. It acts as a warning bell, allowing us to react swiftly to threats, evaluate risky situations, avoid mistakes, and proceed cautiously. Fear has a steadfast companion in doubt, which often emerges when we are in "wait mode." In many cases, fear can give rise to doubt, and doubt, in turn, can intensify fear. Doubt arises from a lack of confidence, worry, apprehension, past experiences, and external influences such as friends, family, and our environment.

Courage, strength, and resilience are the outcomes of facing or, as I like to say, riding your fears and doubts, acting despite these emotions, and, for me now, leaning into my faith. If fear and doubt are integral parts of life and the human experience, then surely it is best to accept them. Perhaps it is even important for us to make friends with these emotions.

My question to you is: How often do you let fear and doubt influence your life, even in the absence of immediate danger or a perceived future threat that may never materialize?

I have learned that by riding the waves of fear and doubt and leaning into faith, we strengthen our resilience and courage, empowering us to face life with confidence. Developing these qualities enhances both our mental and emotional strength, enabling us to confront challenges and recover from adversity. I recognize that navigating life can be daunting, but central to this journey is recognizing the lessons it offers. This foundation proves especially valuable in entrepreneurial pursuits.

I encourage you to make friends with fear and doubt. In your pursuits be clear on your vision. Strategize, plan, execute, reflect, and adjust. Take the leap and don't leave yourself with lingering "what ifs," wondering if you missed out or held yourself back.

It has taken considerable time to reach this understanding, and I am not perfect. I am still, at times, caught in fear and "wait mode." When faced with fear and doubt before applying to write this chapter, I asked myself one question: "What do I have to lose?" My answer was "nothing." I reminded myself, "Who cares if I'm not accepted? Perhaps this is not my path."

"Letting our emotions and what others think dictate our thoughts and actions often steals our joy and success."

#yougotthis

Nytisha Davis

Phillips Mobile Labs LLC
Lab Director/Owner

https://www.facebook.com/phillipsmobilelabs/
https://www.phillipsmobilelabs.com/

I am the esteemed CEO and Founder of Phillips Mobile Labs LLC, bringing over three decades of diverse and enriching professional experience to my role. My journey commenced in Pennsylvania over 30 years ago, where I completed training as a Medical Assistant in 1992. Subsequently, I pursued higher education and achieved an associate degree through the Pharmacy Technician program.

Following the completion of the program, I dedicated myself to working in both hospital and retail pharmacies while simultaneously raising her three children. Returning to my hometown, I discovered a passion for the Behavioral Health field, where I served as a Behavioral Health Specialist (BHS) for several years before returning to the Phlebotomy field in 2011.

My expertise flourished as I worked full-time as a mobile phlebotomist for one of the largest hospitals in Pennsylvania. My commitment to healthcare extended to part-time roles as a home health aide, instilling in my values of patience and kindness in patient care. My professional journey also lead me into working in patient care centers and as a Para-Medial examiner. Annually I engage in projects that allows me to give back to community which has become my passion in life.

Finding Me in the Shadows of Death

By Nytisha Davis

I was left with a dollar and two nickels, shattered pieces of glass from a broken window, and a bruised ego, as I took a long look at the imperfect vision that flashed before me. I mourned the death of my marriage more than the death of my father. By the end of 2014, I was a mother of three adults, just becoming an empty nester, a grandmother of two, and divorced for the third time. Yes, I said third. I was supposed to be living my best life, they say. I'm not a writer by any means, but I feel like I need to tell my story. First, I must tell you a little bit about who I am and how I was raised.

My parents were both born in the South, my mother in Florida and my father in Georgia, to be exact. They both met in a small town in Pennsylvania called Easton in the late 60s. They married in their very early 20s and had me very shortly after their union. When my parents married, my father already had a daughter, who is my older sister, let's call her Shelly. I am the second oldest, and then they had my sister Lynne.

Growing up in a strict Pentecostal religious environment in Pennsylvania during the 70s, I was accustomed to a set of rules that governed everything from clothing choices to social interactions. My childhood was largely spent within the confines of my church community, where familial bonds were strong, but friendships outside of that circle were scarce. We were taught to pray, fear God, and always do the right thing, which also meant "turning the other cheek".

My parents have told me that when I was a child, I always had to have the last word. I was never shy about expressing myself, and I wanted my feelings and thoughts to be heard. As a child, I also seemed to get into a lot of things, which my parents attributed to my being sassy. I guess they were right. I have always been a bit of an expressive person, and I have a tendency to say what's on my mind without thinking it through first. I guess that's just who I am.

Growing up as a darker-skinned child in the 1970s and 1980s was difficult. I was constantly made to feel less favored and unloved, especially when my lighter-skinned sister seemed to be treated better, in my eyes. This bias followed me for years, affecting my self-esteem and my relationships with others. It took me a long time to realize that I was just as beautiful outside as well as inside.

My mother's unwavering faith and commitment to traditional gender roles, reminiscent of the late 70s and early 80s, shaped much of my upbringing. Meanwhile, my father, a talented cook, provided a glimpse of a different kind of relationship. My parents were married, but my father was often absent due to his long commute from Pennsylvania to New York. He was a member of the carpenter's union. When he was home, I loved helping him cook. I was his kitchen assistant, gathering ingredients and learning the secrets of his recipes.

I did not realize until years after becoming an adult and having children when trying to recall certain moments and memories, that I had no memory of holidays as a child with both of my parents. No Thanksgivings, no Christmases. I don't think we have ever sat down to eat as a family together. As far as I could remember, on regular nights, my father ate in the living room in his favorite yellowish flowered patterned recliner that no one dared to sit in at any time while he watched all his favorite shows like the *Andy Griffith* show or *The Beverly Hillbillies* and *Sanford and Son* while my sister and I sat in the kitchen eating our dinner. I can't quite remember where my mother sat while eating dinner. We were lucky to have two parents that were good cooks. My father did most of the cooking and my mother sometimes, but she did a lot of the baking.

My father was always extremely healthy and active. He ate a healthy diet which was no processed foods and was devoted to martial arts and weight lifting. He was very intimidating, and his facial expression always conveyed the idea that it would be unwise to cross him.

I wouldn't say that my father was the most faithful in his marriage to my mother, which is why I have other siblings, totaling four sisters, Shelly, Lynne, Coco, Nene, and one brother Ronnie. My parents divorced when I was approximately 13 or 14 years old. The divorce was hard on me, and I took it hard. I remember at the age of 15, I attempting suicide. I felt torn, wanting to be with my mother but didn't want to leave and disappoint my father. My father made me feel a little guilty for leaving and wanting to move in with my mother, which caused me a lot of stress. I just wanted the love of my father.

My sister Lynn, my mother, and I moved into a small efficiency apartment in Allentown. It wasn't much, but it was our home. My mother worked multiple jobs to provide for us. She tried to give us the best of what life had to offer, considering the circumstances. She sent us to a private school and gifted us with designer clothes and perfume. My mother was a straightforward person who said what she thought and meant what she said. I can see where I got that from. She was a God-fearing woman who loved helping others. She was a very good mother then and now, and I am proud of her, I couldn't ask for a better mother.

My mother landed a full-time good-paying job at a furniture manufacturing company. She worked overnight because that was the only shift available for the new hires. I was now going into my senior year of high school, where I attended a Christian school. During her night shifts, I remember sneaking in a guy from Philadelphia I had met at an amusement park in my hometown. We exchanged numbers and had many conversations over the telephone. He would catch the Greyhound bus most nights to see me. Some months later, shortly after turning eighteen years old, I found out that I was three months pregnant. I was terrified because I thought my mother was going to kill me! My mother always kept a close watch on our menstrual cycles when the time was near. She noticed that I hadn't gotten my cycle, and she asked if I was pregnant. I don't know what possessed her to ask, for all she knew, I was still a virgin. I told her, "No," because I hadn't known for sure, so I wasn't lying, which was something I wasn't very good at, considering I was very outspoken. The day that I decided to go to my doctor's office to take a pregnancy test, we had a youth choir rehearsal at church. I took my best friend Louise with me. We left the office not knowing the results which back then took a few hours for the results. I was at choir rehearsal when I received the call that IT WAS POSITIVE! I WAS PREGNANT! Now, I had to tell her the truth and decided to do so once she asked me that same question again. Terror crossed my face as I played out the conversation in my mind about how I was going to unveil this news. One night before her shift, I laid under her like a cat. She was suspicious. She asked me, and I thought I was going to die! We were taught that premarital sex was not permitted and was a sin in our home life and in our church community. This made this situation even more scary. I didn't know what to do. I just knew that I was going to get disowned. When she asked that question again, I had no choice but to tell her the truth. I dared not lie to my mother. She sat in silence. I can't quite remember her response but I do remember her leaving for her night shift not saying much but I knew she was disappointed. She later told me that, when she arrived at work that night, she cried.

My friends were no longer allowed to communicate with me. Their parents forbade them to engage in any type of friendship with me. I felt alone. Not continuing with the pregnancy was also on the table for discussion at my first appointment with the doctor and my mother. We discussed what not keeping the baby options were. Although we never believed in abortions, that option crossed our minds heavily due to embarrassment to the family and our church family along with what most parents desire, for their child to attend college then get married and have a family. I was doing it backwards. After a doctor's appointment and finding out how far along I actually was, I decided to take that option off of the table and move forward to have the baby.

In my final year of high school, I became pregnant. I was filled with shame and felt like a statistic, but I was determined to complete my education and graduate. The school discovered my pregnancy during our senior class trip, which was a Mexican cruise. The school board called me and informed me that I might not be permitted to attend my graduation ceremony. I was deeply disappointed. However, I did graduate and gave birth to a baby girl a few months later.

I was shamed in front of our congregation at church, that I had given birth to a baby outside of wedlock. The only way to resolve the shame was to get married. I wasn't in love but cared for him and felt like,"Ok, I care about him, we may as well get married." Three months after I had my daughter, I got married to her father. Premarital sex was not acceptable, therefore, we HAD to marry. I was 19 years old, a mother, and now a wife. I still lived at home with my mother and my now husband still lived with his mother in Philadelphia. I would take the Greyhound bus with our daughter to visit. We still lived separately because he worked in another city. He was a professional boxer and trained in a city over 500 miles away.

While attending school to become a medical assistant, I became pregnant with our second daughter. I found out I was pregnant when I was attending a funeral for my then-husband's cousin. During the repass, I noticed, and so did others, that my appetite seemed to have increased. I wanted to take a pregnancy test, but I was afraid, afraid of my mother, afraid of what others would say because I was still young, and so my first child. My daughter was just under a year old. My father was not pleased. Matter of fact, he stopped speaking to me when I announced that I was pregnant with my second child. I was able to complete the first half of the program and earn my certificate before she was born. That same year, in the early part of 1993, the father of my children moved us to Pittsburgh, which was over 500 miles from my hometown. I was very homesick, but I knew I had to make the best of the situation. In 1995, my relationship with my husband ended. We were going in different directions, and he had become very controlling. He moved back to Philadelphia as I remained in Pittsburgh. I lived alone with my two girls until I asked my sister Lynne to move in with me. Her presence was a great comfort, and she helped me through a difficult time.

In 1995, a friend of mine who lived in the apartment building across from me had become ill and needed to go to the hospital. Her live-in boyfriend was away from their home. She asked me as a favor to go to her house when he came home to let him know she was in the hospital. I kept a lookout for him as she requested. When I noticed he was home, I walked over to her apartment to relay the message that she told me to relay to him. He was drunk, but I thought he was harmless. HE RAPED ME! I was trying to do a good deed for a friend. I'm not going to go into the details of it, but I was in shock, terrified, and hysterically crying when running out of there once I got free. I had no one to protect me. I felt lost and afraid. First, because I didn't know what to do, and second, I was afraid of him. I heard he had a reputation as somewhat of a bad boy, and his nickname was "Killer," and from what I heard, he earned that name. I didn't have the courage to call the police because I felt unprotected and feared for my life if I had. I wasn't sure how to handle all the mixed feelings I was having. I also wasn't sure how my friend was going to feel or say. I confronted her and told her what her boyfriend had done to me. I couldn't tell what she was thinking, but I knew she wasn't too happy, and I almost wanted to say that she believed me. I found myself pleading my case to those who had gotten wind of what happened to me in the small apartment community that I had lived in. Some didn't know what to believe. Some said I wanted it. Some said that I deserved it, which I wasn't sure why. This was the most traumatic thing that I had ever gone through, being 24 years old with two young daughters. I felt like everyone had turned against me, and I had no one to turn to. I went through a variety of feelings and emotions. Being scared, angry, defeated.

Months later, I went back to school, majoring in as a pharmacy technician. When I first graduated from high school, I actually was accepted and enrolled in a Christian college until I found out I got pregnant. Getting some sort of education wasn't an option for me due to having two small children to take care of. I was looking for a trade that allowed me to provide for my children at a rapid pace. Taking the Pharmacy tech class seemed like a reasonable amount of time to get a degree, two years, that was doable for me.

At this time, I was single with two children. Halfway into the course, I met a young man on the city bus on my way home from school. He was a very polite young man. Some months later, I would be pregnant with my third child at the age of 25, the day after Thanksgiving break. I liked him a lot, even loved him. We had a 9 lb 11-ounce baby boy. After having two girls, I was ready for a boy. I was a 25-year-old with three children. The girls were six and four years old. He was three years younger than I was but seemed to be very responsible. He moved in with me in my apartment. When our son turned a year old, we got married. We were happy. He treated my daughters like his own. We had many good and memorable times. He was romantic and considerate. We always made the best in not-so-good situations. I met him in Pittsburgh, but he was from Philadelphia. We lived in Pittsburgh for a few years before heading back east of Pennsylvania, back to our hometown. Once we were back home for several months, I found out that he was communicating with other women on online chat lines. We were married eight years before he filed for divorce. He told me, "You're a good mother, you're a good wife, you're beautiful, but I need to find myself." Excuse me!!!! You need to find yourself? And he left out the door. Leaving me with his son, to fend for myself.

I distinctly remember one particular day, when my son was about six years old, the separation was very fresh along with being taunted by my then husband, the father of my son, bragging to me of how much of a better woman the current girlfriend he had, was than me. I knew it wasn't true, but the words hurt! It was a Sunday afternoon after church service. I decided to take my kids to dinner. I can't remember where we went. I parked and sat there for a minute while my kids got out of the car. I was feeling down and low and very emotional. My car door opened. It was my son opening my door telling me it was going to be ok. I broke down and cried. I was broken-hearted. Right then and there, I knew my son had my back.

Going out seemed to be the thing back then in 2006. I was alone and wanted to go to clubs to take my mind off of the breakup. Hanging out with my friends. By then, we all had a few children, trying to get the kids to bed so we could go out. One night I decided to go out to a club in the area. I was out with coworkers hanging out, and I met a man at a club. He offered to buy me a drink if I got the bartender's attention. I did. We talked and swapped numbers. He seemed nice and very respectful. That attracted me. What attracted me was the fact that we were having a normal conversation about life, not him trying to date me or get with me. It was refreshing. After many conversations and the exchange of numbers, we started dating. Some months later, he moved in with me and my three children. He was fun to hang out with and always looked forward to date nights almost every night. But you know when they tell you to look at the signs. I ignored them. He had two daughters as well, but they lived with their mother. At the time, he hadn't had a relationship with his daughters in years. He was a bit arrogant but was a teddy bear behind closed doors but I loved him. After a year and a half of living together, we married. Life was good. He was a maintenance supervisor of an apartment complex. We had our ups and downs, but we were making it work.

He reinstated his position as a police officer from years ago, he loved his job. He was very fair; although he worked with his colleagues who were racist, he would come home and express his concerns and his discomfort. He was a Polish man who married an African American woman. His father loved me, but I wasn't always too sure about his mother. He was so much like his father, outgoing, and did not care what people thought of him. Some seem to think he was a bit bipolar. He had a bit of a mean streak about him. He was very close to his father. During the time we were married, I found out that he experienced drugs. I walked in on him in the bathroom just after snorting cocaine. I saw the residue on his nose. I became infuriated and punched him in his face. I don't think he felt it.

Drinking alcohol seemed to be his drink of choice on his days off. I hated when he would drink because he would become violent. Remember what I said earlier about seeing the signs? I noticed prior to getting married that he would drink and would become this very different person that I didn't know if I liked, but I ignored them. When he would drink, he would push me around and pull my arm behind my back, breaking things including my phones but never actually striking me. Many times I had to leave home during the night with my kids to stay in a hotel. It had become so frequent that I had to start leaving a packed bag in my car for emergencies, and yes, I have used that bag many more times.

He committed to stop drinking. That lasted for about a year. It was great, and I enjoyed my marriage. My oldest daughter was now in her last year of high school, ready to graduate. Our marriage had started getting a little rocky. I noticed his body language and attitude. He confessed that he loved someone else. At the time, I had no idea who it was. I found out the person he was speaking of was actually his boss at the apartment complex he worked at. I couldn't prove that he was having an affair with his boss, but I did see his car parked in his boss's driveway in the middle of the night.

After coming from a college tour with my oldest daughter, I can't recall the events that happened that made me take several sleeping pills. I think I felt like this can't be happening again. Another failed marriage. I felt as if my soul left my body. I have been a good wife, a good person and how and why is this happening to me AGAIN! Especially when he just said," I can't see my life without you." Also said the same thing, " Your a good wife, a good mother but I'm the A**hole!" How am I supposed to feel and think? I was vanishing. I just couldn't take it anymore! I attend church, I pray. WHAT MORE AM I SUPPOSED TO BE? WHAT AM I SUPPOSED TO DO WITH THIS LOVE THAT I HAVE? I'm tired of having love and lost love. Am I supposed to put my heart in a box and push it in the back of the closet? Where was my God that I have always known?

I was rushed to the emergency room at the hospital. I remember getting several visitors from my best friend and her husband, who is now the pastor of my home church and from other family and friends that were concerned about my wellbeing. One visitor in particular I received that I will never forget. It was my oldest daughter. The look on her face was something I couldn't get out of my mind. Right then I knew what I had done and regretted it. I decided that I would never allow a man to affect me in that way again. Everything happened so fast. What was happening? I was told by the hospital staff that I would have to be committed to the psychiatric unit. I burst into tears.No way that this was happening! I didn't mean to take the pills, but I did. I wanted to go home! My time there was very short but seemed very very long. I participated in group and individual therapy. I got visitors only from my mother and my best friend. My husband was a no-show. I tried to call him, I did speak to him a few times before he stopped taking my calls. I wasn't sure why. When I was discharged, I knew our marriage was over and knew we needed to separate for a bit. I rented a moving truck to move my belongings out of the house. To my surprise, the locks were changed. I couldn't get in. I messaged him, and minutes later, a police officer pulled up in front of our house and served me with protection of abuse papers. I was ordered to leave the property. Protection of what? Abuse, against whom? I was shocked and in disbelief. How and why would this man file paperwork for abuse against him? I burst into tears, feeling defeated. I have for the most part tried to do the right thing in life and have tried to do right by others, recalling my upbringing by treating others as I want to be treated. I had to go to my mother's home. Two weeks later, we had to appear in court, let's just say, he didn't win. Case closed. After the court hearing, he wanted to talk. He wanted me out of the house. He had mine and my children's clothing in garbage bags in the garage and wanted me to pick them up.

Some months later, after counseling and many conversations, we started courting again. We did make up and I moved back home along with my children. We rekindle our relationship,with a lot of time spent and effort on both of our parts. But I vowed that I would never allow a man to kick me out of my own home again.

Things took a turn for the worse when we got a phone call in the middle of a snowstorm that his father passed away from a heart attack. He was never the same. He took the death of his father very hard. He was inconsolable at times. I did what a wife does, and consoled him. After his father's death, he became a different person. The fights became more frequent and more violent. I remember a cookout we had at the house. He had been drinking with his buddies. Once everyone left, things escalated. He grabbed me from behind and broke my phone, again, I had to leave the house with my kids. In another incident, he had a sawed-off shotgun, and after a few drinks, he pulled out this gun and threatened to end his life. I stood like a deer in the road, not knowing what to do because I didn't know if he wanted to end his life or mine. I called the police, and they confiscated the illegal firearms. My life flashed before my eyes. I didn't want to be a witness to a suicide, and I didn't want to be the victim of a murder.

He used to say to me every day, "Did I tell you I love you today?" Just out of the blue, he vanished, mentally, emotionally, and physically. He would stay out late and even stayed out all night long. I found out he was with another woman. I asked, and he admitted it. A few weeks later, he served me with divorce papers. I was devastated and confused, and a bunch of other feelings I had no words for. I felt like I was vanishing, losing myself in another failed marriage. I just couldn't believe that this was happening again. I was sinking into a hole. I wasn't eating. Was I affected by failed marriages or the feeling of inadequacy? Feeling abandoned? Similar to the abandonment of my father. At least, that's what it felt like. Have heard many times, "You're a good wife and a good person, but.." What did I do wrong? No one could explain. I was told that again, I had to leave our home. This was the end, the finale. I cried every single day. I felt like a failure. Was I a bad person? I kept asking myself. He left me to be with a woman who was ten years older than he was.

I had made arrangements to move my belongings out of the house for the last time. I arrived at the house to find that he wasn't home and wouldn't allow me to get my belongings until I came with signed divorce papers. I wasn't ready to sign the papers due to everything being so fresh and I wasn't willing to give up on our marriage that fast. I wasn't able to get into the house, so I broke into the house. I shattered the garage window and kicked the door down to find the other woman's belongings in our garage. I was now irate! As I was leaving the property with my belongings, I saw HER. Walking down the street toward my house. The front of my car was heading in her direction with the intention of running her off of the sidewalk. But I didn't. Weeks following, I would dream about the two of them most nights, which would keep me up. Crying and pacing the living room floors in the middle of the night. I prayed every single day in my car. Asking God to help ease the pain and to keep my head up. There were many days I couldn't pick my head up, but I still prayed and sometimes I just sobbed without words. This was the worst feeling that I wouldn't wish on anyone. The feeling of hopelessness, and grief. I felt like not only did my husband not want me, I didn't feel like myself. I questioned myself," Who am I?"

In 2016 I lost my father to colon cancer. I was there when he received the news after he was hospitalized just before Thanksgiving. He was grocery shopping. He almost passed out in the parking lot. He was rushed to the hospital. He had to receive a transfusion. Close family gathered at the hospital. I wasn't ready to accept the news that I had received from his doctor that my father had colon cancer. I was shocked considering that my father always ate well and healthy. The look on my father's face was something that I couldn't explain. It was a very brief look of disbelief then quickly turned into a look of defeat. I can't remember his exact words but it was along the lines of what a superhero would say when ready to battle their villains.My father lived four years after his diagnosis.

I was feeling the grief from all the failed relationships in my life and it weighed heavy on me. I just didn't understand. How is it that you describe me as the perfect wife, but yet, you leave and abandon me? I'm lost in my own world.

God kept me sane and blessed me beyond measure. I am grateful for the people God kept around me that didn't allow me to fall through the cracks. I had friends and family who supported me and made sure

I was ok. I purchased a brand new car when my car was taken.. I did get out into the dating field, just for fun at first, because I wasn't looking for a commitment. I dabbled on dating sites here and there and met some nice men. I became bored with the dating site life and desired to have real and true love. I wanted to allow God to lead and guide me. I decided that if and when I wanted to be in a relationship or find my mate, I wanted to be prepared to bring the best of me to the table.

I got help to fix my finances. I invested in myself. I invested in a personal trainer and a nutritionist that allowed me to be in the best shape possible. I also seeked therapy to help sort out my feelings and emotions. I was determined to find peace even when feeling helpless. I learned what dating myself looked like, I loved and utilized my alone time and kept a close relationship with God. I treated myself to a day of shopping and a movie. I traveled to my dream vacations alone or with friends. I had to realize that I was important and I mattered. I learned to love myself inside and out. I NOW know what that looks like.

I was single for 5 years before finding the person I was meant to be with. I am now happily married to a wonderful, God-fearing man. God led us to each other when we were not searching for each other. He knew what I needed. I am a grandmother of five biological and seven bonus grandchildren. I am the proud owner of Hobo Bay-Be LLC children's loungewear and Phillips Mobile labs LLC, serving as the CEO and Lab Director of my company. It wasn't the tone of my skin, my failure or the loss of a relationship, I was grieving the love lost of me. My grief was my blessing. I wouldn't have known how to find me, and I needed to find her to be who I am today. I AM SHE AND SHE IS ME. SHE IS NYTISHA M. DAVIS AND SHE IS STANDING STRONG!

Tammy Cameron

Calm Strategy
Holistic Educator

https://www.facebook.com/Calm.Strategy
https://www.instagram.com/tammystma/
https://calmstrategy.ca/

Tammy is a compassionate educator with a passion for reading, writing, and all forms of sharing stories.

The stories she writes are stories of courage and connection that engage the reader with new perspectives and a process of inner reflection.

Tammy draws on over 25 years of experience in facilitated classroom, boardroom, and conference room adult education and staff training. She has taught at colleges and universities across North America.

She delivers practical strategies for developing calm spaces where productivity and creativity shine.

Having faced significant health challenges at a young age, she knows struggle and resilience.

She has cried intensely over a dropped grape, focused profoundly on breathing to get through extreme physical pain, and has climbed a mountain in high-heeled sandals because she could!

She most often writes in the early morning, alongside the sunrise, with a view of pine trees and basswood dancing in a gentle breeze.

Change, Challenge, and Treasures Revealed

By Tammy Cameron

September in Canada is usually a time of returning to routines. Summer vacation is wrapping up, travel and cottage plans are complete, and families return to school and work as the temperatures begin to drop and the leaves on the trees change colour, settling into fall. Though sad for fun summer times to end, we dive into this change headfirst, usually ready to tackle a new year.

The September that I will speak about here was nothing like this. This particular September marked the beginning of university for me. This was a big change: a new city, home, schedule, classmates, and there was nothing routine about it. This was difficult but a small challenge compared to what I will speak about.

During my first month at my new school, while orienting myself to university life, I began to experience physical pain in my body, in my abdomen in particular, and this was a pain I had never felt before that brought big fear. At best, I was able to go about my day-to-day activities, moving slowly while feeling nauseated and dizzy. At worst, I was vomiting and crying in the emergency room near my university, unable to stand up straight while walking. Sadly, doctors could not find my problem, and I was sent home. This was difficult, but was a small challenge compared to what happened next.

Unfortunately, my physical pains continued. Bad days grew to outnumber good days, though I pushed forward with every attempt to keep up with my university obligations and a part-time job that I held on weekends. I became a frequent visitor to emergency rooms where doctors continued to not find the problem. I was repeatedly sent home in a state of pain, nausea, and dizziness, confused and scared. A few times, I was hospitalized with pain of unknown cause. There, I was in the care of nurses who passed judgement and freely shared, commenting things like, "You're not really sick. You're just here because you need attention. There's nothing physically wrong with you. You need psychological counselling. You're taking a bed away from people who really need it." This was hard. I won't lie; I can still cry about this today. It was a sizeable obstacle; however, it's not the challenge that I am referring to. I share my story in steps because history gets us to where we are today and is a formative factor in the decisions we make going forward.

Though I never gave up seeking expert help, I faced HUGE discouragement. For this, I had family support. At moments when I was willing to stay at home and suffer versus again make the physical effort it took me to move my body out of the house, into a vehicle, and through the hospital entrance doors where I felt unwelcome, my family provided the nudge needed to encourage me to make the effort. Finally, after many of these trips and a very frank conversation with my family doctor, a 15-minute, exploratory laparoscopic operation was scheduled. Fear gripped me a bit harder.

I have a memory of before the operation. I recall people working around me in the operating room. I recall my family doctor working at my head; he was acting as the anesthesiologist because that's how it worked in my small town at that time. I recall saying to him, "I'm scared." He placed his hand on my shoulder and said, "I know." I asked, "How do you know?" He said, "Your heartbeat is elevated." Momentarily, my fear was replaced with anger because another person could see my heartbeat and know my feelings before I verbalized them. This was difficult, but I had a medical team for support.

I have a memory of after the operation. This is where my resilience story begins. This is where the deep dive into every ounce of courage and strength you could ever muster in your most difficult moment begins. I spoke three words. It took a long time. It consumed all of my energy. "I… can't… breathe." There was a nurse with me. She would respond, "Do you want the oxygen back?" I would answer, "Yes." This conversation repeated. I don't know how many times, but I recall being reassured by the fact that when I spoke, someone heard me, and was there to respond. Though difficult, I got through this.

Then, the learning began. In my operation, they had called a surgeon, unknown to me, who had removed my appendix. I cried. I had a strange doctor, and a team of medical professionals had stolen a body part while I was asleep. I also had a lot of pain. I developed an infection and fever, and this was a hard fight. However, I had a medical team for support.

I was nineteen years old and now in my second year of university. I had a big job to do. I had to heal my body and recover from this experience. I had to study in spite of doctors telling me that I "had to" drop out of school. That was enough challenge for me. However, I was pushed a bit further by nurses, visiting me to say, "Thank God they found that appendix! It's so good to see you walking!" I didn't want those comments. Earlier, the comments were, "You're not really sick. You're just here because you need attention. There's nothing physically wrong with you. You need psychological counselling. You're taking a bed away from people who really need it." These were the same people. To me, this was hypocrisy at its finest, and it was coming to me at a time when my energy was already taxed. I would hear these words, and I would cry fresh tears. I felt angry, frustrated, and sad all at the same time. The time that they had invested in knocking me down in a weak moment could have been spent to help others. The time that they were now investing to try and disguise their true selves with kind words could also be spent helping others. I didn't need or want any words from these people. I had to train myself to try and ignore the comments or to at least cry minimally because I needed my energy to heal. I prayed a lot.

With time, I learned to manage, but the challenges continued. This one operation would turn into four. As I understand it, the ruptured appendix living in my body had damaged the intestine, and in trying to protect itself, my body had developed an abscess the size of a grapefruit in my now 80-pound body. The second operation drained the abscess. The third operation removed a piece of the bowel. When the bowel was connected following this procedure, they used surgical staples. Four months later, I had a fourth operation when the staples did not hold properly. They were all excruciatingly difficult. There are no adequate words to describe this pain, and it's not a place I like to revisit.

It's also only a part of my story. In the years following this period, many were good. Some were not. I began to suffer pain from surgical adhesions, and I began to be hospitalized with bowel obstructions. This continued to happen periodically, was not something I largely understood until recently, and finally resulted in a fifth operation, in a new city, at the end of a pandemic. The environment was ripe with stress and tension for both patients and medical staff. This time, I had the skills to get through it with grace. While I definitely was not able to achieve grace one hundred percent of the time, I was able to make the effort. I was able to support other patients.

This is my history, This is where I come from. Resilience is what I know. In part, it's who I am. There is a huge deep dive into inner strength that happens when you are faced with fear, pain, and trauma. Your boundary of bearable and unbearable will shift and you learn that it can shift. You are not stuck. While you may feel that a tough situation puts you in the place of a victim, it can be temporary. I used to describe my feeling like I was drowning in quicksand. I was trying to swim, but I was drowning faster than I could swim or even tread water. Only my head was above the quicksand. If I reached an arm out for help, no one was there, and the effort would only make me sink further. Then, my head started to sink. If I lifted it, a herd of wild animals would stampede past and trample me down. This was my feeling. It is the most difficult situation I can imagine.

Life is not a one-person show. It's a team effort. When we feel alone, not heard, or abandoned by our team, we suffer, especially when we are in great need. Resilience-building happens in the community. I recovered, not because I'm superwoman with indestructible batteries. I recovered because I had help. Certainly, I could have recovered faster if I had received the proper help sooner, so if you're thinking this, you're not alone. We don't get to control the circumstances that come our way. We do get to control our own decisions, state of mind, and efforts. We are all subject to human weakness and we can all have moments that lack clarity, action, or grace. We have the capacity to forge forward.

In this forward movement, we see our deep, inner resilience shine. We begin to recognize it, to honour it, and to give it a larger place in our world. How you best connect with this inner strength is up to you. For me, it was a combination of prayer, breathwork, quiet, companionship, connection, openness, and persistence. Behind it all, was a desire. I wanted to live my life. I never gave up. I accepted some sacrifice. I'll never go and eat a five-star meal in a restaurant; that's not a safe activity for me. I will enjoy humour and love and good times with my family and friends, and I will engage with my community in other ways.

Community is a big piece of standing in your own strength. In nature, the strongest animal leads the pack, protects the herd, and knows when to take a rest. You are allowed moments of rest and of strength. In your strength, you will understand others. We are all at different stages of development, and all stages are okay. It is okay to be in need of support, and it is equally okay to offer support. Prior to my third operation, I was on the operating table covered in a sheet, and the staff was all bustling around the room. They seemed to be much more "ahead" of schedule in my mind. I said to the staff beside me, "I'm still wearing my clothes." Many heads in the room spun to look at me. "You're still wearing your clothes!?" "Yes." Someone, somewhere, had missed providing a gown and instructing the patient to change. This oversight was quickly fixed; my small sentence made a difference in preparations. When they began to administer the anaesthetic, I began to cry. Everyone in the room was a stranger to me. As I looked around, I spotted my surgeon through a small door frame. I couldn't form words. I reached my right hand out from the sheet and I saw him run and felt him take hold of my hand. I was thinking to myself, "Why is he running? I'm not going anywhere." It was upon waking from that operation that I understood why he ran; he knew that I would lose consciousness quickly. If he didn't run, I wouldn't know that he had responded. This is a connection.

Connect with others to the best of your ability and know that your efforts are enough. This is my advice to you. Many times over many years, people have asked me, "How did you get through this so beautifully and with a sense of humour?" Interesting question. I had to think about it to be able to answer. I don't feel that I always handled every situation beautifully or with a sense of humour. What I did do was show up in every moment authentically myself. I cried, laughed, argued, questioned, and accepted, all without filter. I am healed from some parts of my experience. I continue to heal from others. New things happen. There is beauty in all of this. There is humour in many moments along the way. I have met many people along my life's path who I consider to be stronger than I am. I am blessed to know them or to have crossed paths with them.

Strength is "the quality or state of being strong: capacity for exertion or endurance," as defined by Merriam-Webster. If we want to lift one hundred pounds, we practice daily with light weights and increase increments gradually until we achieve our goal, and then we continue to work until that goal becomes easy. With a similar approach, resilience will become easy. Identify what you want, don't give up, accept some sacrifice, and work to understand others. In understanding others, you will see so much good, and this will build your endurance. Look within, and you will see this within yourself.

When I was a small child, it was decided that we would adopt a family cat. My grandparents had a barn cat who had recently given birth, and we were to adopt one of these kittens. One weekend, we went on a trip to visit these kittens, knowing that they were too young to be separated from their mother. I was pre-school age and super heartbroken to leave with no cat, so my grandfather told my mom to take the mother cat and all of the kittens home. We did. We loved all of those cats for a few weeks until it was time to choose one kitten and return the others. My dad allowed me to choose which kitten to keep. I loved them all, so it was a tough choice. However, one stood out to me. He was the smallest kitten, he was quite adventurous, and he was the one who kept straying away from the mother and siblings. We kept finding him in places where he was not supposed to be while the others were all huddled up in the area that we had set up for them with their mom. When I chose this little kitten, my dad asked me what I was going to name this kitten. I said, "Goodness." My dad asked, "Are you sure you want this one? He keeps getting out of the cat zone. He's bad." I said, "Yes, I'm sure. He's pure goodness. His name is Goodness." The adults saw mischief. I saw curiosity. They saw bad behaviour. I saw adventure. I saw light in his eyes. I saw independence. I saw love.

See your situation, whatever it may be, and as extremely difficult as it is. It's temporary. It can change. You are in charge. Know what you want. Don't give up. Accept some sacrifice. Strive to understand others. Allow a new view to have a greater part of your definition. See curiosity, adventure, light, independence, love, and whatever other treasures are waiting there for you to discover.

I have discovered some of my treasures: I am in the process of recovery, not illness. I am a powerful decision-maker, not weak. I am my path-forward creator, not a victim. I understand that others are innately strong, even when experiencing moments of weakness or defeat.

Rosita Perez

Moving Forward For Life
Founder, Coach & MAM

https://www.linkedin.com/in/rositasellshomestoday/
https://www.facebook.com/rositamovingforwardforlife/
https://www.movingforwardforlife.com/
https://www.youtube.com/@movingforwardLifeCoachRealtor/

Rosita's journey is a testament to the transformative power of faith and resilience. Having overcome significant relationship challenges and childhood wounds, she intimately understands women's struggles in personal relationships—with self, marriage, and children.

Emerging from adversity with unwavering faith in God's grace, Rosita blends Christian principles and practical tools to foster lasting breakthroughs and freedom.

As a coach, Rosita empowers women to master their emotions, conquer their inner critic, embrace their worthiness, and confidently pursue their purpose. With compassionate guidance, women rediscover their strength, reignite their passions, and live authentically with unwavering faith and purpose. Her heartfelt mission is to support women in overcoming obstacles, discovering their voice, and embracing lives filled with faith, resilience, and purpose.

Rising from the Ashes: A Journey of Resilience & Faith

By Rosita Perez

Hello, seasoned midlife beauties! I want to take you on a journey through my life—a journey that is both deeply personal and universal. My hope is that by sharing my story, you'll find inspiration and strength for your own path.

I'm here to tell you that no matter how dark things may seem, there is always a light at the end of the tunnel, and that light is brighter and more beautiful than you can imagine. I hope my story resonates with you and shows you that even in midlife, there's so much more to look forward to.

Every morning, as the sun peeks through my curtains, I start my day with a simple yet powerful routine. I offer a prayer of gratitude. As I reflect on my life, tears often fill my eyes.

Today, I deeply appreciate the loving relationship I've built with myself and the connection my daughter and I are building. My added joy is being a grandmother to my two amazing grandsons. You see, being part of their lives is a precious gift, one that I can fully appreciate because of the healing and growth we've experienced over the years.

Looking back, the relationship with myself was non-existent, which I will share later in my story. However, in the relationship with my daughter, I see the breaking of generational unhealthy behaviors. We're learning our boundaries and sharing our feelings. But our relationship wasn't always this way.

We definitely have had our struggles and we continue to work to understand each other. But through our journey of forgiveness, we're creating a new, loving family dynamic and redefining what family means in this chapter of our lives.

These moments didn't just happen by chance; they come from years of self-discovery and working on our healing—both individually and together, along with a lot of prayer.

Before our relationship could heal, it was imperative for me to humble myself and do my own personal healing work. This step was the only way I would gain the capacity to build a healthy relationship with myself and my family. In my journey, I've learned profound and crucial lessons, one of which is how to prioritize myself. So, a couple of years back, I treated myself to a birthday trip to Hawaii with my sister. I walked along the beach, listening to the waves hitting the shore. I felt the warm breeze going through my hair and the sun kissing my skin. In that peaceful moment, I exhaled and realized I've come to a place in my life where I have truly accepted myself, and love who I am! This newfound self-love, along with gaining the power of forgiveness, has filled me with an unshakable joy that no one can take away.

Today, I am a woman who stands firm in my strength. I have joy deep within, my faith is unwavering—and believe me, this is a stark contrast to who I was five years ago.

Back then, I was caught in storms of heartbreak, feeling as though my life had shattered into pieces. I felt like I was fighting a never-ending series of battles against doubt and pain. The weight of my past wounds and personal setbacks felt unbearable, and I wondered if I would ever find peace again. What I have learned is that in my darkest moments, when I feel so alone, God reminds me HE will never leave me nor forsake me, and I am not alone.

At that moment, I realized I am blessed, and I must move forward because I have been given hope and a purpose. Then a thought filled my mind, time is short, and I need to make the most of what is left.

It's time to get rid of the "stinking thinking" and get busy nurturing meaningful relationships, embrace a joyful life, and live unstoppably. Now that I have the motivation, how do I find this place of peace and fulfillment? To start, I must unpack what has held me back, dig out the roots of my pain, and find the path to my authentic self.

My story is not one of extraordinary heroism but rather of an ordinary woman who chose to face her pain head-on, with Christian faith and a determination to become who I was created to be.

Before I proceed with my story, I'd like to acknowledge that I hold no unforgiveness for anyone, nor do I blame my parents for anything. I believe people did the best they could with the knowledge they had at the time.

My parents were my biggest influences in my life. They taught me strength, to be content whether I am rich or poor, to do the right things, even when the wrong things are being done to me, and to be a survivor.

My journey started on the island of Guam in the early 60s. Born into a large family of 14 kids, I was the twelfth child and the youngest daughter. Before you ask, yes, from the same mom and dad.

To give perspective, Guam is a small island spanning 30 miles long and 9 miles wide. On such a small island, gossip was prevalent. Family secrets were protected fiercely, and the hierarchy demanded respect for elders. This seemed to be the island way and seeped into the familial way.

As a little girl, my dad showed me that regardless of the circumstances we are to gather strength and move forward. The beliefs and narratives were that crying and showing emotions were signs of weakness, that we needed to "suck it up", be strong, and keep going. To me, my dad commanded respect. He was strong and larger than life. My mom was quiet and diligent in her duties as a mom and wife. She was a devoted prayer warrior, a woman of extraordinary faith. Her actions taught me to believe and trust God.

As a child, I was taught children are to be seen but not heard, which often silenced my voice and made me feel undervalued and unimportant. This upbringing planted seeds of self-doubt and unworthiness deep within me.

I learned early on to keep quiet and stay out of trouble; however, as a child, I was inquisitive, and I had challenges adhering to keeping quiet. So, I was labeled "disrespectful". Unknowingly, this label stuck with me and became a limiting belief. This shaped my sense of self-worth and caused me to question my value. "Disrespectful" became my identity. I carried this belief with me into adulthood, and it influenced many of my decisions and relationships.

In the late 60s, our family relocated to San Diego, California, a move that was initially exciting but soon was tainted by tragedy. At fifteen, we suddenly and unexpectedly lost our mom to a massive heart attack. The shock of her passing left me numb and frozen. I reverted to what I had been taught—conceal emotions, suck it up, and keep moving forward. I do not remember crying or grieving. The days following her death were a blur, and it wasn't until years later that I stumbled upon an old photograph of myself at her funeral. The image of my teenage self, hurt and lost, was a stark reminder of the pain I had buried.

With my mom gone, there was a silent expectation that I would take on her duties. I became the caretaker for my younger brothers and dad. This selflessness became my norm, a habit formed of prioritizing others over myself. Unknowingly, this became my default, often at the expense of my own needs. I prioritized others over myself and overlooked my own needs.

This mindset, combined with my limiting beliefs, extended into all my relationships. I yearned for a life filled with love and happiness, and a "forever love" that was shaped by romantic movies and fairy tales.

So, at nineteen, I fell in love and married a man eight years older. However, this dream quickly soured into a painful reality, and unfortunately, my marriage turned out to be brief and abusive. I had a range of emotions—confusion, shame, fear, protective mama bear—how could this be my reality? My self-talk was all over the place:

- How did I let myself be in a physically and emotionally abusive marriage?
- I know I do not want my daughter to grow up in an abusive home environment or think abuse is the norm.
- I can't get divorced, because when you get married, you stay married. But even with abuse?
- I'll be a disgrace, getting divorced in a Catholic family and being a single parent is shameful.
- Can I financially provide? Fears of how I would support myself and my daughter.

Despite these fears and hardships, this marriage brought me the greatest joy and blessing of my life—my beautiful daughter.

Well, my faith and determination won. I filed for divorce. I moved forward to provide for my daughter and navigate life as a single parent. I clung to the lessons of perseverance and emotional suppression that had been instilled in me. I faced divorce and single parenthood with a steely determination. I was no longer a little girl. This marked the dawn of a new chapter in my life.

As a 22-year-old single mom, I was determined to give my daughter all the things I wanted as a child—I vowed to hug her and verbally tell her "I love you", spend time with her, and nurture her. Most importantly,

I wanted to instill in her that she has value, she has a voice and can do anything she is inspired to do. I did my best emotionally, financially, and physically to support what she wanted so she could have opportunities to explore who she was and discover her gifts and talents.

While I did the things I vowed, I inherently parented like I was parented—of course, with love, support, as well as behaviors like stubbornness, pride, parental manipulation, and being controlling.

I did my best to raise her, and as my daughter grew into an adult, our relationship began to be distant. I was clueless as to what the problem was.

One day, my daughter had the courage to speak her peace about our relationship. While I tried to understand, the mom in me was heartbroken. Through therapy, I began to understand how some of my behaviors were unhealthy and caused distance. I learned how I muted her voice, hurt her, and that's why she shut down. Over the years, we still struggle, and with both of us healing, we are building a relationship of acceptance, forgiveness, and respect, as mom and daughter, as two adult women. Learning to respect and honor each other.

While navigating being a single parent and working full-time, I still had a desire to find that fairy-tale love. By my mid-30s, I had a trail of broken hearts and was unfulfilled and exhausted. Seeking a solution, I discovered two patterns about myself in relationships.

One, I repeatedly entered relationships that mirrored my own feelings of unworthiness and inadequacy.

Two, I would keep myself in cycles of self-doubt, anger, and a self-defeating mindset.

These two behaviors kept me stuck. Through therapy, the limiting behaviors from childhood of feeling undervalued and unimportant reared their head.

In relationships, I focused on meeting others' expectations and needs. I lost sight of my true self along the way. But the truth is, I had no idea who I really was, and this uncertainty weighed heavily on me. I grew increasingly desperate to discover my authentic self.

This longing led me to consider going to church despite my initial reservations. I had the perception that I had to change, but honestly, my life was a whirlwind of drama and heartache, and I had nothing to lose.

I began attending a small Christian church. Within a year, I met a man who shared my faith, and two years later, we married. This second marriage felt like the forever love, a beacon of hope, a chance for a fresh start. However, after twenty-one years of marriage, my fairy tale began to unravel. We faced overwhelming debt, growing emotional distance, and intimacy was fading. It was like an open wound that could not heal and incredibly painful. My faith was overshadowed by pain, and I felt like a stranger to myself. I was lost.

We separated. The pain of separation felt like I was tearing apart myself, and spiritually, I struggled with the decision.

During the three years, we decided to salvage our marriage through dating, counseling, prayer, and faith healing.

There were moments where defeat loomed large, and my hope dwindled. In the pit of my pain, I felt like throwing in the towel and giving up on life. In that moment of crisis, I called out to Jesus. Suddenly, my thoughts turned to my daughter and grandsons. I couldn't leave them with this pain, and I remembered how much I valued being a grandmother because I did not have one growing up. My family became my driving force.

So, I began. I recognized how my pain shaped my self-perception. At the same time, I was fully aware I could not face this alone or heal in my own strength. Even though I felt so far from my faith, I turned to God in raw desperation. I surrendered my will to God, and I trusted Him to guide me through the pain.

HE gave me the courage to stop avoiding my pain and realize it's time to confront it head-on. I knew this process was going to be challenging, and the vision of my family's pain propelled me forward. These limiting beliefs and pain plagued me for decades. This time, my wounds needed to heal—period.

I began a season of rebuilding by unpacking, facing, healing from painful childhood memories, and finding the deep-seated roots of my pain.

The resources that helped me were therapy and the Healing Prayer Ministry. I researched practical tools to implement and, most importantly, made a commitment to myself.

For the first time in my life, I took the time to nurture myself and discover who I am. I discovered things I liked and disliked. I reignited my dreams. I paid attention to my needs and connected with the core of who I am made to be.

One important thing I learned was that part of the heartache I experienced was self-inflicted. Because I felt unworthy, I chose from a broken place—my "picker" was broken, and I unknowingly kept the cycles of self-doubt and heartbreak alive!

During my separation journey, I learned how to combine practical tools and my faith to manage my emotions and embrace my worthiness. I surrounded myself with a supportive community of women. I learned to set clear boundaries and heal my heart to rebuild my strong foundation.

Through my faith, I began to transform my mindset and habits. I recognized that I am a unique masterpiece, and there is absolutely no one like me. I attended Bible studies specific to the pain I was experiencing and found support and community. I learned what a healthy relationship is and is not. I stopped seeking validation from others. I kept using the tools to make them a natural process for me. The more I implemented all these things, I was able to manage my self-doubt cycle and be the boss of my negative thoughts.

In my third year of our separation, it became clear that it would take both of us to do our individual work before working on the marriage. I firmly believe it takes two people to rebuild a marriage. Unfortunately, the painful reality is that was not the case. Acceptance of leaving my 24-year marriage was overwhelming.

But God gave me a vision during prayer and a revelation. These provided clarity and courage, leading me to make the most painful yet necessary decision to file for divorce.

At sixty-one years old, I was divorced and facing a new beginning. This was another level of grieving. However, because I chose to do my self-work and heal during the separation years, I had the faith and practical tools to overcome. My sense of self and confidence was restored, and I released the guilt and shame that held me back.

I learned that I first need to love myself and understand my worth so I can make healthy choices as well as give love to others from an authentic place. I accepted that I am not a victim; some choices I made came from a place of brokenness. I accepted that my past does not define who I am. And I hold the power to change my internal narratives.

My faith gave me the strength to persevere during the most trying times. It was my anchor, reminding me of the greater purpose behind my struggles.

Practical tools, on the other hand, provided me with the actionable steps I needed to transform my life. Implementing faith and practical tools brought me a sense of peace, broke down walls, and gave me clarity that I had never known before. This IS my foundation!

Today, I stand proudly in midlife, radiating a profound, unshakable joy. I've overcome challenges and have emerged victorious.

My journey has equipped me with a deeper relationship with God, with practical actionable tools and a mindset needed to step into my inner strength. I have the freedom to be me.

Because of my journey, I have stepped into my purpose as a Mindset Coach. I get to apply my experiences to empower other midlife women to rise above their fears and doubts. I coach them to shed the masks they wear and help them create spaces where they can authentically be themselves.

Every experience, no matter how painful, is an opportunity for growth and transformation. It is imperative to embrace the belief that it is never too late to change the trajectory and narrative of your life. By aligning with your authentic self and trusting in your faith, it is possible to overcome fear and step confidently into your future filled with purpose, joy, and fulfillment.

So, here's to you, seasoned midlife beauty, to your journey, and to the incredible, unstoppable woman you are. Embrace your strength, cherish your worth, and never stop believing in the power of your own story.

The future is bright, and it's waiting for you to step into it with all the courage and love you have.

When you are ready to start your journey, I am here to offer a complimentary Clarity call. During this call you can gain Clarity on your Challenges, identify one goal, and receive 1 HOT Tip to move forward.

To book your complimentary Clarity call go to _www.MovingForwardForLife.com_.

I leave you with this quote:

"Your journey is far from over—it's just beginning;
you hold the wisdom of experience
and the power within to redefine your future."

Louise Borthwick

Empowered Relationships
Accredited Master Practitioner Coach

https://www.linkedin.com/in/louiseborthwick
https://www.facebook.com/profile.php?id=100090617373562
https://www.instagram.com/therapyfreedom.club
https://www.empoweredrelationships.co.uk
https://www.ep-app.online/get-relationship-confident

Louise Borthwick (Dip, FdSc, BA Hons) the founder of Empowered Relationships and The Empowerment Programme. Louise is a highly trained and recommended Accredited Master Practitioner Coach specialising in Relationship Health. The EMB theory and Coaching model has proven success in helping people to have healthy relationships with themselves and others. Louise is a warrior for Mental and Emotional Health Movement. Having overcome adversity in her own life using a wealth of life experience and academic knowledge, supporting others is her life's purpose. Louise had a difficult start in life - adoption, Parental terminal illness, death and sexual abuse before she was 13 years old. All of these experiences disconnected her from herself and her family. This is a story of her journey of self-recovery and healing, a journey back to connection with herself. A journey of rebuilding the relationship she has with herself, becoming her true authentic self free and empowered.

Empowered Relationships

By Louise Borthwick

New Perspective

We, as a society, have social perspectives on people's experiences. For instance, if someone has experienced trauma, society automatically assumes they are troubled. We know this because people can be given some allowances for their behaviour if they have experienced difficulties in the past.

If someone has experienced loss, pain, sorrow, or abuse, we assume that they are fucked up in some way.

Which in my view, is a very limited way to look at it.

Of course, it stands to reason that if we have experienced trauma, we are likely to be affected in some way, however, in my experience it is the attitudes of the wider society that have affected me more greatly than any abuse or trauma.

Society's limited knowledge and opinion of people who have experienced trauma actually keeps the trauma alive, and it is my belief that this is the reason that we continue to react to it as if we are still experiencing it, long after it is over. It is a much-underestimated factor in the mental and emotional health epidemic that is escalating at rapid speed across the world.

As a society, we label people as 'abused' or 'traumatised' or worse still 'victims', and those people go through their lives identifying as such.

We take on that identity and live our lives under the judgements and opinions of those who have not experienced such difficulties. We carry with us the shame, the lack, and the imperfections that our experiences have created. We become a product of those experiences, and society helps that along.

I don't believe that the traumatic experiences that happened in my life were defining of who I am or was, I believe it was society's reaction to the knowledge of those experiences I went through that caused a bigger problem, the lack of my own identity.

In the first instance I was adopted at six weeks old, I started out in this life with a broken connection of my natural path, but was it this trauma that shaped me? Or was it the lies, deception, and secrets that were used surrounding this experience that really caused lasting damage?

There's no doubt about it, that the experience of adoption causes trauma for a child, even if the reasons are legitimate, and for the child's safety in other people's opinions. The deep disconnection from the natural reality with a birth mother causes the adopted person's reality to be damaged. But this is not the only problem adopted children face. Starting a life with an inner knowing that I don't belong where they are is what causes the lasting damage.

For me, it was the deception at the start that also impacted me, going through the first five years of childhood, believing I was with my birth parents only to discover that this was a lie when I was five years old, had a much more traumatic effect on me.

But what is the right way to do it? Tell the child from the off that they are not blood-related? I don't know. I have met people on my journey who have experienced both truth and deception, and they have all experienced imposter syndrome, disconnection, and the sense of not belonging, even if their adoptive family structure had been secure.

Much of society doesn't understand the identity of being adopted, yet it is an identity that can exclude, judge, and generate preconceptions of a person's character and personality. On the one hand, it is an identity, on the other, it causes discord from someone's real identity.

It was society's judgements that affected me so much more than any trauma.

My adopted mother became terminally ill, this went on for four years. When I was a child carer, I witnessed my adopted mother have convulsion fits, develop blindness, swell up with water retention, and become wheelchair-bound over five years from being four years old. I fed my mother from a beaker before I walked to school on my own at seven years old.

I lived in a small boating village. From the age of six, I walked a mile to school on my own. I got myself ready, dressed my adopted mother, gave her breakfast, and handed over to the Home Help Dorothy all before 8am. My adopted father had left for work at 7am.

I would walk the mile along the lane into the village. I went to the local shop where there was a cheese counter. This was my morning visit to the Cheese Lady, who kindly gave me a lump of cheese on my way to school.

As a child, I don't think I knew any difference, I didn't realise at seven years old that my childhood was any different to anyone else's.

It is at about seven years old that we develop a sense of the wider world, we have other interactions with society, and we start to become more aware of other people outside of our family unit.

This is where society gave me the label of 'poor girl'. I was already a victim. Whilst the tea and sympathy were a nice gesture, I believe that this damaged me more than any of the things I experienced as a result of the knowledge of being adopted or my adopted mother's illness.

Being the centre of other people's tea and sympathy isolated me and made me different. I felt like the poor victim, and it reinforced the feeling of not belonging.

I was already isolating myself. I remember building little dens outside under trees to hide in, and I'd sit in there for hours and cry, write my little books, and imagine a different life.

Nobody recognised this, of course, I didn't until much later, but there's no doubt that society's sympathy caused me more lasting damage than the traumatic experiences themselves. Imagine growing up in multiple environments where people feel sorry for you; that put me in the position of the underdog from the off, developing the belief that I was inferior in some way.

My adopted mother died when I was nine years old. I remember sitting on my adopted grandfather's lap and pretending to cry when it eventually happened. I remember the sense of relief in my adopted father, which is normal when a terminal illness comes to an end.

Again the death of my adopted mother put the society spotlight on me. At nine years old, I already wanted to hide away and run away, not from my adopted father, but from the life I had.

I developed some antisocial behaviours. I was lashing out, stealing, and smoking cigarettes, and it was then that society gave me the identity of being 'troubled' or 'trouble'. It's strange I don't recall any support from the people around me.

Behind closed doors, I remember having intense emotional episodes where I would get on my father's lap and sob uncontrollably into his chest. My adopted father did not know how to handle this, but he at least let me cry and held me. I think it gave him comfort, too, in some way. He used to say, 'Stop the world I want to get off'. I think we both wanted that.

Back in the 1970s, when there was a social class structure in the UK, we were middle class, I suppose, although that is debatable. I think my adopted father wanted that status more than he had it.

I sat the entrance exam and passed it, and I was sent away to a private school for a 'good education', and my adopted father set about finding me a new mother, his words, not mine. It really was that practical. He was trying his best in a difficult situation.

He joined an introduction agency and answered some adverts in the newspaper in order to find me a mother and him a wife. Nothing like online dating today; it was very limited and a lot classier than the hookups that occur today. He was basically holding interviews to find the most suitable candidate to be my mother.

That's when he met Dierdre. She had two sons and lived in a farm cottage. I don't think it would have mattered much who he chose, I was always going to hate her, and I did, and the feeling was mutual.

By now, I was getting into trouble, disruptive, stealing money to buy cigarettes, climbing out of my bedroom window in the night to take things from the marina.

I think I was introduced as the 'troubled' one! I was reacting to life; I had already experienced so much, and I was only 11 years old.

In my first year of secondary school, my adopted father pursued a relationship with Dierdre, and my life changed dramatically again.

My adopted father, who I adored, dropped me like a brick into the water for his new relationship. I was no longer important. In his head, I think he thought he'd done his job and got me a mother. Unfortunately, it didn't work out that way.

We moved in with Dierdre. My adopted father sold our lovely bungalow in the village, and we moved away to another village, in a tied cottage, where Dierdre proceeded to work her way through my adopted father's money.

I changed school to the comprehensive, my bedroom was a cupboard downstairs next to the toilet, with a tiny bed in it and that's all. A distorted glazed window led to the cow yard on the farm, and the creepy cellar beneath my bed. I was not allowed to eat with the family, I had to do my chores, and whilst they all sat at the table, I ate alone in the front room with my food on my lap. I then cleared the table and washed up after them all. I was the outcast, the inconvenience, the problem.

With the title and identity of the 'difficult' child at home and at school, I didn't stand a chance.

Of course, I lived up to it. I took it on, the identity, and in some ways, it gave me some power back. Everyone, including my adopted father, expected me to be 'trouble' and difficult by now, so I was.

This meant I was an easy target for predators. I was vulnerable and had no one looking out for me. At this point, I didn't want anyone to either, I was now going solo. So, it's no surprise that I became the target of abuse. My whole persona was asking for it.

I formed an unhealthy attachment to my new older step sibling (that status I give to him very loosely). Little did I know I was being groomed. I just thought it was great that I could smoke in his room and I, at last, could have some friends. His friends tolerated me, I think I was their entertainment, I felt accepted and grown up for the first time ever.

It soon progressed to inappropriate behaviour, touching me sexually, getting into my bed and groping me in the mornings. I didn't have the capacity to know if this was right or wrong. I was told to shush, so I knew it was our secret. I guess it was at that point, and I went along with it.

My adopted father married Dierdre when I was nearly 13 years old. On the evening before their wedding day, in a hotel in North Devon, Dierdre's 18-year-old son raped me. From that moment, my life was changed forever.

I remember bleeding and not knowing what to do, I put toilet paper in my knickers to stop the blood. I felt everyone watching me, so I hid under a table for most of the afternoon.

Little did I know that was just the start of it. I was then regularly raped a few times a week for about three years. I remember the look, sitting in the front room watching TV with the family, and the eyes looking at me, trying not to look back at him and avoid his eye contact, but they were relentless, the eyes that looked upward to the ceiling were my signal to go upstairs for sex.

When I think about it now, I'm not sure why I complied so readily, but I think it was so that I could keep in with the boys, Robert's mates. They were kind to me, I laughed with them, and I felt like they took care of me. Of course, they didn't care at all, but I believed they did.

It was a weird setup. Both my adopted father and Dierdre knew it was happening, but they turned a blind eye. Dierdre was so besotted with her son Robert that he could do no wrong, and I think, in some delusional way, my adopted father thought it was some kind of relationship between Robert and me.

My adopted father was the sort of gentle man who didn't like confrontation. Dierdre manipulated him, and he went along with everything she said.

I look at the pictures of me when I was that age. I look at girls of 13 still now, and I think how childlike I was: grown up in many ways, yet very immature and underdeveloped in others.

I have a poignant memory of my teenage years when we were all down the field at school, when I say all, the girls I hung out with. I suppose we were about 15 years old. They were all talking about kissing boys for the first time, and what they might do sexually.

I remember having an out of body experience where I had to be an innocent 15-year-old girl, but I knew I wasn't. I remember hearing their fears, their innocent experiences, their first kisses. I remember thinking this doesn't apply to me. I have already done all of this.

It was at this point that I became sexually promiscuous. It's a normal behaviour for someone like me, I had no respect or regard for myself. I went for the older boys, I wanted to be the prettiest, the most attractive and fancied. I was very competitive, and I made sure I got what I wanted.

And so that started the nature of more social judgements. I was easy. I used my looks and my body to manipulate people. I learned this very well, I became a professional at it.

All the while longing for that one person who would save me from myself. Someone who would love me. I had learned that the more I gave of myself, the less I would be treated badly, so I did whatever anyone wanted.

Despite being 'trouble', I was a clever and intelligent girl. I'm not sure if that was a good thing or if it just got me into more trouble. I was everyone's frustration, someone with potential but who never excelled; I never had the opportunity to excel.

Only in sports, I was a very good athlete, probably because of my competitive nature. I beat all the school records, I was the best sprinter and the best hockey player, I played for the school and represented my county, but no one did anything to help me. No one wondered why I didn't have the support at home. I could've joined the athletics club, it's what I really wanted to do. I worked hard in the supermarket and bought my own spikes, but I couldn't go, I didn't have the support at home, so I chose to skive school, drink alcohol, and smoke cigarettes instead.

What a waste. A waste of talent, a waste of natural ability.

At 15 1/2 years old, I had had enough. There was an almighty row in the house with Dierdre, and I vowed to leave. I packed my limited belongings into two carrier bags, got my hamster cage under my arm (I loved my hamster), and left for work at the supermarket on that Saturday morning, and I never returned to that house or that family.

I was taken in by a lady who let me sleep at her house. I made up camp behind her sofa on the floor. It was better than being at their house.

When I was 16, a few months later, I got a job living-in at a residential care home. It was like a breath of fresh air, I felt safe for the first time in my life, but this is where the abuse really took hold and became real.

There were a few of us young girls living and working there, it is where I met Shana, my new sidekick. It is where alcohol behaviours were cemented, mainly extreme binge drinking. It is where sexuality was explored and exploited, developing the knowledge that our sexual presence could be used in exchange for what we want. It is where power play was learned.

I went through many ups and downs in this period. Still experiencing episodes of extreme emotional outbursts, when I felt this way, I longed for my adopted father's warmth that I had felt back when I was seven years old, cuddling into him and sucking my thumb.

I wished he would hear me, I wished he would come and rescue me, I wished he would be on my side.

I got in touch with my adopted father when I was 17 to tell him about the rape and sexual abuse and what had happened, why I had left, not that he cared because it had been a good 18 months since I had, and he was nowhere to be seen.

I sat in his car and told him everything, and he said, "I don't believe you".

That was the end of that relationship with my adopted father. He washed his hands off me. I'm not sure why that bothered me. He had done that a long time ago.

Before I had told him my side of things, I suppose there was hope; now it was final, I had no family, not even a dysfunctional one. It was over.

Here I was, a fully prepared adult for the world at 18. I don't think so. All I had known about life so far was how to survive it, and not very well.

I started dating Kevin. He was the same age as Robert and his archenemy. He lived on the other side of the farm, his dad was a herdsman on the same farm as Dierdre was working. They lived in the same country lane, both families were at war.

It probably was a two-finger up to them, my ex-so-called family, I moved in with Kevin's parents. I lived there with Kevin, and we slept together in a single bed. I felt part of a family. His mum and dad took me in, cared for me, and I was accepted at long last.

It would be lovely to be able to say we all lived happily ever after from then on, but that wasn't the case. Kevin got very angry and violent, he had his own issues from being the youngest of six children. Being 10 years younger than his next sibling meant he felt pretty inferior, so I was who he took his frustrations out on.

Both of us lacked any healthy relationship skills, we fought violently. I was in the position of victim again. I regularly supported black eyes and bruises. I remember one occasion when I faked being unconscious to make the beating stop.

But the deal was that I had to endure this dysfunctional relationship to stay in the bosom of this family. A family I loved being a part of, where I felt I belonged.

Even though the relationship was volatile, we also had some deep feelings for one another. I know now that it was a trauma connection and very unhealthy, but at the time, when it was good, it was the best feeling in the world I'd ever experienced.

We got engaged before I was 18, which seems madness now. I remember getting the ring, it was beautiful, a sapphire and diamond gold ring. I was so proud of it. God knows how many times it got thrown across the room, out of a car window, or down the toilet, but it survived the year, and we got married in May after my 18th birthday.

18 years old and married, who allowed that to happen?! In some kind of delusional way, I thought I'd made it, I was grown up. Now I wanted a baby. I was doing it right, married now and then the baby. I will have my own family that no one can take from me, it will be mine. A baby who will love me no matter what, an unconditional bond that can never be broken, a bond with my birth mother that was taken away from me when I was born, I can have it all now.

My first pregnancy lasted about eight weeks, and I miscarried, probably because of the violence. I was heartbroken. It devastated me. I was then on a mission to get pregnant again, it was all that I wanted.

My beautiful daughter was born in August before I was 20 years old. It wasn't a perfect situation, I was still living with Kevin's parents, still sleeping in a single bed, and still in a progressively more violent and abusive relationship.

I was determined to be a good Mum, to get it right. Little did I know there was no right way, but all the same, I used my eclectic skills to observe and learn from Kevin's siblings and their families, who I regularly babysat. I was looking for what I thought would be the best parenting approach, taking in what I thought was good about their approaches and learning from what I didn't agree with. My only focus was to be a successful parent, to love and care for my child was very much a priority.

We got a bedsit from the council in this house share arrangement when my daughter was six weeks old. It was a pretty diabolical environment. Not the dream I'd envisaged at all. Bare floorboards, blankets at the cracked windows as curtains, that sort of thing.

Kevin was still violent, and alcohol and drugs played a big part in behavioural outbursts, abusive and sexual behaviour. Definitely not a healthy environment for a baby to have a settled start in life.

About six months after my daughter was born, we were offered a one-bedroom flat, a ground-floor flat with a garden. A dream come true—my own home. I very soon became pregnant with baby number two. My son was born in October, after my daughter's first birthday.

Still cramped in a one-bedroom flat, things were getting pretty tense. I phoned the council every day pleading with them for a house to live in. Eventually, all of my determination and persistence paid off. A man across the road moved into a bungalow on the street, and his house became vacant. That house had my name on it. I got the three-bedroom house.

I had it all: the amazing house, the beautiful children, and a husband, was this the happy ever after? No!

It was the beginning of the rest of my life. Kevin and I were still fighting all the time. He got jealous very easily, he told me who to talk to and what to wear, he controlled the money, or lack of it. We regularly got into fights, and the police were called.

It had to come to an end. I didn't feel safe, and I had to protect my children. I didn't have a plan really, but I started to sleep on the sofa. On my 23rd birthday, Kevin forced himself on me while I was drunk and asleep for the last time. That was it, he had to go.

I got an inner strength from somewhere and told him to go, and to my surprise, he did go quite easily. This moment of inner clarity and empowered ownership is something that started a new journey for me. Knowing that I had a choice, that when I have inner calm, I have more power.

It was not until much much later I realised the gravity of this revelation, but on reflection, this is where it started. It is where the journey back to me began.

By no means was it the end of the traumatic experiences I was to endure, some were my own creation, some out of my control. But it was at least the start of moving forward away from the traumatised child that I was before.

I had my second son, my third child, very soon after Kevin left. It was partly a concealed pregnancy, not knowing I was pregnant until six months into the pregnancy and giving birth six weeks prematurely. It was a short pregnancy. During this time, I met Colin, Mr Sensible; yes, I went very quickly from a complete life of chaos to a secure relationship, God knows how that happened. Extremes play a big part in the aftermath of trauma. I spent much of my life trying to put right the wrongs of the past. Colin took on my third son as his own from day one, and we became a family.

I then decided I wanted more from my life. I was an intelligent woman with no qualifications and three children, and I was only 23 years old. What could I do? A leaflet came through the door from the local college offering free childcare. I looked through it, and the only course I could do with no school qualifications was a hairdressing course.

This might have seemed a good idea, and it was the making of me, but when I say I wasn't the most suited to it, that's an understatement! I enrolled and turned up with my boy's haircut, chewed nails, no make-up, in a t-shirt, jeans, and old trainers on, I stuck out like a sore thumb with the other girls.

Somehow, I managed to keep going with it, but it wasn't easy in the beginning. But when it came to cutting hair, I was a natural, I realised how creative I was. This gave me so much confidence. I will always be eternally grateful to my tutor Jenny Rickard for taking me under her wing and for giving me some belief in myself. Jenny was a woman with presence, she was so professional and commanded respect, the others feared her, and I wanted to be like her. My first role model.

I spent the rest of my 20s in education. I completed my hairdressing qualifications, computer IT courses, and then went on to do my Cert Ed Adult education teaching qualification.

During this time, I had two more children with Colin. We had an amazing family unit, and I felt safe and secure. I was excelling in education, becoming more and more confident in my trade. I was balancing a large family, education, work placements, and starting my own hairdressing business. I was ambitious and driven.

It was during this time I met my birth mother. It was like coming home, I had two brothers and my family back. Anyone who thinks that was ever going to end well is deluded. For a year, we bonded, my birth mother was involved in our family, a Nan to my children. I loved this time I had a Mum, I married Colin, and got pregnant with my fifth child. We had a proper family Christmas, I celebrated my birthday with my mum, and it was all so perfect, a dream come true.

Her husband was an alcoholic and not very happy about the time we spent together. She felt so much guilt. But my mum was so very happy to be reconnected with her daughter, almost too happy, ecstatic. I was unaware of her mental health issues. She had a manic breakdown, and she was sectioned. I was there when they took her away in the ambulance. With a large family, work commitments, and a house to maintain, I still went to the mental health unit every day to see my mum, and I was supporting my brothers and their father. After six weeks of antipsychotic pharmaceutical treatment, she was sent home. She said she was fine, but she wasn't.

We went back to our usual meetings, and I did the pregnancy test for my fifth child when I was with her, we were so happy. I still have the card she sent me with five babies on the front. It said, this is what five looks like!

I'll never forget this day—the day I took my beautiful mum for granted. On a Saturday, we would meet over at Aunty Pat's. Mum called me up and said she'd rather not go there, but it was closer for me. She wanted me to go to her house instead. I didn't go. I said I wanted to meet at Aunty Pat's because I had the children and work later.

I was at Aunty Pat's waiting for Mum to turn up, and there was a knock at the door, two policemen. My mum had committed suicide.

At that moment, my life imploded again. I lost my mum twice. How could that happen?

For what happened after that day, I will be eternally regretful, a monster emerged in me, I changed. I was self-destructing.

I was a terrible wife to my doting husband, unfaithful and took him for granted. I moved the family away. I was drinking and partying constantly. My marriage ended; how could it survive this? I didn't care anymore. I went from dysfunctional relationship to a dysfunctional relationship.

I was still trying to survive and do the best I could for my children on my own and with the very limited resources both personally and financially. I tried to pick myself back up, I opened a business, created employment for people, and tried to continue with my education to obtain Teaching and Assessors' qualifications, I was till striving for success.

I had a hefty mortgage, I had bought my ex husband out of our home and remortgaged to fund my business, the financial strain was all too much. I couldn't handle it all, my behaviour was out of control, and I didn't care about myself or anyone else.

Throughout my life, I had always been in therapy: counselling started at 16 years old and hypnotherapy in my 20s and other therapy throughout my life. I was looking for an answer and a way to fix it. I tried everything. I wanted to work out what life was all about. It just seemed that my life had been full of negative experiences, life dictated to me, going from one disaster to another, and I never seemed to be able to make it stop. I believed that my experiences had to be for a bigger reason, but what?

What needed to happen to stop this reactive behaviour of mine? Even after everything, I was still reacting. Even though I was aware of my behaviour, I couldn't stop doing it, self-sabotaging, having emotionally overwhelming experiences, and driving myself crazy with negative thoughts, behaving irrationally.

I was so self-aware and self-reflective, I owned all of my faults, I knew what they all were, and I had told my story a million different ways to a million different people, but still never felt heard or understood. I never got an answer; it still never ended. I was stuck in this heightened state of awareness where I was still reacting, and I knew I was doing it like in slow motion. It was like an addiction, I couldn't make it stop.

I got married again and opened another salon still striving, still trying to be successful. I bought another house, and the children were all living with me. I never gave up. Life was back on track.

I had become quite an advocate and adviser for troubled people. I seemed to attract them; they would come into my salon with their problems, and I'd hold counsel with them. I was a natural, so it was not surprising that I'd developed such empathy and compassion for other 'troubled' people with my wealth of life experience.

In 2010, I left my husband, the last of a long line of failed relationships, I packed up and left the salon and decided to retrain. I felt that doing some kind of work in psychological therapy work to help others was now going to be my vocation. I was and still am very passionate about personal development, growth, and healing.

I went to London and attended many seminars on various therapeutic approaches. I wasn't sure what my approach would be. It was a great experience, and I gained so much insight into the approach that most suited me and who I had become. I settled on Practitioner Coaching because it is all about taking action and facilitating change from the here and now, rather than trawling over the old story. I started my diploma in Practitioner Coaching.

In 2011, I met a man called John. He was the only trustworthy man I'd met since my husband Colin. I admired John and respected him. He seemed to understand me, listened to my theories, and told me I was intelligent and clever. I fell in love with John. Whilst John thought a lot of me, he even told me he loved me at one point, he was out of my league, and I knew it. A wealthy man with status, in a completely different world to me. I was still broke and surviving, what could I offer him?

It was in reacting to my feelings of imposter syndrome, inferiority, and not being good enough for John that I eventually pushed John to his limit with my emotional outbursts, and he retracted his interest in me.

It was this final rejection that was the catalyst that I needed for my life change. I cried and cried and drank copious amounts of wine that night. I drank until I passed out in an attempt to self-medicate my emotional state. At 2am, I woke up with a jolt. I felt compelled to write. I got a pen and a notebook and proceeded to write and write for hours until my fingers were sore. I had no idea what I was writing.

I then passed out on the sofa again, and when I woke a few hours later, a little hung over, to say the least, I made a cup of tea and proceeded to read my ramblings of the night. To my surprise, all of my life's questions had been answered. It was right there in black and white, what I had to do to heal myself, how it works, the theory about it and how to reach the state of freedom that I'd always dreamed of.

I set to work on myself, I tested the theory I'd written about, I developed ways to evidence my findings, and I began to see incredible changes in myself, in the way others were treating me, in my confidence, self-belief, and self-esteem. I no longer felt like I didn't belong; I felt free and connected.

I trusted this theory so much because if it meant I'd broken the addictive behavioural cycle in myself and for my children, then it just might work for other people. What I had needed from therapy just wasn't out there, yet I felt I had got the answers now.

I started to put it together into a step-by-step programme. I had to test it. Who would ever believe me?

John and I became firm friends instead of lovers, and with his support and belief in me, I gained the confidence to take the Empowerment Programme into an organisation. As a volunteer, I piloted the Empowerment Programme with 20 service users from a domestic abuse organisation over a 2-year period. I also worked for this organisation as an outreach worker on the helpline during this time. The results of the Empowerment Programme were, to my surprise, very positive. All of the service users who completed the Empowerment Programme changed their behaviour, broke the abuse cycle, and, better still, have sustained those changes to this day.

The Empowerment Programme was pretty primitive back in 2013. I followed my notes written in my little notebook back then, and it was only a six-week model.

In the last 10 years, I have been developing the Empowerment Programme. I went back to education to complete a BA Hons degree in Social Psychology in 2017. I did this to gain more credibility and a better-informed argument for my theory. After all, to many people I'm simply just a hairdresser. I offered the Empowerment Programme for free for many years because I wanted to pay it forward. It is my passion and life's purpose. I wanted to get evidence of its success. I gained Master status accreditation for my practitioner coaching approach first in 2018. This is the approach that I use to facilitate the Empowerment Programme.

During the years that followed I carried on developing the Empowerment Programme, I diversified it into other short personal development course books too, I have polished the EMB theory and I have applied this to all of my work. I have hundreds of testimonials and videos from clients who have turned their lives around and broken free of the behaviour addiction cycle and cleared unresolved childhood trauma.

Fast-forward to 2024, I run a successful Coaching practice, facilitating the twelve week life-changing Empowerment Programme for hundreds of people a year. I have developed a membership platform with a six week Get Relationship Confident Course and many short courses and resources. I have written short self-development course books, and I am currently working on an animation idea to help teenagers and young adults to learn and develop their understanding of mental and emotional health.

I am a warrior for the Mental and Emotional Health movement.

My message is this:

> *"The most important relationship to master is the one you are having with yourself"*

Nicola Brachi

Nikki Brachi Hypnotherapy
Clinical Hypnotherapist

https://www.facebook.com/NikkiBrachiHypnotherapy/
www.instagram.com/nikki.brachi.hypnotherapy/
https://www.nikkibrachi.com/

Nikki Brachi is a Clinical Hypnotherapist, Life Coach & NLP Practitioner. She empowers people to tap into their inner resources and harness their own capabilities to implement positive, lasting and impactful changes in their lives.

Supporting clients to improve their mental, and emotional well-being with a unique and powerful blend of therapies, empowering them to connect deeply with inner calm, and to embody and radiate self-belief and confidence.

Nikki formulates her personalised Hypnotherapy treatment programs and tailors them to the individual, creating a peaceful and safe environment for them to connect deeply with themselves. Guiding her clients on a journey to implement healthy and helpful habits into their daily lives and adopt positive transformations and breakthroughs.

The Power Within: Harnessing Inner Strength to Transform Your Life and Rewrite Your Story

By Nicola Brachi

You have way more power than you realise. You have the power to change your life. To live life on your terms, feeling satisfied and content each day that you are being true to yourself and living with authenticity and honouring your true inner self. To find inner peace. Of course, there can be times when there are gaps between what we want and what we have, finding the strength to choose acceptance, and having the wisdom to recognise what is and isn't within your circle of control. If there are things within your circle of control, direct your energy here. For all those things that are outside of your control, find acceptance, divert your energy and attention away and redirect towards what you can control. The energy and attention will be much more useful this way!

Your dreams and aspirations are in your hands, and you have the power to create the life you want, you get to write your own story. Believe it's possible, put the pen to paper and start writing the script, and more importantly, find your own version of a 'creative writing' practice that supports you in directing the story of your life exactly where you want to lead it. As with any great story, there will likely be some trials and tribulations along the way, but with strong mindset practices and coping strategies in place, the heroine of the story can navigate these and find opportunities through challenges. You can make a choice today. To be that heroine of your own story. To choose to step up and start creating, allowing yourself to steer away from a passive existence in which you feel powerless to steer the direction of the narrative.

For any changes you seek to implement, look within, you have everything you need to make the changes you desire, perhaps you just simply never realised. When you understand the flow of how your thoughts impact your behaviours, which then directly impact outcomes, you can start to understand that every thought you think, and every belief you harbour matter. And these can be changed. Your thoughts are not facts, they are just thoughts, which come and go and can be tapped into and harnessed for your personal power. The vibrational frequency of thoughts is also important when you consider the law of attraction, with each thought having a vibrational frequency. Why not use that frequency to propel yourself towards positive outcomes for yourself?

I am on a mission to spread the word and empower people to recognise these home truths, embody the person they truly want to be and live their daily lives on their terms. Of course, life's challenges will always come and go but recognising that our response to life's challenges is within your control is a great starting place to find coping mechanisms to come through these challenges stronger than ever and embrace learning opportunities along the way. Knowing that a range of experiences and emotions are all part of the whole human experience is the reason that we are walking the earth in this form.

I know all this to be true because I am living proof, I am a prime example of how you can change your entire life from the inside out. Having suffered for many years with a debilitating autoimmune condition, crippling anxiety, and obsessive-compulsive hair pulling (trichotillomania), which became so extreme, I had no hair on my head for several years and had to wear wigs. (In fact, on my wedding day, I got married wearing a full wig!)

It got to the devastating point where I felt so low that I just knew I could not continue like this any longer. That's not to say I felt suicidal, but just that I knew I could not continue to live with the extreme physical and emotional pain and turmoil that I was in daily. I remember distinctly one day breaking down to my wonderful sister and a close friend as I sobbed my heart out and opened up to them about the extremely low place that I was in mentally, and how out of control I felt about everything. In retrospect, this was my 'night of the dark soul'. I'm so grateful to have been able to open up to those two amazing women in my life because it was at that exact moment that it hit me. I HAVE TO CHANGE THIS. THE CHANGE CAN ONLY COME FROM ME. No one else can actually create the change for me. I have to do this, and more importantly, I CAN DO THIS. That realisation somehow liberated me.

For so long, I'd been looking externally for the answers to help me get better, to cure my autoimmune condition, to free me from the shackles of my hair pulling, to release me from the anxiety and fear that plagued my body and mind daily (and nightly). But it was in that moment that the penny finally dropped, it was that lightbulb 'Eureka' moment. I had to be the change, and I had everything I needed within me to do that, I just needed to learn how.

During the recent personal development journey I had begun, I had been reading, absorbing and learning as much self-help information as I could. The things I had been learning from my hypnotherapist, they all made sense. The change comes from within me. I have to choose to commit to change, take action, and embody the change I want to make.

I had always been extremely resilient. When faced with childhood trauma, you learn resilience at a young age. That is a blessing to help you survive, but it can also become detrimental if the trauma is left untreated and unhealed, and living in trauma flight/flight mode for so many years was damaging for me on a physical, mental and emotional level.

I needed to heal. I needed to learn how to feel safe within, find peace and connect with my inner calm.

I had tried so many forms of therapy before, counselling, psychiatrist, medication, CBT, and various different therapists, but I was always open to trying new things to help myself. So when my sister suggested hypnotherapy, finding a therapist and booking and paying for my first session, I gratefully accepted the opportunity to try something new. Although I was a little nervous and apprehensive, as I didn't know much about it and didn't really understand how it worked, perhaps even a little sceptical as I had never found significant benefits from any other form of therapy yet. At that point, I had nothing to lose, and I just had to keep trying, so I gave hypnotherapy a shot.

Being in hypnosis was like nothing I had ever experienced. It was simply magical. It took me away from all my worries and sadness, at least for a short while, and provided me with a safe space within my own mind, where I could just be free. I had never experienced mental freedom like this before, and I knew that I needed more of this. From that very first session, I sensed this was different, I recognised this modality of therapy would be very important and pivotal. I wanted to experience more of the momentary peace that I had discovered while being in hypnosis.

My hypnotherapy journey wasn't linear. It had ups and downs. I tried two different hypnotherapists, which helped a bit, and I would make a small amount of progress, but then experience setbacks. However, I persevered as I knew that if hypnosis could make me feel THAT incredible, then there must be a way somehow of harnessing that feeling and carrying it forward into my daily life. The perseverance paid off. It was when I started seeing the third hypnotherapist that I really began making headway in my recovery from trichotillomania, anxiety and overall poor mental health, fears and lack of self-esteem.

There were many layers that I needed to work through, and I saw my hypnotherapist once a month for about two years. It was like peeling back the layers of an onion, exploring my inner world, thoughts and feelings more closely than ever before, allowing me to create a newfound deeper understanding and compassion for myself.

It was the inner child healing that really turned things around. Helping me to heal that inner child who had been left frightened and traumatised at such a young age by a difficult parental illness experience. By reparenting myself and telling the little Nikki what she would have needed to hear at that time and bringing her into the safety of the here and now, I was able to heal and let go of living in daily flight/fight trauma response mode. I had made peace. I was free. From this point onwards, I began to heal from trichotillomania.

My hair began to grow back, fast-forward to now, where I have been hair-pulling-free for many years and have my own natural flowing curly locks back, and where I feel truly grateful for this every single time that I look in the mirror! Even when my daughter and I joke about how crazy mummy's curly hair looks waking up first thing in the morning! I remember as a child, I had a bookmark that said, 'How can I control my life if I can't even control my hair'. My frizzy, out-of-control locks were always a source of light-hearted laughter in our household. Reflecting on that bookmark now, the significance and poignance of it is profound. Perhaps that was exactly what my hair-pulling was all about – feeling out of control in a world where I was, deep down, still a frightened little girl who felt lost in my own life and feeling helpless to change a thing. If only I'd known, then what I know now. I am the master of my own destiny, and I am fully in control of every aspect of my own life. Even my health to a certain degree. Through acceptance of my autoimmune condition and through making healthy choices that support my health, I can help my body to flourish to its best capacity, recognising that external factors and lifestyle choices will directly impact my physical, emotional and mental health.

Since discovering the power of hypnotherapy and hypnosis 10 years ago, then aged 30, I have spent the last 10 years opening myself up to therapies to help me heal, change, evolve, grow, and dedicated myself to learning the secrets of just how powerful us human beings are and how we can use our thoughts to create a safe haven for ourselves in our own mind. I studied Clinical Hypnotherapy and now run my hypnotherapy clinic, helping people overcome and supporting people who are experiencing unwanted habits, fears, phobias, anxiety and other mental health challenges. If you have any struggles with your mental health, please do not give up. You can find your way to inner peace and calm, too. The strategies and support are out there, and you already have everything you need within you, you just need that extra bit of support to help you connect the dots together.

Reflecting on my life so far, my childhood was often spent living in fight/flight trauma response mode because the world felt unsafe. Then during my twenties, I went into self-destruct mode I didn't know anything about self-care and its importance, and I pushed myself to burn out personally, professionally, mentally and physically. My thirties were the change I needed, I gifted myself the magic of healing and navigated myself into learning and discovering mode. As I enter my forties this year, I am so excited for what's to come. I know in my heart and soul that this next decade will be my accelerated mode, where I implement my learnings and embody the thought vibrational frequency of peace, gratitude, acceptance and love to help attract my dream outcomes and desires and where I can live truly and authentically as me, creating the life that feels just right for me, anchoring inner calm and confidence deep within. To empower, help and support others to become independent powerful people, to be the creator that we human beings were designed and destined to be. You are the creator, I am the creator, we are all creative beings, and it's time for us to remember quite how powerful we are.

Shannon Mott

Founder of Prairie Nova Digital Marketing

https://www.linkedin.com/in/shannonmott
https://www.facebook.com/prairie.nova.marketing
https://www.instagram.com/prairie.nova.marketing/
https://prairienovamarketing.com/

Shannon's journey is a testament to resilience and determination. After her parents divorced when she was just three, she faced a challenging childhood living with her emotionally and physically abusive mother. Despite these hardships, Shannon maintained a positive bond with her father. At age 12, with the support of Child & Family Services, she was able to transition into full-time care with her father, finally finding the peace, stability, and support she needed.

Shannon's drive for success led her to earn a Bachelor of Commerce degree, which paved the way for a successful 12-year career in corporate marketing within the telecommunications industry. Today, Shannon is married with two young children and has channeled her marketing expertise into her own digital marketing business. With a focus on helping small business owners enhance their online visibility, Shannon is passionate about empowering others to achieve success, just as she has in her own journey.

Beyond the Darkness: Rebuilding After Childhood Trauma

By Shannon Mott

A mother's love is supposed to be one of the most powerful forces in the world. It should make you feel safe, nurtured, and valued. That's the image most people have when they think of motherhood: a place of comfort and unconditional love. As a child, I believed that too. I desperately wanted to believe that my mother loved me, that she would protect me from harm and be my constant source of safety. But my reality was far from that.

When I think of my childhood, the first image that comes to mind isn't of a loving, protective mother. Instead, it's of my mother chasing me around the house with a large knife, threatening to kill herself and blame it on me, or shrieking at me from my bedside. I can still feel the cold terror that gripped me as I tried to escape her wrath. I was only a child, trying to survive a reality that no child should ever have to endure. However, this was my normal, and I could see no end in sight, no better life down the line.

My parents divorced when I was three, so most of what I endured began in the late 80s. Back then, mental illness wasn't talked about openly, at least not in my world. People didn't seem to go to therapy or seek help for their mental struggles as freely as they might today. My mother never seemed to consider the possibility that something was wrong with her. In fact, she seemed to believe that everyone else was the problem. She would tell me stories of how her own mother had beaten her as a child, how she had been raped as a teenager, and how my father had apparently treated her horribly in their seven-year marriage. Though from my relationship with my father and his side of the family, none of her stories ever made sense. I felt loved, safe, and happy when with my dad.

However, as a child, I didn't have the capacity to question her version of events. I didn't yet understand the complexities of mental illness or the impact of trauma. But I did know that something wasn't right. Her behavior wasn't normal. I could see that, even if I couldn't fully understand it. As I grew up, I started to question more of her actions and explanations, but I didn't have the confidence to vocalize it much, and certainly not to her directly.

The hardest part of living with her was the loneliness and feeling trapped. As an only child, and coming from a divorced family at such a young age, I felt very alone and scared of having to deal with her on my own. Though my father remained a part of my life, I spent most of my time alone with my mother. There was no one to share the burden of her rage, no one who could understand what it felt like to live in constant fear of the person who was supposed to protect you.

I often envied other children, especially girls who had close relationships with their mothers. I would watch them and wonder what it must feel like to have a mother who loved you unconditionally and who made you feel safe and cherished. I longed for that kind of love, but deep down, I knew it wasn't something I would ever experience. Even as I grew up, watching movies or TV shows that showcased healthy mother/child relationships would make me feel sad and question why I was never given this opportunity in life; one that seemed like a given to so many others.

The memories I have from that time are fragmented, but they are vivid in their intensity. I remember one instance when, after an episode of rage, my mother left the house and took our phone with her so I couldn't call for help—even from my dad. This wasn't an isolated incident—she had a pattern of cutting me off from any means of seeking assistance.

Our house had an open floor plan that allowed for a continuous loop between the kitchen, dining room, and living room, and I remember running around in circles, trying to stay out of her reach. There were times she would chase me with a knife, screaming threats, and the look of a monster in her eyes. To this day, I can still see her face in rage and madness, coming after me like I was some horrible child or an enemy. I wouldn't wish this behavior on any enemies, certainly not children.

Another regular occurrence for her was that she often threatened to kill herself, but not before carving an "S" into her skin—my initial so everyone would apparently know I was at fault. Even as an adult, that idea seems both horrible and ridiculous, but as a child, I was terrified. Her words held power over me, and I felt responsible for her well-being in a way that no child should ever feel. She would say, "Everyone will know you did this to me," making me believe that I would be blamed for her death and that I would carry the guilt and shame of it for the rest of my life.

One of the most haunting memories I have is of her standing at the doorway to my room. I was lying in bed, hiding under the covers, while she stood in the hall, backlit by the hallway light, her silhouette like a dark shadow. She screamed at me, her voice shrill and piercing. Eventually, she would storm into my room, grabbing me, and shaking me as she continued to yell—her spit hitting my face as she screamed at me. I don't remember the words she used, but I remember the overwhelming fear and confusion. I was just a child, desperate for love but trapped in a nightmare.

The psychological abuse was just as damaging, if not more so, than the physical abuse. My mother's manipulation was constant, and she knew exactly how to make me feel worthless and trapped. She would make me feel responsible for her unhappiness and would guilt me into believing that I was a bad daughter. She constantly blamed me for her problems and used guilt as a weapon. One Christmas, I remember her pulling the car over to the side of the road, threatening to leave me there because I wasn't providing the responses she wanted.

But the most insidious of her tactics were the lies and accusations she planted in my head. She claimed that my father and uncle had sexually abused me as a young child, and as a result, I was forced to undergo tests and psychological evaluations at the children's hospital. I didn't know how to comprehend what was going on as I was too young to fully understand the implications, but I knew something was terribly wrong. I felt confused, scared, and isolated. I had no one who could help me make sense of the madness, though I argued that none of this story had actually happened. That was one of many experiences where my mother would make up situations, to the point where she fully believed they happened.

By the time I was ten or eleven, my mother and I began seeing a family therapist. I'm not entirely sure how that came about—perhaps my mother thought I was the one who needed help. But I found comfort in those sessions, especially the ones I had alone with the therapist. I finally had someone to talk to, someone who might understand what I was going through, someone to give me hope that an end to this terror I was living was remotely possible. I was honest with the therapist about my mother's behavior, and for a while, I felt like there might be a way out. However, my mother soon caught on and tried to put a stop to the one-on-one sessions. She couldn't bear the thought of someone knowing the truth.

Thankfully, that therapist was a lifeline for me. She was able to involve Child & Family Services and my father. When I turned twelve, I finally had a choice about where I wanted to live. I chose my father. I chose safety and love. The final weekend I stayed with him as "a visit", I refused to return to my mother's house at the end of the weekend. It was a turning point, the first step toward reclaiming my life. My mother responded with fury, leaving hateful messages on the answering machine and making threats, but I didn't go back. I couldn't. I had endured too much for far too long.

In the years that followed, my relationship with my mother became more and more distant. I visited her occasionally, but the visits felt strained and filled with tension. She never changed. She continued to manipulate, guilt, and threaten me. I tried to set boundaries, but it was never enough. When I was around sixteen, she met a man online and moved to a remote part of Ontario. That physical distance brought me a sense of relief, and for the first time in my life, I felt like I could breathe. But even from a distance, she found ways to haunt me—enter the late 90s internet wave. I was especially thankful for long-distance ringtones back then.

Within the next couple of years, she relocated to Southern Ontario with her now-husband (how she got one, let alone two husbands in life, still boggles my mind). I remember visiting her in her new home when I was eighteen. She had one of her manic episodes, and it was clear that nothing had improved. I knew then that I had to cut ties with her eventually for my own mental sanity. I had already endured enough, and I wasn't going to let her continue to poison my life.

Over the next few years, I visited her only a couple of times, more out of obligation than anything else (and as a young person's eagerness to travel and explore the big city of Toronto). There were still moments when she would spiral into threats of suicide and make unrealistic demands of me, and I would feel that familiar grip of fear and responsibility, but I had learned to distance myself emotionally. I knew I had an out, and I was no longer a child.

In 2006, I made the decision that enough was enough, and I had to sever ties with her for good. I don't remember the exact event that led to that decision, but I knew it was necessary. I couldn't let her toxic presence continue to damage my mental health. Within the next couple of years, she was diagnosed with breast cancer. Most people, when diagnosed with a life-threatening illness, seek support and connection. But not my mother. She tried to use the cancer to manipulate me, and to draw me back into her orbit. I resisted. I had come too far to be pulled back in. She survived the cancer, but she never changed.

After my relationship with my mother mostly ended, I was able to build a life for myself and enjoy the peace of this new life. I was able to travel while pursuing my post-secondary education at the University of Manitoba, Asper School of Business. I obtained a Bachelor of Commerce degree in 2009 and started a career in corporate marketing for a large telecommunications company. As the daughter of a woman who could never hold a job, I was proud of myself for how far I had come professionally, and that I held two jobs long-term as a young adult. However, given my relationship issues as a child and teenager that impacted my trust and security, I have had issues with anxiety and chronic worries that always haunt me and affect my relationships with people to varying degrees.

After over a decade of focusing mainly on my education, career, and many travels, I got married in 2016. I didn't invite my mother to our wedding. I was never sure what the right decision was, but I had to follow my gut. I had to protect my mental health, and I knew that allowing her back into my life would only cause more harm.

During my adult years, I learned that my mother's behavior hadn't just affected me—she had also left deep scars on her siblings. Her two youngest sisters, in particular, had lived in fear of her at various points throughout their childhoods. They told me stories of hiding under their beds to escape her violent outbursts and of fleeing their home on their own birthdays just to get away from her. These revelations made me question why no one had ever intervened. Why had my grandparents allowed her to terrorize all of us for so long? Why hadn't anyone sought help for her? The lack of intervention, especially by anyone throughout my childhood, felt like a betrayal, and it left me grappling with a mix of anger and sadness.

When I became a mother in early 2019, I thought I might feel sadness over the loss of our relationship. I imagined I might grieve the mother I never had. But instead, I felt anger. How could she have treated me the way she did? How could she have put her own child through such pain and suffering? My own daughter gave me clarity. She became my light, and I vowed to be everything my mother wasn't.

In November 2020, I received a message from my aunt that my mother was gravely ill. It wasn't COVID, but a combination of long-standing health issues. We had just moved into a new house, and I was settled into my life. I wasn't sure if I should reach out, but ultimately, I decided to FaceTime her. It was the last conversation we ever had. I even let her see my daughter on screen, something I had sworn I would never do. A few days later, she passed away. On my husband's birthday.

Her death brought with it a confusing mix of emotions. I felt sadness for the relationship we never had, relief that I no longer had to live in fear of her returning to my life, and a sense of peace. She was gone, but the scars she left behind were still there.

I still live with the impact of those years. Chronic anxiety follows me, as does suspected PTSD. The trauma is woven into the fabric of who I am, but it doesn't define me. I built a life for myself—a career, a marriage, and two wonderful children. I even started my own small business to help others achieve their own personal dreams. I didn't become the statistic I was once destined to be. I survived. I pushed forward.

Now, as I raise my own children, I work every day to give them the love and security I never had. I am their protector, their nurturer, their guide through the world, and hopefully, sometimes their friend. I am everything my mother was not. And in that, I find my strength. In that, I find my resilience.

Ashley Ageloff

Your Limitless Health
Thermographer and Wellness Coach

https://www.linkedin.com/in/ageloffa/
https://www.facebook.com/yourlimitlesshealth
https://www.instagram.com/limitlesshealthashley
https://yourlimitlesshealth.com/

Ashley Ageloff has a bachelor's degree in Education, and is certified as a wellness coach, yoga instructor and thermography technician. She is also a mom of two young kids, runs a holistic mommy and me group, and is passionate about creating community.

Ashley merges her skills of teaching, and knowledge of health to educate people about thermography and wellness. Her passion of spreading awareness about health modalities that can effectively help others, came from her personal experiences of overcoming her own health issues using natural life style changes to regain her now vibrant health. Through coaching she uses various modalities to help people heal. This includes emotional work, meditation, stress reduction exercises, and nutrition.

Ashley dealt with trauma, stress, and anxiety in her younger years. This is why she is so passionate about helping others heal through various unique modalities.

The Imprisoned Mind

By Ashley Ageloff

We all come into the world innocent—a blank slate. Then, based on experiences, the blank slate gradually disappears, and we lose sight of where we came from. We adopt belief systems based on what other people have told us, start to take things personally, learn to make assumptions, and turn ourselves into "meaning-making" machines. We make things up about everything we see. We even make up our own "story" based on past experiences and define ourselves in the present by that image.

We all have made-up stories based on past experiences that we say "happened to us," which now shape our lives in this moment. Of course, sharing your past stories can be therapeutic and healing, but the key is not to get enmeshed in them.

For a long time, I defined myself as my story. What other identity would I have, if I were not my past? In my mind, this was what life was, and it felt like I could not escape the confines of what I believed. I felt like I was floating through life. I thought this feeling was normal, until I began an incredible journey, finding that there is much more to life. Have you ever felt that who you were in the past is a completely different person? This is exactly how I feel. I feel that I have lived many lives in this one lifetime.

I hardly remember anything from the age of 7 and under. When we experience trauma in our lives, our brains do whatever they can to block it out. My childhood had many dysfunctional moments. This is not to say I did not have great memories. I know both my parents loved me, I know they did the best they could with the tools they were given. Yet, no matter how much, as an adult, I logically knew this, it didn't change the energy I felt as a kid. As a child, I could not logically comprehend what my parents were going through. I learned through what they told me but mostly learned from the energy I felt being in that environment.

My first vivid memory was when I was 7 years old. I was in my room playing when I heard my parents screaming. My mom had sprayed some kind of chemical in my dad's eyes, and my dad had thrown a chair at my mom. I was standing at the top of the stairs screaming for them to stop. I was crying, and yelling for what seemed like hours. They did not stop. They just escalated. All of a sudden, a white van showed up and took my mom away. At this age, I felt very close and protective of my mom. No one explained to me what was happening. I interpreted this as if it were my fault. I realize now that this was one of the first moments I made up that my voice was not worthy because no one cared what I had to say. I became extremely shy. I never did extracurricular activities at school because I wanted to stay with my mom. I would never have playdates or sleepovers because I felt this internal need to constantly be there for her.

The white bus that day when I was only 7 years old took my mom to rehab. At the time, I had no idea where we were. No one explained it to me. I now realize that as kids, we pick up all the energy and emotions around us. If the energy is overwhelming, we can take that on, and if we do not have the tools to regulate ourselves, we internalize things. If our feelings are not validated as a child, we believe we are not worthy. I now know I have to be aware and conscious of my energy at all times. I am a mother of two small children, and when I get overwhelmed or when my nervous system is off, I am quick to react, yell, or say things I regret. I strive to learn from my mistakes and teach my children that we all make mistakes, but always repair when I do. For instance, if my daughter, who is 5, drops a glass and it breaks, my first habitual response is to say, "Why did you do that, what's wrong with you?" This only makes her feel bad, and she runs off crying and I am left with glass to clean up. Now when this happens, I say, "I love you. It was a mistake. Let's take a deep breath and clean it up together." If I do not sleep or I am feeling dysregulated, it takes more awareness and breath for me to remember to stay calm. When I do remain calm, it nourishes my child, and the outcome is completely different. I did not get this as a child. No one explained to me when I asked questions, no one validated me, and no one remained calm in the midst of chaos. My hope is that I can be aware enough to change this cycle for my children.

An archetype I quickly became drawn to as I grew was the *fixer*. With being a *fixer*, I quickly became a people pleaser. I wanted to help everyone else and would do everything for everyone else while limiting my own potential. I was like a chameleon, adapting and fitting in so I could be liked by everyone around me. Once I started my personal growth journey and looked deep into my habits, I learned that this was exhausting. Plus, I was not being true to who I really was. I now know I can not fix anyone, or please anyone. Not everyone will like me, and I am finally ok with this. All I can do is work on myself. I can be who I truly am, and life will show up for me how it's supposed to.

Many life events have shaped who I am. Due to the trauma I experienced, I began to question everything from a young age. As a child, my parents fought so much. There was a lot of verbal abuse between my parents, my sister, and me. The yelling was a normal part of life, and I did my best to drown out by isolating myself in my room. My parents even called me "Room Girl."

When I moved to Florida at the age of 9 from New York, I felt like an outcast. It was not until sixth grade when I started to have a nice group of friends that I felt I belonged. Quickly after moving to Florida, my parents got divorced. I had to go to my dad's on the weekends. At first, this was really difficult for me, but I began to enjoy it because my dad was fun. I started to become close to my dad. When I was 12 years old, only a few years after moving to Florida, my whole world turned upside down. Every summer, I would go to the Hamptons with my dad. It was the most magical experience of my childhood. There was a full house of people, tons of friends, and activities going on constantly. I could just be a kid without anxiety. I felt energy deeply from a young age, so this particular summer, I could tell something was off with my dad. One day he took my sister and me for a walk on the beach and told us that he had to go away for a while. We sat there, we all took it in, and we all cried. I knew my life was about to change, but I really had no idea how much.

At age 14, I got picked up early from school, and my life changed forever. We flew to NYC, and the next day, I was in the courtroom with family and friends, watching my dad get sentenced to 5 years in federal prison. As the tension from the prosecutor was getting heavier, the judge advised all children to leave the court room. As we stepped outside, my sister and a few friends were all playing. I could not play. I knew he was going to be taken away. I asked my dad's friend, who took us outside, to be honest with me. He still said it was going to be okay. It was not okay. Twenty minutes later, everyone walked out of the room. I heard the prosecutor say, "We got him. We finally got him." They were laughing. I turned around and screamed at them. I felt so angry and so sad. That same day, we flew back to Florida. I returned to school the next day, pretending that nothing was wrong, sharing with no one the inner turmoil that just turned my life upside down.

High school was not easy for me. It was a struggle living with my mom. The weekends were spent visiting my dad in Jail and lying to my friends about where I was because I was too scared to tell them the truth. Senior year of high school, things got very bad with my mom, so I moved in with my dad's girlfriend while my dad was still in Jail. He would be home in less than a year, and I was so excited. I became really close to my dad even though he was away. We had deep conversations, and he was in a good mind space. He sent me self-help books to read and remained positive despite his circumstances. This inspired me and encouraged me to do well in school so I could make something of myself.

Then at age 19, something terrible happened. The FBI raided my house while I was asleep in my bed. At age 20, on my birthday, my dad got sentenced to another 5 years in Federal Prison. I was in the courtroom that day. I prayed so much for him to get released. As much as I believed in God, I started to doubt him. Why would this happen? Why couldn't he just come home? I did my best to surround myself with positive people so that I would not dig myself into a deep hole, however, the inner turmoil began to be too much.

In 2010, I knew I needed a change. I decided to move to NYC on a whim. I decided to take a course called Landmark. During this course, I did a lot of work around forgiveness. I called my mom, and we spoke for the first time in months. She shared how hard her life was when she was younger, and how much guilt she had for everything she put me through. This conversation led to healing and forgiveness. I was finally ready to look at what caused her to act in certain ways, and I had so much empathy for it. Living in NYC alone made my life flourish. I became independent and found purpose and meaning. I no longer was bound by family obligations or felt like I had to please anyone. I could actually focus and find out who I was, what I enjoyed, and what I wanted out of life. I lived in NY for two years and grew more than I knew. In 2012, my dad was getting ready to be released, so I moved back to Florida so he could live with me.

I had an expectation that my dad would come home, and be grateful, full of life, and humble. Only, it was not like that at all. This is the moment I realized that the mind is what really traps us. It is not so much where we are, but how we think, and how we regulate our emotions, and nervous system. The mind is what imprisons us, and I saw it firsthand. Have you ever been somewhere amazing, like on vacation, but still seemed to be upset or sad? This is because our subconscious mind is running us.

The same year my dad moved in with me, I developed Hashimoto's. I was extremely fatigued and experienced joint pain and brain fog. I ended up going to a functional medicine doctor and learned of my thyroid and gut issues. I started to heal myself through diet and stress reduction exercises. This helped me, but it was not until I worked through deep emotional trauma that I began to truly heal.

I became so intrigued by how nutrition and nervous system exercises can heal you that I went back to school for it. I quit teaching and started my own business doing wellness coaching and teaching yoga and soon after that opened up my own thermography practice. I no longer wanted to play small in life and knew I had to just do it, even if it was scary. Then in 2016, an opportunity to work at a Drug and Alcohol Center fell into my lap. I have always been interested in this field from having family members struggle with addiction. I created a holistic program teaching self-development, yoga, and other practices that can help shift your mind. The most profound lessons were the groups I facilitated about not being a victim of the circumstances in your life. We all have a choice at any given moment on how we show up. It is more difficult to show up enthusiastic and kind when we feel broken, or when our nervous system is dysregulated. This is why the nervous system works along with the mindset work is key.

Once people understood that even though the cards they were dealt in life were not a great hand, they could reinvent themselves by stepping out of the victim mentality. This was a huge growing and learning experience for me, and I was so grateful I could share this with others. I transformed in those few years of working there. I saw some people have remarkable changes—shift their entire life from doing the work. I also experienced grief like never before. Over the time I worked there,

I probably lost around 15 clients to overdoses. These lessons taught me that all I could do was show up each day by being the best version of myself. If I modeled the work I was doing, and they were ready to do the work, then I was doing my best. I learned I could not save everyone, nor was it my job to.

Another practice I implemented into my daily life and the groups I ran was a gratitude practice. When I am feeling a bit off or sad, or in need of comparing my life to others, or feel like where I am at is not good enough, this practice helps shift my perspective. It helps me focus on what I have rather than what I lack. A limiting belief system I adopted as a kid was that I was not smart and not good enough. When I shift my perspective and work on my limiting belief systems, I stop playing small.

My favorite quote is by Wayne Dyer: "Change the way you look at things and the things you look at change." I have been taught so many lessons, I have grown in unimaginable ways and triumphed over many of life's struggles. I look at things in a different way. I create my own reality. Yet, the learning never ends. The challenges still come. The old unconscious habits still arise. I notice I still complain and can go into the victim mindset. Only now, I come out of it quicker. I have more support, more tools, and much more awareness. I am a different person now. Every stage of life for each of us is different. Each is a stepping stone. Each is a realization for us to reflect upon and make a different choice. We always have a choice. We can focus on problems or solutions. We can be a victim or champions of our circumstances. We can focus on what we have to do, or what we get to do. I hope this little chapter here helps you find some distinctions on how you get to show up in life. When life gets hard (and it will), slow down, and tune in to yourself. You are your own greatest teacher.

I still go through moments of disconnect, sadness, and overwhelm. I am a mother of 2. I yell, I get frustrated. The biggest lesson I am going through now is to not go into the low vibration of emotions of shame and guilt. There are moments when I yell, and say things I do not mean. I do my best to repair it with the kids. I can do this because I have done a lot of inner work. I have the nervous system tools to calm myself down and help my kids regulate their own emotions and nervous systems as well. I know I am constantly a work in progress and will continue to grow each day.

These are the biggest lessons I have learned in my life:

- Communication is key. Do not assume things, or take things personally. The book *Nonviolent Communication* is a great place to start.
- Don't be a victim of your life circumstances. No matter what has happened in your life, you can heal, and create the life you want.
- Do not let the beliefs you were taught dictate or run your life. Ask yourself if those beliefs are true or if your subconscious mind is running you.
- Forgive yourself, and others for yourself. Holding on to resentment is like drinking poison and expecting the other person to die. In the end, holding on to any low-level emotion will only hurt you.
- Let go of shame and guilt. These emotions do not and will not ever serve you.
- In every new moment, we can change our lives if we want to. I hope this chapter helps you shed light on any situation you are going through, and make conscious choices as you go through your life.

Nadia Sheikh

https://www.linkedin.com/in/nadiasheikh1/
https://www.instagram.com/sheikhnad2025

Nadia Sheikh was born and raised in Calgary and currently lives in Whitby ON She works in the Finance industry for reputable Finance company. She can speak three languages.

Nadia had been volunteering since the early age of ten. She had achieved a black belt in the discipline of Shotokan Karate at the age of Fifteen. She had participated both in the Nationals and the Alberta 98 Winter Games. She was the first student for her karate instructor to achieve a black belt and had set a Standard for the Japan Karate Association at the time. In the last two years she had loss her husband to Cancer June 23rd, 2022. As a dedication to her husband and not letting anyone know she had participated in a Grassroot Pageant Women Empowerment with a Social Cause in the name of Novacosmo Worldwide and had won the title as Ms Novacosmo Worldwide.

Forever In My Heart

By Nadia Sheikh

Now this is a story about a girl who had met her soulmate and thought she would have her happily ever after. After having an arranged marriage, I never thought I would get married again. When I used to see one of my friends in how happy they were as a couple and how they would do everything together. In my mind, I said that is what I want! I had put a wall up. I had said whoever is going to be with me will have to like me for who I am. What I also learned was never to say never. How they had first met is an interesting part. After my training class, one of my colleagues introduced me to him, saying they had previously worked at a different company together. When he told me he had lived in Calgary and had gone to the University of Calgary, I was like, no way!! That same day, we had our company quarterly meeting. The rule of our quarterly meeting set by our CEO, whoever was the late one, would have to sing in front of the whole company.

That very same day, he ended up being late to the meeting. Our CEO had told him, "You know the rules." So, he started singing and dancing at the same time, which I thought was so cute.

After the meeting, as we were walking out, I told him I thought he was so funny.

He said, "I knew you were there, so I thought I would just add on the dance to make it more entertaining." I didn't think much of it at that time. After that day, we became very good friends. Daily, while at work, I would come by his desk, and we would have our little chit-chats, and he would tell his jokes that would always make me laugh. Our first lunch together was at the food court downstairs at Freshii. I had never tried couscous in my life prior to that. Since he had introduced me to it, I had been hooked on that particular couscous recipe.

We were just hanging out when one day, he asked me, "Would you consider marrying outside of your religion?" At that time, I was very traditional, and I said no. He said, "What happens if I convert to a Muslim?" Then I said, "Well, maybe." That night I went home and started thinking about the conversation that we had. I was contemplating back and forth whether I should give up a chance to be with a guy that I just had an internal feeling saying this person was for me just because he wasn't from the same background. Do I want to give up what I knew could be so beautiful? That night I made the decision to give it a chance.

A couple of weeks later, he asked me out, and when I said yes, he was taken aback that I had said yes. So, on our first date, we went to the Hard Rock Café. He was like, "What would you like to eat?" During that time, I was in a phase of eating Macaroni and Cheese. So, on our first date, we shared a plate of Macaroni and Cheese. After our dinner, we went walking along Yonge Street, and we stopped to watch a magician do some tricks. Then we spent the night talking, and he walked me to the GO train station to get back. The first date was a night to remember.

He was known as the 'clown" of the department. He loves to make everyone laugh or just be a goof. So, the next day he went over to everyone's cubicles and switched the name plates around. Both he and I were working the evening shift that day. So, when everyone was gone, he stood on top of his desk and started to shoot elastics at me. I was like, "Hey, watch it."

I said, "I am going to start shooting elastics at you." And he was like, "I would like to see you try." He was right. When I tried to shoot the elastic band, it just went a short distance.

He just laughed at me. I gave him the look, and he just shrugged. A couple of weeks later, one of our colleagues asked us if we wanted to play basketball after work. I was like, hell ya. That evening, we went to play basketball with our colleagues. I was the only girl that had been playing. I was extremely competitive. I was guarding well, then suddenly, I tripped up and hurt my knee. All the guys stopped to see if I was okay. They went to get some ice for me. Nick dropped me off at home. The next morning, he called me and asked how I was doing. I was unable to go to work that day. Nick also decided to take the time off and take me to the doctor. He came over to my house and drove me to the doctor. The whole time he was holding my hand to make sure I was okay. Without me even asking, he was just there.

During the first couple of months we were dating, I had a wall up, which he knew about. Most of our dates would be eating at restaurants and walking around different parts of downtown. He was very persistent in getting my full trust. From walking around downtown all around the city that was when we got to know each other well. That is how we built the foundation of our relationship, and that was how I knew he was the one for me.

Eight months later, on May 22nd, we decided to take a day trip to Niagara Falls. The first thing we did was head over to the falls together. It had been raining; however, when we stood there for a while, the rain stopped, and the sun started to shine down on us, and a rainbow appeared over the falls. We both took that as a sign. Once we were done with the falls, we headed over to Clifton Hills. We went to Ripley''s Believe It or Not. After Ripley's Believe it or Not, we headed to the Wax Museum. It was so much fun while we were there, he would go behind each of the celebrities and start to imitate their voices. When we came to the section for the Wizard of Oz, I stood behind Dorothy and started singing "Somewhere Over the Rainbow." He chimed in, and we sang it together. We had a blast just singing it. As we were singing it, he had captured the singing on video. We also did the 4D ride. After the 4D ride, we went over to this place, where we decided to do a wax hand sculpture. It was an interesting experience. What they did was put our hands in ice until our hands were completely frozen and numb. Then we held hands and dipped our hands together in the hot wax. They then peeled the wax off our hands. It was nice; we had a beautiful holding hand sculpture with a heart on it. After we had eaten our dinner, we just sat on the lawn together and then passed out. When I woke up, I was like, "We must get going," and he was like, "Not yet." Suddenly, the fireworks started going. Nick and I wanted to go see it, so we ran through the crowd down Clifton Hill to the falls to watch the display of fireworks. Once the fireworks display was over, we continued to watch the falls. As he was holding me from behind, he started to say the sweetest and kindest words. He then took my hand and turned me around, got down on one knee, and kept saying more kind words. I had tears in my eyes. He was still saying the sweetest things, and then he asked me to marry him. I said yes. The people that were around us started clapping and congratulating us. My heart was singing, and I was overcome by joy. It was one of the happiest moments in my life.

During that time, we had so many different experiences. We would try new restaurants. We went to Medieval Times, the Monster Truck Show, and the ROM. One day at our workplace, they were recruiting a team for the United Way Stair Climb. I said, "Let's do it." At first, he hesitated because the CN Tower climb was 144 floors. Eventually, he agreed. So, we would prepare by climbing 22 floors of the apartment building.

On the day of the stair climb, the team had gathered, and we were all just chatting away. Then we found out they were not letting anyone take a water bottle. We were like, what in the world, why not? They had let us know due to water spilling on the staircase, it could be hazardous. We all just looked at each other and wondered if we really wanted to do this. We were close to the stairs, so it was pretty much the point of no return. So, then we started the climb one step at a time. At first, we thought we were going to dread the climb. As soon as we started, we were pacing ourselves. As soon as we got into the rhythm, we were like, this is not bad at all. When we got to the top, we had an adrenaline rush. We couldn't believe we had climbed the CN stairs. Not only did we climb it, but our time in reaching the top was 16 minutes and 24 seconds. We were so proud. Once we had gotten to the top we had so much adrenaline. We took the elevator down, and we started running back to the entrance of the tower. We had another adrenaline hit.

Fast-forward to the day before our civil wedding. I was getting ready for our wedding day. Nick's parents had come in from Calgary, and his plan was to spend time with his brother and his parents. So, I was just running errands and getting the things I needed to get done beforehand. He kept texting me throughout the day to see what was happening and where I had been going. Each time I would ask him, he would be like, I am hanging with my parents and brother, or he is yawning and stretching. In my head, I am like, why does he keep bugging me, why isn't he spending time with his family? So, I was at the salon getting my nails done. Then, I got a text message from him asking where I was. At that time, my foot was being soaked. So, I messaged him back, letting him know I was at the salon. As I was speaking with the manicurist and I was getting my nails done, suddenly, there were flowers that came from behind me, and he put the flowers right on the table.

As soon as I saw him, I got up and gave him a huge hug. I was in shock that he was there.

Can you imagine he had walked all the way from Toronto's downtown all the way to Markham to a nail salon? I was surprised and felt so proud, and my love for him had grown even more.

I asked him what made him do that. He said he wanted to mark it as a memory of a lifetime.

The next day was our civil wedding. It was beautiful with our families around. After our civil ceremony, he took so many pictures. After our civil wedding, our families had a celebration at the Mercatto at the Eaton Centre. I ate the butternut squash ravioli, and after that, I was hooked, so whenever we would go to the Mercatto, that was my signature dish. A week after our civil wedding, our ceremonial wedding was happening in Aruba at the Riu Palace.

On Oct 16th, we arrived at the airport. We were waiting in line to get our bags checked in. In front of us, there was this couple. We introduced ourselves and started talking. We asked them where they were going to stay. They said, the Riu Hotel and then we let them know we were going there, too, for our wedding. They had told us, "Congratulations." We all became fast friends and continued to speak until it was our turn to check in. When we arrived in Aruba, we were looking for our bus to take us to our resort. Once our bus had arrived at the resort, I was like, wow, this cannot get any better. When we arrived in our room, we were met with rose petals all over the floor with candles and a towel in the shape of a dove. Once we checked out the room, we went straight to the ocean for a swim. Nick wanted to swim out far. When I looked at the waves, I told him, "You go for it, I will wait for you to hear." The reason why I wanted to stay behind was because when I was younger, I almost drowned in the waves. After getting the water in my nose, I panicked. He told me, "I am not going to leave you behind." I told him, "You know the reason why I don't want to go swimming so far." He did. He is like, "I am not going to leave without you." I told him he should go. However, he was very adamant about not leaving me. He said, "I will swim with you on my back." I was like, "You are crazy." He asked me, "Do you trust me?" and I said, "Yes, of course." So, I got on his back, and he swam in the choppy waves with me on his back. It was one of the best experiences I had ever had. Three days later was our wedding ceremony. As I was getting ready, my brother-in-law was taking pictures. He was our photographer as well. He came into the room, and he was cracking jokes.

Then it was time. We walked through the lobby of the hotel to the stairs down to the resort. A man from the window yelled out, "Congratulations Nadia!" As I continued to walk through the resort, the people who were both in and out of the pools started cheering, clapping, and yelling, "Congratulations!" I felt nothing but love and happiness. We arrived at the place of the ceremony, where I met up with my dad. As soon as the song started to walk towards Nick, everyone started to cheer again. When I got to the altar and met up with Nick, he took my hands and we were just gazing into each other's eyes. I remember as we were saying our vows, I just had that glow in my heart. After we said our I do's, we had a big cheer from the whole crowd at the resort. When we had our couple's dance the whole crowd at the resort was watching. At that moment, as we were dancing, all I remember was just being in the moment just being in his arms. As soon as the song ended, there were more claps. When the wedding was over, and we were returning back to the hotel room, the whole resort was clapping and yelling. We thought that would die down. For the rest of our time spent at the resort, we also felt like celebrities. As we went for our dinner, it was another special moment after we would cut our cake. We had both put icing on each other's noses. Our wedding planner for our wedding named me "The Princess of the Riu Hotel." We went for a day out. My brother-in-law and my in-laws had rented out a jeep for us to use for the day, so we drove around the island. The first stop was at the lighthouse, then we drove in the desert, and we also did some parasailing. We got to see the island all in a day. As we got back to the hotel, we had a lot of people still saying, "Congratulations," and they loved how we looked as a couple. They said ours was one of the most memorable weddings at the resort.

On the last morning, before we had to return home, Nick woke me so we could watch the sunrise together. We went to the balcony to watch the sunrise. He held on to me from behind as we watched the sunrise. It was one of the most memorable sunrises together.

After the sunrise, we met up with the family to have our last brunch together. We had our laughs and our jokes, and then we headed towards the airport. And then we had to say farewell to Aruba.

One of our favourite pastimes is cuddling up together and watching TV or movies together. While we would watch a show or a movie, I would just end up passing out. The sweetest thing about Nick was he wouldn't wake me up. He would just pick me up and bring me to bed. He did that pretty much throughout the time of our marriage. The other sweetest thing was he would spend every other weekend with me at my parents' house. The funniest thing was when we would be watching TV with my mom, I would always end up falling asleep on the couch; however, he would stay up and watch the *Home and Garden TV show* with my mom. The next year, we got our Siberian Husky, Akitla. Our little furbaby. Walking has always been one of our favourite pastimes. That's how we had gotten close. We had the most amazing things happen on our walks. Once, we accidentally walked on a taping of Warehouse 41; another time, we found out there was a Jan Arden concert going on. And then all the general Summer and Winter festivals. One of my favourite memories was when Kwai Leonard made the shot for the Raptors, and we won. We all were screaming from the balcony at the top of our lungs. Then we were like, "Let's go," and we went out on the intersection between Yonge and Bloor and when the lights would turn red, everyone would run to the middle of the road and jump up and down and then run back. We had brought our dog to the madness. After we marched, yelling at the top of our lungs, "Let

Go, Raptors." We were walking and yelling all the way till we got to Yonge and Dundas. Everyone was all being sweet and also giving way to Akitla.

When I was going through my rough patches at work or had any complaints about anything, Nick was always there to console me, always bringing the positive side to everything.

When COVID hit, I had been let go from my job, and Nick offered to go to Calgary, and I agreed. It would be a good change of pace, and we would be able to spend time with his family. So, we packed our things and drove to Calgary. It was my first road trip across Canada. I loved it, but it was really cold, and because of COVID, we had limited places where we could stop. However, I still enjoyed the whole trip. When we arrived in Calgary, his parents were excited to see us as I was excited to see them. I loved his family more than anything as well. So, it was great that we had the opportunity to stay with them for a long time. My mother-in-law was like since you guys are here, and my brother-in-law was in Vernon. She was like, I won't be traveling anytime soon, so let's move to Vernon. So, we ended up moving to Vernon. Our place was so beautiful, especially the view. We had mountains in front of us and a mountain trail behind us. The people we had in our neighbourhood were amazing. They were very welcoming. When we had moved to Vernon, I didn't have too much to worry about, so I was like, why don't I get into something that I have always wanted to try? So, the first thing I did was work at a Ski Resort as a Reservations Agent for a season, and I loved it. Then, I started working as a PSW with eleven people with disabilities at a Senior home. Also, I started working part-time with a family with a mother who was in the initial stage of dementia and a father who had been paralyzed and had other diseases. Also, I started working with a twenty-two-year-old non-verbal girl who had constant seizures and sleep apnea. However, I loved working with them all.

Nick and I loved Vernon a lot. We were doing a lot of walking and swimming. I felt like I was in paradise. He had always treated me like a queen and had not let me lift anything for ten years. I was like, I am so grateful I now feel like Nick and I have finally come to a phase where we can just start to do what we love and also just be. Everything was turning out to what I would have considered as being perfect. As soon as I had felt that way, all of a sudden, things had turned for the worse. Nick and I had both come down with COVID I started to feel better; however, Nick wasn't bouncing back as fast. We were certain it would just take a little more time for him to heal. After a while, Nick did heal, however, he seemed like he was always feeling tired. We were going for walks, but after a while he was like, "I don't have energy, you go." I didn't really think too much of it. I felt like he was just being lazy. I was asking him why he doesn't just go to the doctor. He didn't want to, so I also said why don't you go to the hospital just to check things out. Nick was refusing to go because he had PTSD since the time of his childhood with leukemia. His stomach was hurting. All he would tell me to do was purchase cabbage or any food that was good for healing the stomach and the gut. I kept pushing him to go to the doctor, but he was always stubborn about it. I also told my mother-in-law about it. He wouldn't even listen to her. One day my mother-in-law asked him to run into the bank for her. He couldn't go into the bank because he didn't have the energy to walk in. That is when my mother decided to take him to the hospital. This was two days before my birthday. They decided to keep him at the hospital to run tests. During that time, because we weren't vaccinated, we couldn't go in with him. My brother-in-law could go in to visit him, and we were anxiously waiting at Tim Horton's to hear the results. After an hour, we got the dreadful news. Nick called us and told us he had been diagnosed with cancer, and they had given him three weeks to live. Our hearts just dropped. My 40th birthday was bittersweet. He made sure he was discharged from the hospital and that I had my favourite food.

I loved that he had made it back; however, I was also heartbroken to know that this would be my last birthday with him. We all knew we couldn't cry, we all needed to make sure we stayed strong. All I could do was just hug him.

So, for his treatment, he decided to try this diet for fasting, thinking it would help. We did some Holistic remedies with tinctures and the Tesla frequency healing. He was still debating on doing radiation. Because he was afraid of not being able to use one of his legs, he decided to go for the radiation. It was so hard to see him go through the whole process. Watching your husband go from being so strong and independent to a deteriorating phase was one of the hardest things you could go through. As we were going through the process, we made sure never to cry in front of him. And he was so strong and trying to show everyone he was okay. Despite the pain he was going through, he was always making sure his family and I were always okay by trying to stay happy.

On his last day, he made sure he didn't take his last breath in front of me. The moment I had stepped out was the time he had taken his final breath. I sat with him for an hour after he had passed and watched the whole process until he had been taken away to the funeral home. Nick passed on June 23rd, 2022, at the age of 42, of stage 4 cancer. My prince charming had been taken away from me. I felt my fairytale ending had been taken away from me. I literally felt like half of me had been taken away, and I was half empty. It was so hard to go through the grieving process. I moved from Vernon to Toronto to be back with my family. Then three months later, my dad ended up with a collapsed lung and was intubated for a month. Two months laterI found out the girl who I was looking after was very close to her sister. I found out her sister had passed away. As all this had been going on, I didn't really get to have my full grieving period until February of the following year. I was able to isolate myself and do some meditation, chakra healing, sound healing, and prayers, plus, being out in nature helped me gain my strength. However, what gave me strength and peace was my faith. Also, I knew he was no longer suffering, and most of all, I was proud that whatever his purpose was, it had been fulfilled.

As a dedication to my husband, I decided to participate in a Grassroots Pageant, which supports women's empowerment and a social cause. When I participated in the pageant, I didn't even tell anyone. When some of the girls found out I didn't tell anyone, they were all shocked. I let them know this was more of a thing for my husband and me. I ended up winning the National Title. This was like a symbolic meaning of him always treating me like a queen. And I won the Queen National Title as Ms Canada Nova Cosmo Worldwide. My goal is to keep his memory alive. Both he and I used to want to have everyone be positive around us. So, for the rest of my life, I am going to try to be the change and to lead a life with Love.

Dorothe Philippe

Mentor in intuition and telepathy

https://www.linkedin.com/in/dorothephilippe/
https://www.facebook.com/dorothe.philippe?locale=fr_FR
https://www.instagram.com/dorothe.philippe/?hl=fr
https://www.dorothephilippe.com

Dorothe Philippe is a mentor in intuition and telepathy with over twenty years of experience. She is German living in France, mother of four grown up children and a passionate rider since her young age. Her journey started when a healer saved her family from a tragic destiny and taught her how to tap into her intuition, an innate capacity we all possess. Dorothe then got chosen by Volcano, a young former stunt horse difficult to approach. Volcano taught her, how we may become more conscious of our thoughts, emotions, actions and the language we use, so we may be aligned, succeed and lead a happy life. In addition to her work as a life coach, animal psychologist and healer, Dorothe engages today to share valuable information about our inborn abilities of intuition and telepathy, in order to allow us to know more and expand our true potential.

Listen and Align

By Dorothe Philippe

It was a hot sunny day in September. I had gone into the garden to hang up the laundry. The sun was touching my back, illuminating everything around me. Birds were singing, there was a soft breeze, and still the lovely smell of summer in the air. Yet, despite the strong warm sunrays, I felt as if I was only surrounded by darkness and cold. I shivered, and fear grabbed my heart. There had always been light in my life. Light triggered by an inner knowing that no matter how bad things look, somehow, all will go well. Not so this time. There was only darkness - the silent, oppressing lack of light and hopelessness, which surrounds a forgotten prisoner in a fortress's deep, damp hole.

I had a happy life. I was born and raised by loving parents in Germany. At the age of thirty, I left my country to move to Paris to marry a wonderful French man and give birth to four healthy children. However, life is not always smooth, and sometimes it may take us through quite some loops. When I was a student, my mother had been diagnosed with cancer and six months of survival. She was able to live another seventeen years, though, and she even survived my dad, who was never really sick. When I was pregnant with my second child, my husband went through an impressing brain problem which was fortunately repaired without consequences. As a baby, my second child survived two life-threatening situations. As I reviewed these and other difficult moments of my life, observing the play of sun and shadow around me, everything inside of me just started to yell and rebel: "This cannot be. There must be a way out.", I screamed inside of me, and at that very moment, I heard the word: "Sophie." I went inside and phoned my best friend. She listened attentively and gave me the following advice: "Call Michel. He is a friend and a healer. But he just moved to the Reunion. If you want his help, you will have to bring him over."

Some weeks prior, our youngest child had been hospitalized in one of the best children's hospitals in France. Instead of getting better, though, our son's health deteriorated alarmingly. As he seemed to be resistant to traditional treatment, my husband and I were offered two solutions: risky surgery, or having our child enrolled in a test study for a new medication. We declined both. My intuition told me so.

A few days after my conversation with my friend, the doorbell rang. At its sound, my heart shrunk. All of a sudden, I was afraid. What if I had done the wrong thing? What if I had put my son's health even more at stake? I had the courage to blindly follow my strong inner call. Neither surgery, nor the test study had felt right and safe to me, and as doctors had to agree, I had not hesitated one second to get our child home to search for another solution. I had also not spent one single thought on the idea that the medical staff could prevent me from doing so. I just did it, knowing that this was the only and right thing to do. So, what was it that I was afraid of now? Why did I tremble to open the door and let Michel, the healer, in? Was it fear of the unknown? Fear of not knowing what was awaiting our family? Yet, wasn't it a risky surgery, or taking part in a test study without knowing its outcome the unknown as well? So, why all these doubts? What made my heart beat so strongly now? A quote by Hermann Hesse, my favorite German poet and novelist, shot into my mind: "How many opportunities do we miss out in our lives, just because we are afraid of our own courage." I shook myself, stood up, and opened the door, not knowing that I was opening it to a new world. Thanks to ancient healing techniques, which are mostly transmitted within families, or by a healer to someone of his choice, our son became healthy again. At the same time, I discovered that intuition and extrasensory faculties such as empathy, clear-hearing, and clear-seeing are not only innate, but rely on how I may tap into them on demand. In practice, I then quickly realized that we actually bear all within. We are born to be self-sufficient. We are born to thrive.

We are able to know what is the best for us, and how and where to find it. We are coded to do the impossible and to constantly outgrow ourselves – if we just learn one single thing: listening to ourselves.

In his book *The Reality of ESP: A Physicist's Proof of Psychic Abilities*, American laser physicist and co-founder of the Stanford Research Institute (SRI), Russel Targ writes that "many people find that their first introduction to psychic abilities is life-changing." I may thoroughly confirm this. My whole established knowledge and belief system were crushed within a few hours, at the same time that a whole world of new possibilities emerged. Michel had invited me to do a number of exercises. In reading Targ's book many years later, I realized that we have been doing what Targ had coined as "remote viewing". Wikipedia defines remote viewing as "the practice of seeking impressions about a distant or unseen subject, purportedly sensing with the mind. A remote viewer is expected to give information about an object, event, person or location that is hidden from physical view and separated at some distance." Yet, remote viewing is actually much more than experiencing distant locations and finding and sensing a target. Targ himself describes remote viewing as "a process in which you can quiet your mind and inflow information from anywhere in the world." According to Targ, remote viewing is also implied in other enlarged perception techniques, such as intuitive medical diagnosis and distant healing, to find mechanical and safety problems, sources of human error, environmental hazards, and so on.

I was amazed to learn that from 1975 to 1995, the CIA, NASA, and other US government organizations sponsored Targ and his partner, Harold Puthoff, and their work in the $20 million Stargate Project, in order to do research and determine potential military application of psychic phenomena and gather intelligence information about worldwide activities during the Cold War. Over the years, the SRI team found a downed Russian bomber in Africa, reported on the health of

American hostages in Iran, described Soviet weapons factories in Siberia, located a kidnapped US general in Italy, forecasted the failure of a Chinese atomic bomb test, identified by name the kidnapper of American heiress Patricia Hearst and described and located the kidnapper's car to name just some outstanding outcomes. Besides being an outstanding scientist, Russel Targ is also an ardent student of Tibetan Buddhism, which led him to discover that psychic abilities were already described in great detail in two-thousand-five-hundred-year-old Buddhist and Hindu writings, particularly in the encyclopedic Buddhist meditation The Flower Ornament Scripture and the Yoga Sutras of Patanjali. In our days and our culture, however, receiving psychic information is more or less considered a mysterious and paranormal phenomenon. In working with Michel, I learned that we use our extrasensory capacities naturally as children. As we grow up, we are told that some of what we see, feel, or hear, does not exist. As a consequence, doubts arise, we stop sharing our extrasensory sensations, and in the attempt to adapt to our cultural, religious, and educational environment, we finally end up ignoring ourselves. Our natural abilities of empathy, clairvoyance, and clairaudience, however, never leave us. We are born with them, and we die with them – no matter, if we use and accept them, or not. There will always be moments in our life where we may see into the future, have information from the past, or hear a voice that tells us what to do, or not – and this mostly in times of danger and severe problems, and as soon as there seems to be no solution on hand, as showed my story.

I was not familiar with the terms clairvoyance or clairaudience, which are both of French origin and mean "clear seeing" and "clear hearing", or other extrasensory faculties, and so that may be you. I remember to have had premonitory dreams and sensations from childhood on, and that they had always perturbed me a lot. I also remember not starting into a crossing, though the light had turned green. A truck then burned his red light at high speed. If I had not listened to myself, it would probably have hit me. It is not uncommon that we are guided by a vision, a voice, the famous gut feeling, the hunch out of the blue, and you certainly have a similar story to tell. You may also remember to have woken up at night with a message coming out of nowhere. But would it not be helpful to know more, so you may make more use of your innate capacities?

The word intuition derives from the Latin word intueor, which means "to look at, consider" from in- "in, on" and tueor – "to look, watch, guard, see, observe". When you start to pay attention to your intuition and learn to call upon it on demand, you will quickly state that it has a lot to do with increased awareness, and what happens inside your body.

So, the first thing to do is to pay attention to yourself. I always ask my clients to sit at the place they feel drawn to. Being seated where you feel the best allows you to be more anchored and aligned. You will concentrate, express yourself, and work better. Pay attention to anything that makes your energy shift. Note when and where you feel at ease, happy, passionate, energetic, and dynamic, or when and where you feel tired, drained, or bored. This helps you to identify aspects of your life in which you are in alignment, and in which you are not.

Go through your home, office, or workplace. Feel if things are in their right place; if not, arrange them better. Find out which supports your personal energy, and which does not. Have the courage to separate yourself from that which feels or seems negative or does no longer correspond to your evolution. Little actions like this make energy flow and create a resourcing and harmonious atmosphere. You may apply the same principles to all aspects of your life.

To further train yourself, focus on a task. Make it a habit to note what comes first to your mind. This gives you access to additional information and guidance.

Here are some characteristics, which help you identify intuitive information from your reflected thoughts: Psychic abilities manifest naturally and on their own. No effort is involved. The received information seems to come out of the blue, or from "nowhere". We do not know "where it comes from". The information seems to download immediately or suddenly. So, intuition is distinguished by the speed at which it happens. As intuitive information is fast and subtle, it may be hard to catch. Know, however, that the more you pay attention to yourself and to what is manifesting in your environment, the more you train your intuitive capacities and gain experience, insight, and guidance. Extrasensory capacities are like muscles. You can train them.

Intuition may involve non-verbal processes, sensations, and feelings, which may be difficult to put into words. Make it a habit to not ignore your body. Emotions, pain, and other body reactions like having a headache each time you see a particular person, or go to work, are there to give you valuable information. Take note of what comes up. It will guide you in one way or another.

What you feel and receive, is often accompanied by a sensation of certainty, or inner knowing. You cannot explain the why nor the how. "You know." That's all. Make the "Knowing" your inner compass. It will guide you in any moment of your life.

The received information may be completely new to you. You may never have learned, seen, or heard about it before. What you receive, may be of astonishing, or surprising content and may even seem irrational to you. Do not doubt. Do not worry. Welcome, embrace, and trust whatever comes up instead.

Your psychic abilities may manifest in the following ways:

- Clairvoyance, or clear-seeing, implies having visions, seeing images, scenes from the past or the future, words, symbols, metaphors, objects, places, colors, and so on.

- Clairaudience, or clear-hearing, implies hearing a voice, or voices. This is my favorite. Nothing is more evident than a "don't go there", "leave it", "do it", "go", "what are you waiting for?", and so on.
- Clairsentience, empathy, or mimicry implies sensing the pain, feelings, and emotions of others, an animal, a situation, or an environment in your own body.
- Guidance, answers, and solutions may also manifest through precognitive or premonitory dreaming. Yet, don't be afraid of bad dreams, or visions. The future is made up of many possibilities. Your subconscious mind may have sent you a strong message, so you may express and choose deliberately what you want for your life. Clearly state, plan, and visualize what you want instead. Take note, however, if your vision includes a particular warning.

You may "tune in" to intuition by intention, or simply thinking of a person, an animal, or an issue. In case, you have problems, try the following:

- First, remember, every child knows how to do this. So, relax. Be a baby. Know nothing and all at the same time.
- Second, to rapidly obtain a state of "no thought", Dr. Frank Kinslow, founder of the Quantum Entrainment Healing Method, recommends first looking intentionally at the ground and then at the ceiling. He explains that between those two intentions, there is an empty space in which you stop thinking. Check it out.

To make your intuition work, think of asking yourself logical questions.

- Note what comes up.

- Watch out for the "I know" feeling. It confirms that you are on your right way.
- Take nothing for granted.

Question what sounds wrong or not logical to you. Ninety-five percent of the Universe is unexplored. What has been scientifically proven before may already have been rectified, or will be defined differently tomorrow.

- Be a keen observer of yourself and your environment. Learn from life, nature, animals, and anything that inspires you.
- Do not forget to be patient with yourself. Trusting yourself is a learning process.

But my story does not end here. The same year I met Michel, Volcano came into my life. Volcano is a grey Lusitano gelding. He was born, raised, and trained in Portugal before he was sold to France and worked as a stunt horse in an attraction park. When he was six years old, his owner went into severe depression, and my friend Sophie bought the horse, who was known to be hard to catch and to approach. I fell in love with Volcano at first sight, and as he chose me as the only person to put hands on him, Sophie sold him to me a year later. An incredible journey began, with my horse becoming my mentor and teacher.

Neuroscience states that 95 percent of what we think, do, say, and feel happens out of our awareness. Animals are great at catching our state of mind and what is going on in our hearts and over the years, Volcano trained me how to become conscious of limiting beliefs, patterns, and behaviors, which did not serve me. I learned to correct things for myself, and how to help others. Animals are very aligned. When they have a thing in mind, they go for it, and unless there is an obvious reason, they never give up and do everything to succeed. Humans tend to want to do a thing, but then say, do, and feel another. Your needs, wishes, and desires, however, are of an incredible force. They are the stepping stone for your future. Your thoughts, actions, feelings, and emotions then give them life, or not. The language we use is important, as well. Every word has an impact. If you wish to realize a goal but then say things like "I hope", "we'll see", or "not sure I will succeed", you contribute to unsure outcomes.

So, if I resume the teachings of my horse in a few words, it is all about alignment:

- Do what you judge is important and necessary for yourself.
- Watch your thoughts, actions, feelings, and sayings to give yourself the best support.
- Never give up on a dream or heart wish.
- And, of course, never forget to listen to yourself.

I hope that the above will serve you in one way or another so you may navigate best through your life. Remember, all this demands quite some courage and persistence. So, stand strong. Be not afraid of the illimited being you are. Simply be yourself and make use of the gift life gave you.

Charu Seth

Founder of Thrive Transform
Life Coach

https://www.linkedin.com/in/charu-seth-0b8b631/
https://www.facebook.com/profile.php?id=61561085026288
https://www.instagram.com/thrivetransform/
https://thrivealter.com/

As an ICF Certified Life and Relationship Coach, I am passionate about empowering individuals to unlock their full potential and create meaningful connections. With a compassionate and supportive approach, I work with clients to identify their goals, overcome obstacles, and cultivate a sense of purpose and fulfillment.

My coaching style is grounded in somatic practices, which utilize the body as a tool for transformation. By addressing physical sensations and emotional patterns, I help clients uncover limiting beliefs and develop healthier coping mechanisms. Whether you're struggling with stress, anxiety, relationship issues, or personal growth, I am committed to guiding you towards a more balanced and fulfilling life.

Fearless and Limitless:
A Journey of Resilience

By Charu Seth

I've always been a fighter. Even when I chose to become a stay-at-home mom, leaving behind my dreams. I saw it as a different kind of battle – a battle for love, family, and a life well-lived. I dedicated myself to nurturing my family and supporting my husband's career. But over two decades, the lines blurred. As the years passed, the emotional disconnect and lack of partnership eroded my self-worth and left me questioning the direction of my life. My partner's career soared, while mine seemed to dwindle.

I became a shadow, unseen, unheard, and unappreciated!!!

Chapter 1: The Shattered Pieces

The day I realized my marriage was irreparably broken; the world seemed to tilt on its axis. I had spent two decades building a life around my family, believing that my role as a wife and mother defined me. But the reality was starkly different. I was a ghost in my own home, a silent observer of life that was no longer mine.

This realization hit me like a physical blow, leaving me reeling. I had traded my my dreams, for a love that had turned cold. The emotional disconnect was palpable, a chasm that seemed impossible to bridge.

Unheard! Unseen and Unappreciated!!

The decision to divorce was agonizing, a choice that would forever alter the course of my life. I was terrified of the unknown, of the uncertainty that lay ahead. But I knew that staying in a loveless marriage was not the answer. It was a dead end, a path that would further lead to unhappiness and self-destruction.

They say there's always a lull, a certain kind of calmness before a storm, but what about the storm that's brewing within? A storm that never ceases to stop, it engulfs you to the point where you are fighting for SURVIVAL.

Did I just want to survive? What's the point in surviving this kind of loveless, unseen, unappreciated, and unheard life?

What's the reason behind forcefully living a disconnected life? Is the pursuit of career, success, fame wealth the only purpose in life? What is the trade off's when we choose material success and gains over authentic connections? Why is the "giver" always celebrated? Why do we accept and glorify a toxic work culture, that shakes the very core of many families? Why can't we have both, a career and well-balanced family life? Why is work-life integration frowned upon in the corporate world? Why are we normalizing the rise in number of divorces in families due to this unhealthy work life imbalance?

The Asian women are thrust upon the patriarchal view to uphold the families together; coupled with unrealistic high expectations of being the nurturer and holding them responsible for building their families. In the meanwhile, the men choose to focus on better things "career, power, wealth success," since they are the providers, and are not required to nurture their families. They are given a choice, whilst for women the decisions been made. How can we choose to ignore this bias and be ok with this imbalance?

As a South Asian woman, can we hold our south Asian men accountable for the generational trauma that's passed onto their spouses? Why are we celebrating men as the providers and lowering their standard of expectation in nurturing a family and relationship(s)? When can we stop accepting the least effort from the "receivers" in the name of them being the "providers." Why did my spouse get a choice at financial freedom and pursuit of career without judgment, whilst my choice, (and our joint decision) to raise our family, was always frowned upon, and questioned. As a result of this emotional trauma, their thinking, actions and attitude made me feel less worthy of myself, stripping away my self-worth gradually. There began my tryst with validation and self-worth.

What did my nurturing do to me? How much of me was LOST? Where was I? Where was US?? These questions hounded and perplexed me. It sent me into deep despair and depression, where I sometimes contemplated if living was even an option.

The black hole, kept sucking me in, wanting to take control of me. Oh boy! It rightfully did so. With sweaty palms, breathlessness, anxiety and panic attacks, lying on the bathroom floor, coiled in a fetal position, afraid, and dejected. My mind was in constant war, and all I could do was curse myself for not holding my family together.

The voices in my head grew louder each passing day: "Can't you keep a marriage and a family intact?". Why can't your partner reciprocate your feelings, acknowledge your presence and appreciate you as a partner? I knew I had more questions than answers. What had I become? An absolute mental wreck! The boisterous voice of judgment taunting me of my unworthiness, my inability to be a "good wife, and a good parent to my kids." Shame, and disgust became my companions, as if mocking every waking hour, "Look at you, neither could you keep a marriage intact, nor are capable of being a wife and mom?"

The infamous words- "I am checked out?" Now what does that even mean? I assumed our world revolved around each other and our families. I thought we genuinely cared, loved and had the best partnership in the world! Who was I kidding? There were many red flags, but I chose to ignore, because I believed in US, the purpose of this partnership. It takes two to tango; it takes both to make and break any relationship. They say falling in love is easy, but staying in love is the true testament of a healthy marriage. Our relationship was plagued with the greed for material success and misplaced priorities. It was no longer the unit of a family with combined vision, and goals. He made a choice to grow independently for I was seen as a cog in a wheel, since I highlighted my unmet needs. A 20-year marriage that was initially built on values, purpose, support, and love somewhere lost its path; It became fake, and burdensome. The relationship evolved for the worst for me and our family. As a spouse my questions were aplenty:

"When did you become so individualistic and self- centered to have prioritized material success over family and relationship?"

"Why did you stop including me in decisions that impacted us?

Why did you unilaterally decide the future of our lives?"

"Why did you decide to stop nurturing this relationship and walk out on us?"

"Why did you stop being my partner during challenging times?"

"When the going got tough why did you stop working on us?"

"Why did you create distances between us that made us strangers?"

As if almost screaming; "Where am I in this new picture of life you have?"

"Is the family and our marriage not a priority for you?"

"Did you think about the emotional trauma and impact this decision would have on our 13-year-old and 11-year-old boys?"

I had assumed we were each other's strength.

These conversations and more echoed in my head for a couple of years:

"My work is my priority"!

"My work's my life and wife"!

"First comes my job"

"Then my kids".

"Then YOU"!

Aghast, disbelief, angry, and very painful to listen and see, I was last in the pecking order. These were the red flags that I kept ignoring for years in the garb of "he's extremely busy,", he's to focus on his career", "I, knew I was his home, because he would come back to me at the end of the day. Was this stupid foolish love or over confidence in the feeling of love and US? I was living in a make-believe world (mentally) for I ignored what he was showing me and chose to believe what I wanted to see. Reality bites! I heard myself calling: "Could you please help me? I'm drowning here!"

My mind went into a flashback, finding reasons where I had erred. Plagued with low self-worth, and confidence, emotionally abandoned, ignored, and invisible, I took the sole the responsibility for the disintegration of our marriage and family. I had called it on myself. Or did I? My realizations dawned on me during my introspections of my behavior, attitude and my share of faults that led to this. I did the work, and knew I had a role to play. To be alone is a choice but living lonely in a relationship was not only unacceptable but disrespectful to the partner in my opinion. This self-awareness gave me the strength to voice my needs and stand up for myself. I was given the choice of quid pro quo (to live life as is, as long as we were together as roommates until he achieved his career success and kids left home), but I had endured enough, and this fake offer wasn't the path to my happiness nor did I want to be in someone's life who truly didn't value me for what I brough to the relationship. It was one- sided, and I didn't want any of this anymore! If a conversation can rattle the foundations of a marriage, remember the foundation was never strong. A healthy marriage is bult on such conversations, to grow inwards.

The doubts that were very critical to me at one point, no longer mattered to me. Doubts like:

"What really brought this change?" "Was I not enough?"

"What else could I have done to have had a different outcome?"

Was my marriage disposable? No, I am disposable, until someone else takes my place.

Self-realization is a powerful tool as; it paves the path to clarity. My clarity helped me focus on my happiness, and voice my needs, and dissatisfaction. To take charge of your life is an empowering and liberating experience, but there come consequences with it. I was ready for those penalties. I was no longer ok! With breadcrumbs, and receiving the bare minimum – time, effort, care, joy, partnership, understanding and love. Accepting my love relationship was one sided and based on needs of person was tragically heartbreaking but true.

A healthy relationship requires both navigating and steering the course of the relationship to bring it to fruition.

My friend, partner, and my idol was afflicted with ego, blinded by misplaced priorities, and allowed his generational traumas to impact our relationship. I wasn't responsible for the actions and inactions on his part, and he was accountable for the choices he made. I no longer wanted to be his shadow, because by doing so, I diminished my light and compromised on the person I was becoming. This was growth to me. Acknowledge and Acceptance the powerful tools of growth.

My refusal to surrender, and to forge ahead by picking up the shattered pieces of my life was as much anxiety driven as rebuilding and creating something afresh. In the depths of despair, I found a glimmer of hope. I realized that I had the power to shape my own destiny. With unwavering determination, I embarked on a journey of self-discovery and healing. During the darkest hours of my life, I chanced upon Michelle Obama's book Becoming as if speaking to me to wake up, recognize, take power back, and become the authentic person we are supposed to be in our relationships. She became my guide, positive voice and steered me from heartbreak to being hopeful. This book became came at a defining moment of my life, and Michelle Obama became my mentor, and inspiration for life going forward.

The decision to divorce is never easy, even though I was trying to repair my so-called one-sided marriage, it was an agonizing process that engulfed me physically, emotionally and mentally. After making peace with this decision that took a whole lot of my emotional energy, I knew it was the first step towards healing, rebuilding and shedding the OLD ME. My 45th birthday was a tumultuous year grappling with feelings of inadequacies, and fear, but never have I ever felt more resolute to forge forward and reclaim my new identity. I made a promise to take a step on my birthday and do good by ME, even though with an uncertain future and clueless about where to begin.

I knew that I had to start somewhere. Yes, start! No more Pause in my life for anyone or anything…

Chapter 2: Finding Myself in the Fragments

With a heavy heart, I began the process of rebuilding Charu 2.0. It was a daunting task, like piecing together a shattered vase. Each shard represented a part of me that had been lost, a piece of my identity that had been chipped away by years of neglect and emotional abuse. The road to recovery was long and arduous. I sought therapy seeking guidance and support from a therapist who not only helped me navigate the emotional turmoil, but encouraged me to pursue and rewrite my new chapter.. Through therapy, I began to understand the underlying causes of my low self-esteem and the fear that had held me back for so long. Therapy became my lifeline, a safe space to explore my emotions, heal my wounds, and rediscover my lost self.

I learned to embrace vulnerability, to acknowledge my pain and imperfections without shame. I discovered the power of self-compassion, of treating myself with kindness and understanding. I began to see myself as a whole person, not just a wife and a mom.

As I worked on healing my inner wounds, I also began to explore new possibilities. I enrolled in a life coaching program, driven by a desire to empower myself and help others. I wanted to prove to myself, and to my children, that I was capable of more. I poured myself into learning, acquiring new skills, and pursuing certifications that would empower me and hopefully help others navigate their personal struggles.

Becoming a Life Coach was more than just a career move; it was a declaration of independence. I wanted to prove to myself, and to my two young boys, that I was capable of growth. I wanted to show them that life, despite its twists and turns, offered endless possibilities.

I wanted to take a chance on myself, and from there came my strong belief: "We all have choices/decisions to make. The decision(s) we take alters the outcome of our lives."

"My Choice – Chance on ME, and My Outcome – To Thrive"

Chapter 3: Navigating the Single Motherhood Journey

Raising two adolescent boys as a single mother presented its own challenges. They were used to seeing me as a stay-at-home parent, but now things were different, I was a single working mom. It was a new learning experience for me as much as it was for them: setting boundaries for myself, and for them to respect my time, value our commitments, and learning to adjust as a unit. These were soft skills that my boys were learning.

Both my boys coping mechanisms were different. My older was mature, and pragmatic without any judgment and respected my choice, whilst my younger took it hard, had challenges accepting, and believed in the vision of a family, was the most disappointed and hurt. This at times would come out as lashings or projections during his emotional outbursts. "But why did you guys get divorced and ruin my life?" "Couldn't you have waited after I finished high school, and saved me this trouble?" Earlier, my eyes would swell up at these outbursts, felt guilty at my decision, that left me speechless, but as I grew stronger, and healed, I understood I had to offer compassion to myself as well for the guilt I carried far too long. I provided him safe space to vent out, during the initial years, ensuring he was listened and understood, but as he grew older, there were more open and honest conversations and communications about my expectations from a relationship and marriage. It was important for him to know the decision to divorce wasn't an easy one for me, but I had to for my peace, and happiness.

The guilt-ridden feelings for a decision freed me from the bounds of a fake, and unloved relationship. I had finally come on my own. Being assertive with my son did not mean I wasn't compassionate with his pain, it meant that as much as I acknowledged his trauma, I equally had a right to be life a fulfilled, loving, joyous and a thriving life.

Our connection, even though fragile at times, was reinforced with a constant reminder that despite the changes in our family dynamic, they could still feel safe with me, and express freely, without being judged. We went through a very difficult phase during pandemic when we were going through separation and my son's academic struggles and mental health crisis was at its peak. As a parent, it was painful to witness my son's struggles, but this also was a big wake-up call to acknowledge and take charge of behaviors that stem from mental and emotional health concerns. The past 4 years have been a roller- coaster ride as a parent, and this experience has largely influenced me to become an advocate for the mental and emotional well-being of our youth at schools. I am passionate and determined to normalize this taboo conversation.

As the men in my life the lessons for my young men were to love, care, appreciate, acknowledge, understand, listen and respect their loved ones in their lives. Every relationship and a partner deserved this. Nobody was worth compromising on one's identity, self-worth and self-respect.

The transition from a full-time stay-at-home parent to a single working mom comes with its own challenges, and it's a work in progress. Whereas co-parenting with my ex was a minefield. His absence during the initial phase when children need a father figure meant them relying on me for their emotional, social, physical and academic needs. Now I found myself at crossroads to give away enough for him to be father to our kids. Navigating this complex dynamic, meant I had to unlearn many past behaviors, and patterns, and learn to be assertive, enforcing boundaries and demanding respect. A new battle every day for it was a new territory for us, and I was no longer the same woman he left me. Things had changed, my expectations were different, and I could no longer be manipulated or taken for granted. Eventually with constant reminders and boundaries in place, we are deftly learning the playbook of co-parenting where the importance of compromise and flexibility are paramount.

In challenging situations, especially when we did not see eye to eye on certain things. I also learnt the listening technique that didn't hold me hostage to accept or agree. There wasn't any more of people-pleasing, silent treatment, gaslighting or arguments. I'm sure this shift wasn't an easy one for him to see and accept, but it liberated me from years of being a "YES, SIR!" and "My way or the highway" expectation. I realized that while I had the right to be heard and respected, I also had to be willing to meet my ex halfway. By focusing on what was best for my children, I avoided engaging in unnecessary conflicts.

Chapter 4: Finding Solace in Nature and Connections

To maintain my mental and emotional health, I turned to nature. Hiking and running became my solace, providing a much-needed escape from the chaos of daily life. The beauty of the natural world helped me to find peace and perspective.

I discovered the power of mindfulness, journaling and meditation. These practices helped me to calm my mind, reduce stress, and connect with my inner self. I learned to appreciate the present moment and to savor the simple joys of life. Connecting with community and being involved at the local temple helped me gain clarity, find peace strength and purpose. My deep-rooted friends, became family, some closer than ever before, formed a sisterhood bond that raised me to a high level, caught me on check when needed, and also became my biggest critics and cheerleaders in life. I learned to sift through people who I could rely on and count on. Meaningful connections and conversations helped me grow as a person, when in doubt or unhappy, I had my tribe to listen to me patiently or lean on. Now more than ever, I engage in building solid connections, that inspire, uplift, encourage and motivate me. It's become a symbiotic relationship with a handful because they truly believe in my growth and are authentic.

Chapter 5: The Road to Financial Freedom

This road represents more than just earning an income – it's a path towards self-empowerment, independence, and a renewed sense of purpose. While the transition has been intimidating, it's also a profound opportunity to reinvent myself, build new goals, and achieve financial security on my terms. Re-entering the workforce has triggered both excitement and fear. It's a continuous process to manage the emotional aspect of this transition by recognizing and working through self-doubt and anxiety. While I might view myself as "out of the loop," skills like organizing and multitasking are highly transferable skills. Studying Organizational Behavior, Positive Psychology, and Life Coaching, equipped myself with life skills that has enabled me to look at my new 2.0 chapter with vigor, zeal, excitement, tremendous growth and opportunity. With my emotional intelligence, intuition, resilience, and problem-solving traits being the bedrock of my professional career, I look forward to empowering and enabling many people stuck in their life's journey, fearful of transition and wanting to lead a fulfilled and purposeful life.

Chapter 6: The Power of Resilience: A New Beginning

My story is a testament to the limitless potential within each of us. Through it all, I learned that strength is not the absence of fear, but the ability to overcome it. My journey has been one of resilience, of overcoming adversity, and emerging stronger than ever.

I believe that everyone has the potential to overcome challenges and live a fulfilling life. My hope is that my story will inspire others to embrace their own journeys, to believe in themselves, and to never give up on their dreams.

I am a survivor, a fighter, and a woman who refuses to be defined by her circumstances. I am Limitless and Fearless, and ready to embrace whatever the future holds. Until then, I hum "Que Sera Sera"- by Doris Day- Whatever will be! will be!

My Takeaways:

What is meant to happen will happen!

Remember, if things didn't work out, that means it wasn't in your best interest!

Do not be with people, in spaces/ lives where you don't belong!

Do not force conversations, relationships, people, love, laughter, or connections!

Your self-respect and self-worth are non-negotiable!!! Respect your boundaries, before you expect from others.

Do not dim your light to be their lightness. Authenticity comes from being vulnerable.

Expression is a sign of strength, don't let anyone tell you otherwise.

Your values set the boundaries of how your life should be. Do not change your values for others who do not value you.

It's not your job to change yourself for others, but their responsibility to see and accept you for who you are.

Stop making more withdrawals and begin depositing more.

It's ok! To be alone, but dangerous to be lonely in a relationship.

There's no right decision but decide right!

Authentic connections are based on being your true self, and not compromising yourself.

If any disagreement or communication causes a rift, then remember the connection was one-sided

Generational traumas break the foundation of a relationship and self.

Do not compromise on your values, because that defines your character and integrity.

Nurture your personal relationships just as you would your work, relationships, it should never be an Either/ Or.

Time and effort are the only two strengths of a relationship. It will either blossom and grow, or wilt and wither away.

Some people in your life come as a lesson, learn to accept it, because experience is the best teacher.

Remember, what did not work out for you, worked out for you!!

My mantra: Being LOVED is minimum. I'm making sure I'm also valued, respected, prioritized, desired, heard, understood, and supported

I do not have expectations anymore, I have standards.

Respect my time, effort, match my energy, keep your promises, and be consistent. These are my non-negotiables!

With this, I'm sending a note to my future self that I'm currently focused towards: "Leave a currency of love, joy, laughter, togetherness, compassion, generosity, belonging, effort, respect, and values- the true measure of WEALTH."

Yuliana Francie

Intuitive Leadership and Prosperity Catalyst Coach

https://www.linkedin.com/in/yulianafrancie/
https://facebook.com/yulianafrancie
https://www.instagram.com/yuliana_francie//
www.yulianafrancie.com

Yuliana Francie is a corporate strategist turned best-selling author, coach, and spiritual mentor, passionate about guiding ambitious women to unlock their highest potential. With a deep commitment to helping women embody their feminine energy and achieve success on their own terms, Yuliana empowers them to pursue personal and professional goals while staying true to their authentic selves.

As an intuitive leadership and abundance coach, Yuliana is dedicated to catalysing change among those who seek not only personal success but also a meaningful impact on their communities and the world. A fierce advocate for elevating global consciousness and eradicating violence against women, Yuliana stands as a champion for both individual empowerment and collective transformation. Her mission is clear: to inspire women to embrace their inner power and lead with purpose, driving positive change on a global scale.

Aurora's Resplendent Promise

By Yuliana Francie

"With Aurora's grace, resilience blooms, promising a luminous hope of a new beginning." —Yuliana

Congratulations on being here, beautiful soul. Each word in this chapter is a reminder of your unique significance. Out of eight billion souls, you are here because you were born with a special mission. You've felt it, haven't you? That persistent tug at your heart, whispering that something greater awaits you.

But doubt creeps in, whispering, *"Who do you think you are? You can't even manage your own life, let alone make a difference."* If that resonates, know that you're not alone. Countless others have faced this doubt, yet it doesn't have to define your journey.

Pause for a moment. Close your eyes and think about the last time you felt truly aligned with your purpose. Maybe it was fleeting, or perhaps you're still searching, feeling stuck in unfulfillment. Wherever you are, know this: That voice of doubt is not your truth. Set it aside and consider the possibility that you're reading this chapter because the Universe, Spirit, or God is guiding you to remember your infinite power.

The Universe is perfect. If there's infinite power behind every creation, would there be a mistake in placing you here, in this lifetime, with a unique mission? Like a flower blooming to enrich the world with beauty, you were created to evolve into your greatest self, contributing to the transformation of this world in ways only you can.

Your current reality might not yet align with your destiny, and that's okay. Evolution is a journey, not a destination. As you grow and learn, the path to fulfilling your destiny will become clearer. Every experience, every challenge, is guiding you toward your highest potential. Lao Tzu said, *"Life is a series of natural and spontaneous changes. Don't resist them; that only creates sorrow. Let reality be reality. Let things flow naturally forward in whatever way they like."* Your destiny, your core essence, was written in the stars long before you arrived in this physical world.

I know this because I've walked this path. Today, I live a life overflowing with love, abundance, and energy. I get to live on my terms and fulfil my mission of helping other women create their own prosperous lifestyles. But it wasn't always this way. My journey was far from easy. I've faced despair, battled demons, and struggled with doubt. There were times when giving up seemed like the only option. But each time I fell, an unwavering belief in my potential kept me going. I knew, deep down, that I was destined for something more—something extraordinary.

My battle with doubt began early. As a child, I lay awake in a small room in Indonesia, staring at the plain white ceiling, asking, "What am I here for?" I never felt like I fitted in—family, society, or friends. I spent most of my first 40 years chasing perfection, pleasing everyone, and adhering to rules that felt foreign to my soul. I never allowed myself to meet my true self or fulfil my desires.

Yet, the Universe offers us opportunities to take that first step, creating a new path. We rarely know where the path may lead, but we must have faith that life will work itself out. All we have to do is follow our soul's calling and take the leap of faith!

> *"Let yourself be drawn by the stronger pull of that which you truly love."* —Rumi

At 18, I took such a leap. With no grand plan but a deep trust in spiritual guidance, I immigrated to Sydney, Australia. A university lecturer saw my potential during an accounting competition and suggested I further my studies in Australia. This wasn't something I had ever considered, but Spirit had other plans for me.

I arrived with one large suitcase, little knowledge of English, and a heart full of hope. My job as a cashier barely covered rent and food. I remember the gnawing hunger as I scraped together my last dollars for lunch. A small miracle happened—I found a $50 note in a public restroom. Tears of joy streamed down my cheeks—I had enough money for food until my next paycheck. That night, I felt a deep sense of love and support from an invisible force guiding my life.

Day by day, my life improved. I graduated from university and achieved my dreams. By 27, I was a successful corporate strategist, managing a $500 million business and owning multiple properties. I was married for 15 years and had two beautiful daughters. To the outside world, it seemed like we had it all. But Spirit had a different plan.

My 35th birthday marked a turning point. I had my first astrology reading with Jonathan Quintin, a visionary artist and seasoned astrologer. His words were like a key, unlocking something deep within me. "Your destiny is to inspire change in this world. Your soul's purpose is to make an impact on humanity." His reading answered the question I had been asking since I was 13: "What am I here for?"

A strong calling arose within me—a yearning to find a place where I could be loved and accepted for who I am. A place where I no longer had to beg for affection, attention, or love. I wanted to live life on my own terms.

A week later, I was tasked to write my autobiography by Kelly, my business mentor. I didn't expect much, but it was life-changing. I reflected on my childhood and past, realising I was a scared little girl lost on her life journey. As a Chinese, female, Catholic who grew up in a small village in Indonesia, I ticked the trifecta of the minority. I was a people-pleaser, accepting less-than-equal treatment, too scared to speak my truth.

But the Universe was trying to show me the source of my frustrations and nudge me onto a new life path. During a Monday meditation, I saw Jesus and Mary in a beautiful meadow. With love and affection, they gave me a warm hug and handed me a baby lamb. Jesus said, "Go forth on your new life, you are my shepherd."

Six months later, I left my job and ended my marriage just before our 15th anniversary. My friends and family were shocked. No one saw it coming. But my soul needed to be revived.

Even though I had a successful career, owned a thriving business on the side, three properties, and a beautiful family, my heart was empty. I was merely existing. I felt disconnected from the excitement life had to offer.

The ambitious energy of living in a "not good enough" belief system drove my ambition. My upbringing shaped me into being a highly competitive achiever, with an end goal of attaining success, social status, and a sense of security in life. The baby lamb symbolised the courage to leave all the success and comfort of my old life behind and start a new chapter.

The first breakthrough was getting a divorce. I married a man like my father, and I was turning into my mother. I could see my marriage heading toward dysfunction. Getting a divorce was my first major step in the "unbecoming" journey; a road less travelled. In my community, divorce is seen as a failure, but I chose to prioritise my happiness and model that choice for my daughters.

My healing journey would end the ancestral karmic lessons passed down through generations. Our souls have sacred contracts to grow through the lessons we need to master in this life. For me, manifesting a love relationship was a major area of growth and learning. This coincided with the dysfunctional family my soul agreed to be part of— a journey to find a secure place within myself that allows me to give and receive love unconditionally.

Without self-love and self-acceptance, I am not whole and complete. Others will mirror my "self-rejection" patterns. Hence, I felt I had to choose between love, wealth, or myself. Each time my career and business reached a new level, I faced significant relationship challenges. I struggled for years to find the pathway to the life I wanted and loved.

Life challenges are workshops designed to help us uncover our superpowers to help others and fulfil our purposes. My life challenges became my newly found passion in life—empowering women to own their power within the vessel of divinity so they can design a life worth living.

I truly believe we can have it all if we have a little more courage, conviction, and commitment to the life we dream of. As Rumi said, "Beautiful days do not come to you. You must walk towards them." So, be brave enough to dream, ask, and follow through. Feel worthy to receive it and stay resilient when life takes you on a roller coaster journey.

Every single one of us has encountered opportunities to rewrite our story and strive toward a greater version of ourselves, but all too often, we choose to stay put. The reason? Transformation requires us to face our fears. But through transforming ingrained beliefs, we are authenticated, and our truth is validated. It's a fundamental change to our existence; similar to demolishing our home without knowing if there's a new roof above.

Albert Einstein once said, "We cannot solve the problems with the same mind that created them." Therefore, to transform, we must first deny our current identities and beliefs about who we are, regardless of our resistance.

Our spiritual journey is like the lotus flower, growing through muddy waters to bloom. The lotus symbolises purity, resilience, and rebirth, reflecting our own spiritual evolution. Our spirit, like a lotus seed, has infinite potential and can overcome challenges. Through self-exploration and shedding limiting beliefs, we realign with our true selves and manifest our power.

And so, my journey continued. Each step, each challenge, each moment of doubt was part of my evolution—part of my journey toward becoming who I was always meant to be. As I reflect upon my path, I realise the journey is never truly over. We are always evolving, always growing, and discovering new depths of our own potential.

Always remember why you came here—your life is sacred! Embrace the challenges; for they are catalysts for growth. Trust in your inner strength to create the life you deserve. Seek out those who believe in you more than you believe in yourself. Stand strong and let your light shine brightly—the world needs your light.

In your darkest hour lies the opportunity to become all you can be. Your worst moments can be your greatest teachers. As you emerge from the shadows, you'll see that you were born to bring light to this world in a way that only you can. The power you seek lies within, waiting for you to awaken it.

Trust in the divine plan. Life is a dance of change and growth. Embrace the rhythm, step into the flow, and let your journey unfold with grace. The Universe is conspiring in your favour. When you look within, you'll find that all the answers you seek are already within you.

In the end, the journey is the destination. Each day is a new beginning—a new opportunity to grow, learn, and become more of who you are meant to be. Life is not about the destination; it's about the journey, the experiences, the growth, and the person you become along the way.

So, take a deep breath, dear soul. Step into the light of your own truth, knowing that you are guided, loved, and supported every step of the way. You are on a divine path, and your journey has only just begun.

I have found beauty in simple experiences, like a sunrise. Each dawn is a sensory symphony with golden rays painting the sky, and birds heralding a new day. Sunrise symbolises new beginnings and an opportunity to rise above our fears.

Often, we're conditioned to limit ourselves, told not to ask for too much, or to trade self-love for approval. We are taught to trade self-love in exchange for desires of love and acceptance.

Life has come full circle for me. After feeling isolated and unfulfilled, I've learned to create a life by design. I am now deeply connected to my soul and supported by my spirit. I embody the essence of feminine energy, blooming like a lotus from the mud.

I'm living proof that it's possible to rise above adversity and shine. My mission is to empower other women to live unapologetically and authentically. Embrace your inner warrior. Resilience is about choosing your own destiny, despite setbacks. You alone are enough at any stage in life.

By sharing my story, I hope to inspire your journey of self-discovery and transformation. Embrace your challenges as growth opportunities. Trust in your power and remember: Your personal opinion is the only one that matters. My affirmation is, "I am a powerful woman, and I love that about myself."

Trust in the belief that you were born as the light on a dark path. You are the seed of change that seeks to emerge. Own your power, speak up, challenge the norms that seek to confine us, and be that powerful woman. Power stems from your inner soul; being internally validated, internally motivated, and owning your truth. Most importantly, remember that the only opinion that matters is your own.

After six years of spiritual development, psychological studies, research, and personal life experiences of overcoming racism, corporate bullying, harassment, toxic relationships, and challenging the status quo, I emerged with three steps of achievement.

The Unbecoming project comprises a three-step process: unlearn your limiting conditioning, uncover your true self, and unleash your creative power over 21 days of daily reflections. It is a step-by-step process to "unbecome" from our childhood conditioning and societal programming, so we can become exactly who we are born to be.

"Wherever you go, go with all of your heart."—<u>*Confucius*</u>

<u>"Unbecoming is the process of revealing your authentic, loving self – a self once rejected out of shame and the belief that you weren't 'good enough' to meet others' expectations."</u>

JOIN THE MOVEMENT!
#BAUW

Becoming An Unstoppable Woman
With She Rises Studios

She Rises Studios was founded by Hanna Olivas and Adriana Luna Carlos, the mother-daughter duo, in mid-2020 as they saw a need to help empower women worldwide. They are the podcast hosts of the *She Rises Studios Podcast* and Amazon best-selling authors and motivational speakers who travel the world. Hanna and Adriana are the movement creators of #BAUW - Becoming An Unstoppable Woman: The movement has been created to universally impact women of all ages, at whatever stage of life, to overcome insecurities, and adversities, and develop an unstoppable mindset. She Rises Studios educates, celebrates, and empowers women globally.

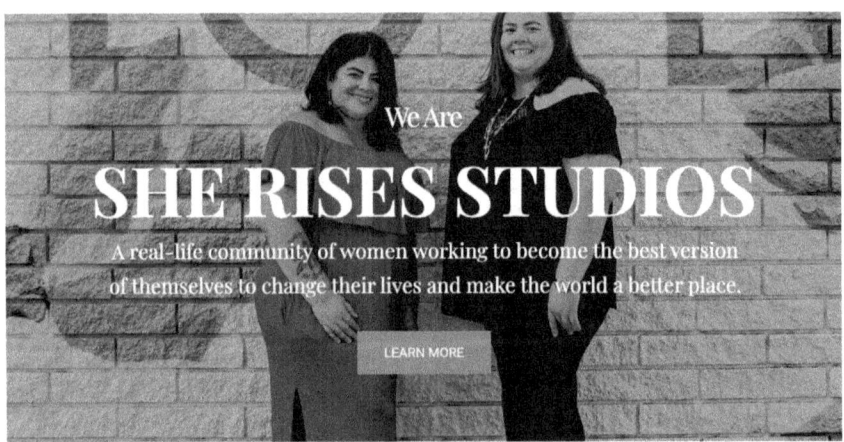

Looking to Join Us in our Next Anthology or Publish YOUR Own?

She Rises Studios Publishing offers full-service publishing, marketing, book tour, and campaign services. For more information, contact info@sherisesstudios.com

We are always looking for women who want to share their stories and expertise and feature their businesses on our podcasts, in our books, and in our magazines.

SEE WHAT WE DO

OUR PODCAST

OUR BOOKS

OUR SERVICES

Be featured in the Becoming An Unstoppable Woman magazine, published in 13 countries and sold in all major retailers. Get the visibility you need to LEVEL UP in your business!

Have your own TV show streamed across major platforms like Roku TV, Amazon Fire Stick, Apple TV and more!

Learn to leverage your expertise. Build your online presence and grow your audience with FENIX TV.
https://fenixtv.sherisesstudios.com/

Visit www.SheRisesStudios.com to see how YOU can join the #BAUW movement and help your community to achieve the UNSTOPPABLE mindset.

Have you checked out the *She Rises Studios Podcast?*

Find us on all MAJOR platforms: Spotify, IHeartRadio, Apple Podcasts, Google Podcasts, etc.

Looking to become a sponsor or build a partnership?

Email us at info@sherisesstudios.com

SHE RISES
STUDIOS

www.ingramcontent.com/pod-product-compliance
Lightning Source LLC
Chambersburg PA
CBHW070905120626
46546CB00001B/148